Holy

Holyrood
The Inside Story

Susan Bain

Edinburgh University Press

For Nichol

'The Beginning of a New Song' by Iain Crichton Smith for *Collected Poems*, Carcanet Press, 1996. Reproduced with the permission of the publisher.

© Scottish Parliamentary copyright material is reproduced with the permission of the Queen's Printer for Scotland on behalf of the Scottish Parliamentary Corporate Body.

© Susan Bain, 2005

Edinburgh University Press Ltd
22 George Square, Edinburgh

Typeset in Adobe Minion by
Servis Filmsetting Ltd, Manchester and
printed and bound in Great Britain by
The Cromwell Press, Trowbridge

A CIP record for this book is available from the British Library

ISBN 0 7486 2065 6 (paperback)

The right of Susan Bain to be identified as author of this work
has been asserted in accordance with the Copyright, Designs
and Patents Act 1988.

Published with the support of the Edinburgh University Scholarly Publishing
Initiatives Fund.

Contents

Contents

Preface

IN 1998, FOLLOWING our first visit to Holyrood, independent documentary producer Stuart Greig and I sat in a coffee shop on Edinburgh's Royal Mile. 'Make the most of this coffee,' Stuart told me, 'I've a feeling it's the last chance we'll have to sit down for a while.'

In the six years that followed, our lives have completely been taken over by the Holyrood building. 'This is not a seven and a half hour a day job,' EMBT/RMJM's Brian Stewart told us, 'this embraces everything. It just is something that is totally absorbed into your life . . . there's barely a day goes past but there's something in the *Evening News* . . . it's just been constant.' For Enric Miralles, the relentless scrutiny left him feeling 'almost naked in front of everybody'. And for us, the entire process has been exhausting, frustrating, exhilarating, rewarding and deeply angering.

Over the last half-decade, Holyrood has become far more than the story of a building. It is the story of a long-anticipated new democracy, its new home hamstrung by political game-playing, its story seriously misrepresented by sections of the Scottish press. If the story played out in the public arena has been damning, the real tale is far worse. This book is a chance to give a full account – drawn from the BBC footage of *The Gathering Place* documentaries, and my comprehensive research and contemporaneous notes collected throughout the length of our filming project.

During the making of the films, I have met my husband, married, and had two children. My colleague Stuart has married, Enric has died, and so has Donald Dewar. There has been the murder of Sarah Payne, 9/11 and a war in Iraq. But inside Holyrood, there has been a profound sense of isolation. The building has been everybody's primary focus, and defending it has become as time-consuming as actually building it.

There are many people I'd like to thank for their help and contributions over the last six years. In particular, I'd like to thank John Gibbons – without whose efforts there would be no parliament building – and Brian Stewart, Alan Mack and Hugh Fisher, each of whom we have seen put through hell and back as Holyrood took on an increasingly political focus. I'd also like to thank the Holyrood Progress Group, who gave me free rein to attend its meetings over the years, enabling a far fuller understanding of the process than would otherwise have been possible. Also, Mick Duncan, Benedetta Tagliabue, Barbara Doig, Alan Ezzi, Sarah Davidson, John Spencely, Joán Callis, Ian McAndie, David Steel, John Kinsley, Dick Mulholland, John Hyne, Eddie McGibbon, John Clement, Bill Armstrong, Janice Mack, Margaret Hickish, Sue Wilson, Marie, Margo MacDonald, Donald Gorrie and all those on the Holyrood Project Team, particularly Judith, Mary, Ginny and Jim, I'd also like to thank Donald Dewar and Enric Miralles, neither of whom survived to see the building. I'd also like to thank my colleagues at Wark Clements and the BBC, and a special mention goes to Stuart and his determination that the Holyrood story be told. This list is by no means exhaustive, and the contributions of everyone we have spoken to, either on or off camera, have been greatly appreciated. The views expressed in the book, however, are entirely my own, as are all conclusions drawn.

It is important to stress that all those who spoke to us were representing their own views, not those of any business or organisation for which they worked. For ease of reference, the Barcelona and Edinburgh ends of the joint architectural practice EMBT/RMJM are referred to as 'EMBT' and 'RMJM' when spoken of separately. This refers solely to the two ends of the joint venture, and not to the pre-existing businesses of the same name. Similarly, UK newspapers referenced in the text are Scottish editions, where available.

For my own part, I would like to thank Nicola Carr, my editor, who allowed me to tell the story straight, and was of enormous help and support, especially in the last few difficult weeks, and Eddie Clark and Stuart Midgley at EUP, both of whom were endlessly patient. Violet and Tom Shannon have proved invaluable. I would also like to thank my parents, Ranald and Judith Bain, and my parents-in-law, John and Bronwen Wheatley, all of whom have helped shoulder the burden of this project as it has grown larger and heavier. Most of all, I would like to thank Nichol, and our children Finn and Lily. The last six years have been enormously difficult, and, without their love and support, I simply wouldn't have got through it.

Chronology

4 April – Information session for MSPs prior to debate.
5 April – Second Holyrood debate.
31 May – Departure of Project Sponsor Barbara Doig.
28 June – First meeting of Holyrood Progress Group.
3 July – Death of Enric Miralles.
1 August – Barcelona visit.
13 September – Resolution of architects' leadership.
11 October – Death of Donald Dewar.
13 November – Alan Ezzi's employment as Project Director commences.

2001

10 May – Third Holyrood debate.
19 June – Announcement of Alan Ezzi's departure.
21 June – Fourth Holyrood debate. Sarah Davidson replaces Alan Ezzi as Project Director.
Late August 2001 – SPCB/Progress Group fall out over Barcelona trip.
13 November – First report to Finance Committee. Estimated final cost £241 million.
26 November – Progress Group meeting with EMBT/RMJM directors.

2002

January to April – SPCB/Progress Group disabled access row.
12 March – Report to Finance Committee. Estimated final cost £266.4 million.
8 October – Report to Finance Committee. Estimated final cost £294.6 million.

2003

16 January – Letter from David Steel to Finance Committee. Estimated final cost £323.9 million.
1 May – Election.

10 June – Consultants' fee capping meeting with SPCB. 'Fat cat' fallout in the press.

12 June – Lord Fraser appointed to conduct inquiry into Holyrood Project.

18 June – Report to Finance Committee. Estimated final cost £375.8 million.

23 September – Report to Finance Committee. Estimated final cost £401 million.

October – BBC/Fraser inquiry tape row breaks.

2004

26 February – Report to Finance Committee. Estimated final cost £431 million.

31 March – Debate on BBC Holyrood tapes.

7 September – Parliament meets at Holyrood for the first time.

15 September – Publication of Lord Fraser's report.

22 September – Debate on Fraser Inquiry report.

9 October – Opening ceremony.

The Beginning of a New Song
Iain Crichton Smith

Let our three voiced country
Sing in a new world
Joining the other rivers without dogma,
But with friendliness to all around her.

Let her new river shine on a day
That is fresh and glittering and contemporary,

Let it be true to itself and to its origins
Inventive, original, philosophical,
Its institutions mirror its beauty;

Then without shame we can esteem ourselves.[1]

1. Poem read at the opening of the Scottish Parliament, 1 July 1999.

1

There Shall be a Scottish Parliament

'Parliament is a mental place.'
Enric Miralles, concept design presentation

IT'S 17 JUNE 1999, and two weeks before Scotland's first parliament in nearly 300 years opens its doors, it's D-Day for the Holyrood project. After New Labour swept to a landslide election victory in May 1997 and a decisive referendum result delivered devolution, serious questions have begun to be asked about the new building to house the fledgling democracy. What will it cost? Why is the timescale so tight? Is eccentric Catalan architect Enric Miralles the right man for the job? And, crucially, why is it being built at Holyrood – opposite a royal palace, in the shadow of Arthur's Seat, and slap bang in the middle of a UNESCO world heritage site? For most of Scotland, the obvious place for a parliament had long been the Royal High School on Edinburgh's Calton Hill. The potent icon of Scotland's aspiring nationhood, site of a lengthy vigil for a parliament, and even converted for the purpose by the Labour government ahead of the 1979 referendum, its credentials had never seemed in doubt. So how come it got ditched? And why have we ended up at a site no one has even heard of, with an architect who hails from Spain?

For many of Scotland's new MSPs, the answer is simple: politics. Less than six weeks after their election to office, it's already clear many opposition members are feeling disenfranchised and angry. With all the major decisions about their new home already made, suspicion is rife that Holyrood is a New Labour stitch-up, and that cheaper, more practical, more *symbolic* solutions have been deliberately and cynically dumped. Voices in the press too are being raised – with First Minister Donald Dewar's credibility in particular having been questioned. He announced the site;[1] he headed the panel which chose the architect, and it is he who has been the public face of the building's rising costs. These costs – first quoted as £10–40 million[2] – have now grown to an overall total of £109 million, and press and politicians are voicing outrage. For the Scottish public, the parliament they voted for in unprecedented numbers already seems to be losing its gloss. It appears that Holyrood is spiralling out of control before even a single brick has been laid on site, and nobody seems to know why.

Today – perhaps – should be an opportunity to get some answers. For the first major gathering of Scotland's new parliament, veteran Liberal Democrat campaigner Donald Gorrie and maverick SNP 'voice of the people' Margo MacDonald have tabled a debate on the building project. The topic for discussion? Whether to press ahead with the decisions made under Donald Dewar's stewardship, or back an amendment calling for a delay to reassess potential sites and revisit the current budget and timescale.[3] Whatever the outcome, this debate is hugely symbolic. For a new democracy founded on principles of openness and public accessibility unprecedented in British politics, Holyrood has already raised some serious questions. And although no one yet knows it, what the debate itself will reveal will raise even more.

For the team charged with making Holyrood happen, it's been a whirlwind seven days. Despite press stories focusing on Miralles and Dewar, the man who's really in control at Holyrood is John Gibbons, an urbane sixty-something Englishman whose relaxed academic air belies a steely focus and determination. An architect by training, he has spent over thirty years in the civil service, emerging as Chief Architect at the Scottish Office and Dewar's right-hand advisor on the parliament building. He is funny, charming, incisive – and a massively skilful and experienced political operator. Furthermore, he is the man who knows what's really going on. While Dewar assured the public five months ago that 'there is no question at this stage – and I hope at any stage – of [Holyrood] being over budget or at any stage of it being delayed',[4] the story from within the project is somewhat different. The complex nature of Miralles' concept design has introduced a greater level of unpredictability than anticipated. And the budget and time-scale are tight. 'We are sitting here today a few weeks behind programme,' explained John Gibbons in May 1999, to Stuart Greig and Susan Bain, the documentary crew charged with charting Holyrood's history, 'but a few weeks that are quite recoverable . . . so we're sitting relatively comfortable [sic] at the moment. The great dangers I think we face are probably those that any project faces, of changes of mind or any unpredictable events in the next two years: unpredictable weather, unpredictable site conditions. We've done everything we can to minimise the risk of a delay to the project but that's where we are.'

Although Gibbons couldn't possibly foresee it, unpredictable weather would be the least of the hurdles Holyrood would face over the coming years. Over the next twenty-four months alone, the catalogue of unpredictability would run as follows: the architect would die, Scotland's First Minister would die, four political debates would be held on the building's future, there would be an independent review, an audit investigation, numerous battles for control, four different project directors and a rising wave of public hostility. That Holyrood was about to become Scotland's most controversial – and politically damaging – building project was beyond doubt. Yet in May 1999, all this was still unknown. Devolution had arrived, work on Holyrood was underway, and within the building team everything appeared, for the moment, to be relatively straightforward. Holyrood certainly had its problems, but nobody anticipated any obstacles that could not be overcome.

However, with the decision taken to press ahead with the new parliament building before the parliament itself was up and running, the team was already having to adjust to some inevitable changes. Information was constantly filtering in about the administration's developing needs, leading to adjustments, size increases and the inevitable cost rises. A fast-track construction management contract had been adopted to manage the changes starting so early would entail, with the intention of allowing the building to evolve and develop at minimal cost. And with the newly elected parliament due to take the project over from Donald Dewar and the Scottish Office, there would be a change of 'client'. From summer 1999, Holyrood would be run by a new board of directors, the Scottish Parliamentary Corporate Body – or SPCB – a cross-party group chaired by Presiding Officer Sir David Steel, and comprising a member from each of the four main political parties. A change of client in the middle of any project is a risky enterprise. On a high-profile, publicly funded, fast-track political project, it is a potential recipe for disaster. And although no one yet knows it, the seeds are already sown for a political scandal of catastrophic proportions.

As Scotland's new politicians gather and chat in the black and white corridor outside the parliament's temporary chamber, it is already clear that the mood is angry. A week ago, David Steel circulated a paper to all members explaining the current state of play at Holyrood, and further information has since been put out on the project's history, management and costs. But in the light of what's been appearing in the newspapers over the last few weeks, some MSPs aren't in the mood to believe it. Stories are circulating that builders have been ordered to use cheap foreign materials in an attempt to keep soaring costs down. Lino – it is said – will replace carpets, imported hardwood will substitute for Scottish sycamore, and granite will be replaced by spray paint.[5] 'They are giving us a Mini instead of a Porsche,' complained Margo MacDonald, who would emerge as Holyrood's most vocal and persistent critic, 'A Mini is useful, but it is not the sort of showpiece we want for Scotland.'[6]

Margo's anger certainly seems to have struck a public chord. But while the new cost-cutting allegations have sparked outrage, they have also served to compound some far more serious worries. The year 1999 has also seen news break that Bill Armstrong, Project Manager at Holyrood and the man who wrote the brief for the building, has resigned claiming that the project is over budget and behind schedule. Worse still, the news of his departure has been accompanied by accusations that all his warnings were ignored, and cost escalations were buried in order to avoid political embarrassment. The Scottish Office response that everything remains on track has done nothing to quell fears: if anything, it has made matters worse. It claimed that Armstrong retired: he immediately denied it, saying he resigned in protest when it became clear he was no longer allowed to do his job.[7] With some MSPs seemingly concerned that contracts for the building will be finalised deliberately in order to 'fix' the debate by ensuring massive cancellation costs, a ten-day freeze has been ordered on all new Holyrood contracts. The mood is far from one of national celebration. Many MSPs clearly feel that they have been given insufficient facts and figures to make a fully informed decision on whether the scheme should press ahead. But if this is the case, it raises one fundamental question. If politicians *really* feel they are seriously short of information, why did only half of them turn up to the information sessions specially laid on for their benefit by Holyrood's design team?

It is 10.30 a.m., and the angular, slightly stooped frame of Donald Dewar rises for the Scottish Parliament's first major debate. It's been a long road to devolution for the new First Minister; the culmination of decades of campaigning, and the fulfilment of a fiercely held political and personal mission. But this is not the start to the parliament that he must have envisaged. His usual wry humour has been replaced by a controlled anger. With Dewar publicly backing a parliament at Holyrood, news from the SNP camp this morning has come as a shock. Unexpectedly, the opposition is whipping, so today's debate on a matter of national and symbolic importance will now be decided not on the merits or shortcomings of the project itself, but by party politics.[8] With the Scottish

Tories likely to side with the SNP in voting for a pause, the future of Holyrood is in serious peril. And Dewar is incandescent. He is convinced that Holyrood is the right solution, and that any U-turn now will be disastrous. But for his opponents – and the public – it is clear that things have gone badly wrong already. Without consultation, a site, an architect, a cost and a timescale have been decided for a supposedly democratic parliament, and there seems to be no guarantee on the final cost. For at least one leading member of the opposition, Dewar's uncharacteristically passionate speech suggests only one thing: the First Minister's anger may be driven far less by a burning passion for architecture, and far more by a desire for getting his own way.[9]

As politician after politician rises to speak, a deeply disturbing picture rapidly emerges. With suspicion about Holyrood rife, few on the opposition benches seem to have much faith in the official information they have been given, and some appear to believe newspaper accounts over material presented by those directly involved. Fact is being confused with fiction, mischief is being made, and the result is a morass of information, misinformation, speculation, concern and propaganda, through which it is almost impossible to navigate. However, this is nothing compared to what is about to happen. Shockingly, a minority of Scotland's brand-new MSPs begin to bed down into opposing trenches regarding what was actually said at the design-team information sessions, while others reinvent questions already answered to distance themselves from knowledge they clearly possess. 'After the debate when I spoke privately to the people [involved],' confided an incredulous John Gibbons, '. . . they both knew the answers, so what they went through was some sort of theatrical demonstration . . . And I mean it was political and it was using the parliament as a political football.' The facts about Holyrood seem to be being twisted for party ends, and for those relying solely on what they are being told in the chamber today, it will be impossible to evaluate who is telling the truth, and who is lying. Scotland's new parliament is only six weeks old, and already the building intended to embody a new form of 'honest' politics has become a political weapon.

As the votes are counted, Donald Gorrie smiles, shrugs and nods his head. With calculations at lunchtime suggesting that there were only two votes in it, a huge effort has been put in throughout the afternoon to convert the marginals and floaters. Holyrood has won the day, but only by the slimmest of margins. And John Gibbons, who has been in touch with Miralles in Barcelona all afternoon and most of last night, is ringing him again with the news.

Miralles, a difficult but prodigiously talented designer, has found the fuss surrounding his building bewildering. As much artist as architect, he is a charismatic and unexpected blend of the cerebral and the roguish. His tendency to characterise his work in metaphors – he has already variously described the parliament design as upturned boats, giant leaves, an onion, potatoes and tumbling rocks – has proved confusing for the public, and is easily caricatured by Holyrood's opponents. This has been compounded by his infuriating and mischievous tendency to 'forget' he speaks English when questions about the project become too dull, too irritating, or too intrusive. Today's debate has caused the architect enormous distress, and – as he will privately confide to the documentary team – the vagaries of a political environment are creating massive uncertainty and confusion. Private discussions with MSPs have been both welcoming and friendly, yet in public, these opinions have become, he explains in worried bafflement, 'completely opposite and contrary and contradictory to the same conversation you have had an hour before'. Despite this, the threat of significant changes has finally been lifted. Or as Miralles will rather more colourfully put it, 'In a way it's like . . . you are running . . . the 100 metres run, and then somebody in the middle . . . tells you, "Now you should do swimming and parallel bars!"'

Miralles is immensely likeable and hugely frustrating in equal measure. But whether he is the man who can deliver

Scotland's new parliament on time and on budget is a question that has been brought increasingly into focus. His attitude is unquestionably unusual. As he explains from his eclectic and vibrant offices tucked in a back street of Barcelona's old town, 'I think in a way it's a kind of game . . . Someone says, "This needs to be done in three weeks," and I think the role of the architect is saying "Yes!" But then everybody understands if it's possible or not. I think in a way saying yes and being positive is quite important. I never found in any project we have done that the client has not understood that we need more time . . .' However, Holyrood is not solely Miralles' responsibility. He is part of an architectural consortium, EMBT/RMJM, formed by a joint venture between his company – EMBT – and Edinburgh-based architects RMJM Scotland. He may be the public face of the project, but he has three co-directors, RMJM engineer and managing director Brian Stewart, RMJM architect Mick Duncan, and Enric's own wife, Benedetta Tagliabue, memorably described by Donald Dewar to a colleague as 'all legs and teeth'.

It is the marriage with RMJM that has given Enric's practice the resources to deliver Scotland's new parliament. But some newspapers have already been noting that the two companies make an unusual – and inflammatory – combination, and stories abound that the partnership has been rocked by a series of massive rows. Enric's Scottish partners are everything that Miralles is not. While EMBT is all flamboyance, charisma and artistry, RMJM has a solid reputation in delivery of fast-track projects. And Miralles and Brian Stewart, RMJM's key player, could not be more different. Tall, handsome and greying where Miralles is bear-like, Latin and roguish, Stewart is fiercely analytical and has an overwhelming sense of duty. For him, the overriding responsibility on this project is for a quality product to be delivered within the client's defining requirements of budget and timescale. However, if today's debate has proved anything, it's that quality seems very far from the top of many MSPs' agendas. Brian Stewart is appalled. Much of what has been said in today's debate, he confides in disbelief, 'was actually more than distorted. I mean it was actually, you know, quite wrong. Some of the things that were being said were the exact opposite to the facts and what was presented to them. I mean, all this [about the] environmental issues . . . It's completely outrageous! . . . What made him say that?'

Today's result has been, at best, a Pyrrhic victory. After a week of preparing presentations and a full day of MSP information sessions, all of which have deflected the team from the process of actually developing the building, this morning has been a shocking eye-opener. Holyrood's key players seem, effectively, to have been accused of professional incompetence. And the ammunition used to direct this charge has been either untrue, or aimed to sink a political target, catching the Holyrood team in the crossfire. After a year of working at maximum capacity, the group is utterly demoralised, and even John Gibbons, fiercely and personally devoted to the project, has been reconsidering his decision to stay on as architectural advisor to the new board of directors, the SPCB. The threat of a political client made up of 129 competing individuals has clearly caused him serious alarm. However, with the battle won, he is – for now – both relieved, and magnanimous. 'Well, I think to be charitable, these are early days . . .' he mused, back in Holyrood's headquarters overlooking Edinburgh's historic Royal Mile, 'I'm prepared to be charitable and say, "Well, this will improve, this must improve."'[10]

With the handover from Dewar to SPCB now complete, responsibility for Holyrood has passed to a body that should be able to represent – apolitically – what the parliament and Scotland really needs. Today, the group has been given a mandate of what needs to be done, and top of the list is a redesign of the debating chamber. The original brief for the parliament building had specified a horseshoe-shaped forum, but Miralles' design has opted for a more flattened layout – still in line with the consensual politics the envisaged parliament aspired to. What has become clear over the last few weeks is that some of Scotland's press and new politicians don't like it, variously describing the design as a coffin, a boomerang, a banana and 'suitable only for a ferocious debate on flower arranging'.[11] Work will now focus on developing this part of the design out of sequence. But Holyrood, crucially, has been given the go-ahead: completion should occur within the current cost estimate of £109 million, and current timescale – ending autumn 2001.

However, there are two factors underlying Holyrood that will prove twin time-bombs ticking under the project for the next five years. Under the fast-track construction management contract selected for the project, no guarantees of final cost or timescale can be given until the building is completed. And, worryingly, Holyrood's current cost estimate is *not* the figure given to the parliament today, but – according to the cost consultants' figures – £27 million more. These two issues will underpin every single twist and turn yet to unfold in the extraordinary tale of Holyrood's soaring costs over the coming years. And although no one can possibly predict what is about to happen, the project has just stepped into a whole new area of political mire. Holyrood's new board of directors – far from making things better – is about to make things a whole lot worse.

Notes

1. *Scottish Office Press Release* no. 0029/98, 'Scottish Parliament to be built at Holyrood: Dewar opts for new building in historic heart of Edinburgh', 9 January 1998, http://www.scotland.gov.uk, http://www.holyroodinquiry.org
2. 'Because of the range of sites under consideration and the variety of funding methods potentially available it is necessary to express the cost as a range of between £10m and £40m.' Scottish Office, *Scotland's Parliament*, Edinburgh: The Stationery Office, 1997, p. 32.
3. Motion S1M-52, amendment S1M-52.1, http://www.scottish.parliament.uk
4. Quoted in Paul Riddell and Elizabeth Quigley, 'I quit as Holyrood bill soared towards £100m; Donald Dewar faces storm over rising cost of the new Parliament', *Scottish Daily Mail*, 16 January 1999.
5. 'MSPs cash in on perks: Parliament votes itself big pay deal while cutting £10m of the budget for new building', *Daily Record*, 9 June 1999; Ian Swanson, 'Parliament suspends all Holyrood contracts', *Edinburgh*

Evening News, 9 June 1999; Ron McKenna, 'Parliament in a mobile home: Labour accused of ruining Holyrood building', *Scottish Mirror*, 9 June 1999.

6. Quoted in Ron McKenna, 'Parliament in a mobile home: Labour accused of ruining Holyrood building', *Scottish Mirror*, 9 June 1999.

7. Ian Swanson, 'Behind schedule and over budget', *Edinburgh Evening News*, 15 January 1999; Paul Riddell and Elizabeth Quigley, 'I quit as Holyrood bill soared towards £100m; Donald Dewar faces storm over rising cost of the new Parliament', *Scottish Daily Mail*, 16 January 1999; Alexander Linklater, 'Project manager for Parliament building resigns', *Herald*, 15 January 1999; Shirley English, 'Builder alleges £20m over-spend', *Times*, 16 January 1999; Andrew Walker and David Scott, 'Holyrood Parliament row as Project Chief resigns', *The Scotsman*, 16 January 1999; Ian Swanson, 'Cost "cover-up" at Holyrood', *Edinburgh Evening News*, 15 June 1999.

8. 'I agree with Donald Dewar on one issue: the site is a parliamentary issue. Why, therefore, is he making us vote on an Executive motion? That is an outrage and has caused what may be a disproportionate response from another party.' Donald Gorrie, *Scottish Parliament Official Report*, vol.1, no. 10, col. 526, 17 June 1999, http://www.scottish.parliament.uk; Lord Fraser's inquiry report would give the background to this issue, *Holyrood Inquiry*, (SP Paper No. 205), Chapter 9, para. 9.35, September 2004, http://www.holyroodinquiry.org

9. Mike Russell, *Scottish Parliament Official Report*, vol. 1, no. 10, col. 530, 17 June 1999, http://www.scottish.parliament.uk

10. John Gibbons' concerns were modified by his observation that it appeared MSPs did not yet seem comfortable or *au fait* with their environment.

11. Dorothy-Grace Elder, *Scottish Parliament Official Report*, vol. 1, no. 10, col. 558, 17 June 1999, ibid.

2

But Where Should it Be?

'A little knowledge is a dangerous thing . . .'
Samuel Butler

THE ROYAL HIGH school at Calton Hill casts a long shadow over Holyrood. Built by Scottish architect Thomas Hamilton in 1829, its hold over the Scottish spirit has grown both potent and unassailable. For five and a half years following the Tory election victory of 1992, this neo-classical masterpiece, based on Athens' Temple of Theseus, was the site of a vigil calling for a parliament of Scotland's own. Eighty thousand signatures were collected from members of the public. And when New Labour won a landslide election victory in May 1997 with a promise of devolved government, it seemed the settled will of the Scottish people would – finally – be realised. The Royal High, refurbished prior to the failed 1979 devolution referendum, sat ready. All that was needed was the nation's new MSPs.

So when Donald Dewar announced on 9 January 1998 that the Scottish Parliament would not be going to Calton Hill but to Holyrood, the news was met with a mixture of fury and disenchantment by his political opponents.[1] Both the SNP and Scottish Lib Dems had worked closely with Labour on the devolution referendum, and both were bitterly disappointed. What caused the greatest outcry, however, was not the news that Holyrood had been chosen but the apparent reason. The site had been seen as a favourite since it publicly entered the race – late – in December 1997. And with the news of its success leaked ahead of Dewar's announcement, the location of the new Scottish Parliament was probably the worst kept secret of the entire devolution process. What really caused an uproar were reports that Calton Hill had been discarded because it was a 'nationalist shibboleth' whose rejection would be 'a poke in the eye for the Edinburgh establishment'.

The source of these statements – quoted in the *Herald*[2] – was variously identified as Dewar himself, his 'close allies', a 'Labour insider', and 'senior Labour sources'. But Donald Dewar denied that he was the man responsible for the comments, privately confiding, 'I actually think – if I remember rightly – that the first time I ever [heard] that it was in the mouth of a Conservative councillor in Edinburgh. Certainly, they were words that I never uttered.' Whatever their origin, the remarks provoked an angry reaction from SNP leader Alex Salmond, who wrote to Dewar protesting that the 'clear consensus' in favour of Calton Hill had been broken. 'The *Herald* report reinforces suspicion that the motivations behind this decision have had little to do with proper considerations,' he argued, 'and that an aversion to Calton Hill has been running through the entire process . . . This is hardly acceptable criteria for such an important decision, which should be arrived at on the basis of consensus.'[3]

Liberal Democrat MP Donald Gorrie was equally outraged. In a letter to Henry McLeish, he argued that an 'evasive' answer given in the Commons 'confirms my worst suspicions that the decision on the site was a typical, old-fashioned stitch-up', and that 'the rhetoric about being open, consultative and consensual is just a sham'. 'I know many Scots in Edinburgh and elsewhere,' he argued crossly, 'who feel it is an outrage that the site of a Nation's parliament should be decided by one man.'[4] In a letter of 6 January, he delivered what would prove a prescient warning. 'If the choice of site is a personal decision by you, is clearly contrary to overwhelming informed public opinion, and is not justified by rational and open argument, [then] you can expect the most vigorous opposition possible from those interested in the matter, especially the people of Edinburgh and their representatives, including me.'[5]

*

13

So how did Scotland's new parliament end up not at Calton Hill but at Holyrood? And how did the decision itself become so controversial? For the answers to these questions, one must travel back to summer 1997, with Britain still bathed in a post-election Labour honeymoon glow. May 1st had seen an extraordinary election win for the Labour Party under the leadership of Tony Blair. And in Scotland, where the party had campaigned on a platform of devolution, the result was seen as a firm endorsement of a new Scottish Parliament. With New Labour pledged to enact legislation to allow a swift referendum on devolution, Dewar and his team were under pressure. But while the hard work was still unfolding, another consideration was beginning to grow into a pressing concern. With a new Scottish Parliament at last almost a reality, where was the government going to put it?

Within a month of Labour's election win, John Gibbons received a call from Dewar's office. Would he meet Donald Dewar, his team and members of Edinburgh Council to have a look round the Royal High School? No one yet knew where – or what – the new Scottish Parliament would be. All they did know was the Royal High was the obvious starting point. 'We assume that [you] will wish to minimise costs,' the briefing for incoming Ministers had declared, 'not to exceed (and perhaps not even to match) Westminster standards ... [the Royal High] is available under the City of Edinburgh Council's ownership and we assume that [you] will want that to be the Parliament building.'[6] Despite problems of space and flexibility, the High School offered two – very obvious – advantages. 'Use of the building would avoid a potentially difficult debate about alternative sites,' the paper had stated sagely, 'and it is likely, in the short term, at least to be cheaper than purpose built new accommodation.'[7]

Whatever the advantages of the Royal High, however, by mid-May the option was coming under question. Under the high-speed timetable set by Labour, the building seemed the cheapest – probably only – credible option. But both practicality and politics raised issues for the 'obvious' choice. Within the Scottish Office, fears were raised that 'gut feeling' alone couldn't justify recommendation – perhaps 'political' reasons should be given over economic ones.[8] And already, the political will was not turning out as had been thought. 'Resigned acceptance' – rather than enthusiasm for the building – was the message coming back from new Ministers.[9] And Donald Dewar, it seemed, had got reservations of his own. Over the last years of Conservative rule, he had come to associate Calton Hill with increasingly depressing journeys from Edinburgh's Waverley Station to St Andrew's House, an A-listed building dating from 1939, which sat across and along the road from the Royal High. St Andrew's House had been office to Tory Secretary of State for Scotland Michael Forsyth. And for Dewar, the entire area was now not the symbol of the bright new beginning he had spent so much of his career fighting for, but the physical embodiment of everything that had been wrong with the past.

After two hours of touring the Royal High to assess its potential, one thing would become absolutely obvious. Regardless of Dewar's personal prejudices, the Royal High School was too small, too expensive to maintain, and had appalling disabled access. 'I suppose the overriding view which he came to very very quickly,' John Gibbons would tell the Holyrood film crew, '[was] that moving to the Royal High School or St Andrew's House was going backwards. And it was really at that time that he did – or we – coined the phrase "the new beginning". And that really cemented in to the whole approach at the time, to finding a new home for the Scottish Parliament – that it had to be symbolic of a new beginning.'

As the publication of the devolution White Paper came closer, the inadequacies of the Royal High School were increasingly highlighted in the press. Magnus Linklater, chairman of the Scottish Arts Council, was the first to argue that the building was too cramped, too confrontational and entirely symbolically wrong for a modern devolved parliament. Perhaps, he suggested, an international architectural competition to design a new building would be the best option.[10] By the time that Dewar publicly announced on 16 July that that was precisely what would happen, the Scottish press was resoundingly on side. But two journalists sensed potential problems in the way the news was being put forward. Neil Baxter, writing for the *Herald*, argued that the necessity of a new building had clearly been realised some time ago, claiming, 'The public relations process of weaning us away from the Royal High . . . has been careful. The Press has been led around as if it were a privilege and allowed to point their cameras at the building's manifold inadequacies.' In *The Scotsman*, Iain Macwhirter had different worries. 'It's unfortunate that no-one thought to prepare the ground . . . for this announcement a little more carefully,' he argued bluntly. 'If the Royal High School really was inadequate in 1979, why has it taken this long to realise that another venue would be necessary?' Those in the know may well have realised all along that the building wasn't suitable. The problem was that the Scottish public had not.[11]

Behind the doors of the Scottish Office, Dewar's trip to the Royal High School had certainly triggered a rethink. Before the visit, broad alternatives had been tentatively 'sketch[ed] out'.[12] By 6 June, the options were starting to take shape.[13] And within a week, the goalposts were starting to settle. 'If there is to be a change from the generally held assumption that the Parliament will meet in the [High School],' a minute of 12 June stated, 'it would clearly be desirable . . . to announce a decision . . . in the White Paper or at least before the referendum.'[14] Within days, Donald Dewar's aspirations would be clear. 'The Secretary of State noted that a new building would make an impact on public perception,' a minute of 16 June recorded, 'and would help to symbolise the new approach which was being taken to Government in Scotland.'[15] In the evolving devolution White Paper, a brief change would highlight a seismic shift in approach. Under a section blandly headed 'Accommodation', the call for the Royal High was placed in parentheses. The new title? 'A Home Fit for a Parliament.'[16]

By late September 1997, with the referendum delivering a decisive endorsement of devolution, the search for the parliament's headquarters stepped up. A site search had already been underway in conjunction with City of Edinburgh Council officials,[17] and with Calton Hill, Haymarket and Leith now on the shortlist, consultants Jones Lang Wooton were brought in to provide fuller advice. Holyrood – the eventual winner – was already out of the running. Several options within the area had been considered, but with some land unavailable and the rest thought 'very constrained', the decision had been taken to ditch it. For one observer though, the location had seemed rich in potential, and the suggestion was made that an eye should be kept on the site. Despite this enthusiasm, it was clearly not a view shared by everyone. 'In general,' declared a minute in mid-August, 'it was not felt that [the location] had the scope to meet the needs of the new Parliament.'[18] Within weeks, all that was set to change.

In September 1997, a chance meeting on the Glasgow–Edinburgh train would alter the entire course of events. John Clement, a striped-shirted, smartly dressed commercial surveyor with D. M. Hall, was returning from Glasgow when he fell into conversation with passengers from the Scottish Office and the government's property procurement arm PACE.[19] The search for a parliament site – he heard – was hitting problems, and as the conversation unfolded, an obvious solution would emerge.

Clement had a long-standing, non-retained business relationship with Gordon Izatt, Scottish and Newcastle's group property director. Furthermore, he knew that the company had been undergoing modernisation throughout the 1990s and was potentially looking to relocate. An urban regeneration plan was already underway in the area for which Scottish and Newcastle had donated land, and with access due to be closed up as part of the strategy, traffic would be redirected – a potential security advantage for a parliament building. Any normal development at Holyrood would face problems. A royal palace sat just across the road, raising serious limitations on how the brewery land could be developed; and with the brewery in the middle of a UNESCO world heritage site, planning restrictions on the area were likely to be tight. Scottish and Newcastle's Chief Executive too had been man and boy at the location, and only a very, *very* good reason would persuade him to move. What better reason could there be, Clement wondered, than the building for the new Scottish Parliament?

The more Clement thought about the problem, the more his solution seemed to offer the answers. Before 1997, Scottish and Newcastle had bought Queensberry House, a Grade B-listed seventeenth-century town house on the edge of the Holyrood site to help bail out the trust which owned it. Incorporating this into the area, the company now owned a suitable-sized piece of land. Scottish and Newcastle's own buildings were not listed, so could easily be demolished. And the brewery's location, under the shadow of Salisbury Crags and on the edge of Holyrood Park, offered both a dramatic and historic backdrop for what could clearly become an iconic building. Holyrood, certainly, had potential. The only question was, could John Clement persuade Scottish and Newcastle to part with the land?

When he raised the issue with Gordon Izatt, Clement inquired if it would be appropriate to promote the property to the Scottish Office. Izatt, though, was wary of being drawn into a political and media minefield, and refused to make any initial move himself. If the Scottish Office wanted to come to him and talk about Holyrood, however, he would be willing to consider the options. With Scottish and Newcastle chairman Alistair Grant 'blacklisted' as someone Donald Dewar would not ring up due to his anti-devolution stance, it was clear some mediation was required to get the two sides together. How, wondered John Clement, could it be done?

The solution was for Clement to ring the Scottish Office, and then gradually, skilfully, bring the two sides together. Despite an initial lack of eagerness from civil servants, within a fortnight more information would be requested.[20] And on 8 December 1997, Holyrood would be added to the shortlist. 'Part of <u>historic fabric </u>of town. (Always) Worth having. Now a possibility. So let's include it,' stated a scribbled note on the draft news release. Then, more naively, 'New build – which gives a measure of predictability on costs/timescale.'[21] Ultimately, Holyrood offered everything that Donald Dewar wanted: the chance for a new building on a central, historic site. Despite a strong showing by the St Andrew's House option – which almost tipped the balance back towards Calton Hill – Dewar ultimately could not get past his dreadful memories of meetings there with Michael Forsyth. And in this sense, Dewar's decision *was* political, although it was a reaction against a hated Tory past, not a feared SNP future.

Holyrood was bought for under £4 million, and on 9 January 1998, the official news of its success was made public.[22] Despite the myth that evolved into 'fact' from 1998 onwards, Donald Dewar never called Calton Hill a 'nationalist shibboleth', though it seems he was the man responsible for the 'poke in the eye' jibe. As Alan Robertson of Jones Lang Wooton confided in a *Herald* article of April 1998, 'I've no doubt that if there had been a four acre clear site available on Calton Hill that there would have been no hesitation, Calton Hill would have been the destination for the Parliament.'[23]

So if that was the story behind Holyrood's selection, one question remains. How did the conspiracy theories and rumours of dark political intrigue surrounding the project take hold? The answer lies in the months between Holyrood's re-emergence into the site race, and the parliament's first debate on the building in June 1999. Holyrood's addition to the shortlist had been surprising but, with its historic links, city-centre location and Donald Dewar's clear enthusiasm behind it, it had quickly been installed as a leading contender. The manner of its emergence, however, had raised some questions.

On 8 December 1997, a minute had come down from Dewar's office. The previous afternoon, Holyrood had been added to the shortlist, and instructions were now in hand to make the decision public. 'Ministers decided that the addition of a fourth site . . . should be announced as soon as possible,' the minute had stated, 'so that it did not appear an implausible rabbit from a hat at a later stage.'[24] The damage, it would transpire, had already been inflicted.

Holyrood's inclusion on the shortlist would receive a broad welcome. But in some reports, there were hints that things might not be as transparent as they appeared. 'Just as Calton Hill looked set to get the nod over its two rivals . . .' wrote David Scott in *The Scotsman*, 'Donald Dewar pulled the fourth contender out of the bag.' In the *Herald*, Robbie Dinwoodie's take would be similar. 'At a stroke, a compromise candidate ha[s] emerged from nowhere,' he observed, '– satisfying some of the strongest feelings which ha[ve] polarised the debate between the previous front-runners . . . Calton Hill and . . . Leith.'[25]

In political circles, the focus was somewhat different. On 4 October, the SNP's National Executive Committee had formally backed Calton Hill as the site for the parliament building. 'The Parliament will operate as the heartbeat of the nation,' a press release had stated, 'and must be located in the heart of our capital city. The Calton Hill site . . . is a symbol of Scotland's desire for self-government, and offers scope for exciting development along modern lines . . .'[26] Constitutional affairs spokesman George Reid had prepared a report on the shortlisted locations, and – unsurprisingly – the SNP's favourite had come out on top.[27] In the document's preamble, emerging tensions around the site issue had been apparent. 'In the course of the Referendum, the Secretary of State repeatedly stressed the need for consensus,' the report had argued, '. . . Since the Referendum result, [he] has – unlike the Secretary of State for Wales – declined to continue any formal mechanism for consultation'.[28]

By 17 October, with Dewar having agreed to political opponents taking part in discussions, the focus of some on the Calton Hill option would be clear.[29] Donald Gorrie of the Liberal Democrats was pleased by developments. 'This is a victory for public opinion over private briefing,' he declared memorably. 'I welcome the news that Donald Dewar hasn't plunged into Leith docks and I am quite sure that he will be satisfied that Calton Hill could house a working parliament.'[30] For the Scottish Nationalists, Dewar's 'concession' was equally welcome. 'The SNP will enter into these consultations in a positive manner and will present the strong case that a consensus can be built,' responded George Reid, 'for Calton Hill.'[31] Only the Tories would sound a sour note on proceedings. 'It's not the business of Oppositions to try to extract Secretaries of State from holes of their own making,' grumbled constitutional affairs spokesman Michael Ancram. 'I find it quite staggering that, at this stage, Donald Dewar and his colleagues are still undecided about where the Scottish parliament should be.'[32]

By 23 October, a briefing ahead of the consultation had gone to Dewar. In a very tight timescale, with both SNP and Liberal Democrats backing Calton Hill, the risks of delay or public disagreement were obvious worries.[33] Yet an additional factor was beginning to emerge in the wings. Three weeks earlier, a letter had arrived from John Clement, and, in it, Clement had confirmed that a potential four-acre site might be available on Holyrood Road.[34] By 15 October further information had been requested, and a day later a meeting had been held to gauge Historic Scotland's views.[35] Within a fortnight, Clement was updating Gordon Izatt. 'It would appear that they are wishing to keep Holyrood Road in the "background" and let the press and public speculation continue to concentrate on Leith and Calton Hill,' he wrote. 'They have realised that your site has substantial benefits and potential and are continuing to do their own work and research on it . . .'[36]

The emergence of Holyrood had come at the worst possible time for consensual politics. With press speculation intense, opposition pressure on, the site still not a formal 'runner', and potential negotiations for Scottish and Newcastle's new home likely to be damaged by fevered publicity, it was clear that Holyrood was not yet an option for open discussion. Yet in the political world, a move promoting consultation was being announced. By 3 December, the new option site would seem possible, and a minute was looking forward to what might be done. 'Our current assessment is that [Holyrood] ought to be feasible . . .' the minute stated. 'We need to consider with Ministers whether, and if so how and when, to bring it into the public domain and how to manage the reactions of other interested parties.'[37] If Holyrood wasn't a political stitch-up that would soon run into serious problems, it was certainly doing a good job of looking like it was.

Or was it? Although political opposition to Holyrood had always been inevitable, in the wider world there were other powerful factors at work. Within Edinburgh, the Calton Hill site was still clearly a favourite, and there was disappointment and anger that public and architects felt excluded from playing a role. Commentators, newspapers, political opponents and interested parties all had strong opinions on the subject, and with the situation apparently going from bad to worse, almost every aspect of the parliament building was up for debate.

Both Holyrood and Miralles offered rich pickings. The selection of the brewery site would beg the obvious question of whether the Scots could organise a 'piss up' in one,[38] and Miralles' eccentric descriptions of his design invited snappy quipping – or snide comment – from those inclined to give it. During 1998, reports concluded that the parliament would be sited 'under a capsized Spanish trawler', that Dewar must hope that 'Miralles' boats don't turn out to be Labour's Titanic', that the theme was 'a metaphor for shipwreck, a capsized constitution and Titanic economic decline', and that Enric's design was 'one hull of an idea'.[39] All of this was par for the course and mostly harmless. But on a project that was to last far longer than typical news stories tended to run, and in a political environment where soundbites could have devastating impact, comments of this sort would have a hugely damaging cumulative effect.

Pithy opinion would prove a powerful weapon. On 15 January 1998, Tory councillor Brian Meek had written an article in the *Herald*. In it, he argued that there was no prominent professional figure supporting the Holyrood option, and that Donald Dewar had been operating the 'ABCH agenda –

anywhere but Calton Hill'.[40] It was a superb soundbite – and it was one that was also shared with the pro-Calton Hill SNP.

In March, with a row erupting over whether the temporary parliament should be housed in Edinburgh or Glasgow, the SNP's George Reid would volunteer the following. 'The Strathclyde House option has been thrown in like Holyrood was, so that the Scottish Office can stick to their ABC line – Anywhere But Calton Hill.'[41] In October, the phrase would emerge again – this time in connection with the cost issue.[42] And on 17 June 1999, it would be heard during the first Holyrood debate. 'We know that the attitude of the First Minister was ABC,' the party's Fergus Ewing would declare in the chamber, 'anywhere but Calton Hill.'[43] The slogan was no longer the shared opinion of Holyrood critics. Now, it was political fact.

As the Holyrood project developed, it would become almost impossible to separate views which had originated in the newspapers and been politically adopted, or political views which had been reported in the papers and become 'truth'. In the media too, the story of Holyrood could look very varied. In January 1998, the *Herald* would report the following: 'Scottish architects, in conjunction with a leading international partnership, are seen as the best bet to win the design award for the new parliament at Holyrood.'[44] In the *Sunday Times*, the message had been somewhat different. 'Although Scottish architects will be encouraged to apply,' it declared, 'Dewar is determined the design should be world-class.' 'The design is expected to stand favourable comparison with the most distinctive buildings in Scotland . . . However, it is unlikely to be designed by a Scot.'[45]

By spring 1999, just weeks before the parliament was due to debate Holyrood's future, the situation was both damaging and misleading. 'Halt Holyrood,' screamed a *Scottish Daily Mail* campaign, while the *Sunday Times* had declared, 'Spare us the Holyrood cringers who don't want Scotland to stand tall.'[46] 'What I am trying to do now is to understand the Dr Jekyll and Mr Hyde logic at work here,' explained Enric Miralles,[47] while

for his Edinburgh colleagues the situation was utterly demoralising. There seemed, explained John Gibbons, 'a campaign to
feed into the public domain all sorts of erroneous information',
while Brian Stewart was 'not sure really [of] the source [of it] –
whether it's political or what it is. And really, because it's so
extreme it's actually quite difficult to counter.' For another colleague, misinformation was causing great frustration. 'The way
the escalations in cost have zoomed up and down – it's almost
as if we're not here,' he explained. 'I don't know where half of
the information appears from . . . I don't know, in percentage
terms, there must be 70 per cent of the information out there is
just absolute garbage. But I don't know where it comes from, or
how it gets out into the market.' 'You can sense from that that
it's very difficult from our side to keep the team motivated,'
John Gibbons told the Holyrood film crew ahead of the debate.
'It's crucial that the work continues, the programme continues.
This is still a tight programme. We have to maintain that
progress, yet at the same time, we have to deal with a lot of
extraneous flak.' Scotland's new parliament – 300 years in the
coming – was only a few weeks old. And already, its new home
at Holyrood was shrouded in myth.

Notes

1. *Scottish Office News Release* no. 0029/98, 'Scottish Parliament to be built
   at Holyrood; Dewar opts for new building in historic heart of
   Edinburgh', 9 January 1998, http://www.scotland.gov.uk, http.www.
   holyroodinquiry.org
2. Catherine MacLeod and Murray Ritchie, 'Dewar set to be first among
   equals', *Herald*, 7 January 1998.
3. Alex Salmond to Donald Dewar, Letter, 7 January 1998,
   http://www.holyroodinquiry.org
4. Donald Gorrie to Henry McLeish, Letter, 23 January 1998, ibid.
5. Donald Gorrie to Donald Dewar, Letter, 6 January 1998, ibid.
6. Robert Gordon, *Labour: Briefing for Incoming Ministers. Additional
   Costs of the Scottish Parliament: Accommodation, Staffing and Related
   Costs*, pts 4,10, May 1997, ibid.
7. Ibid, pt 10.
8. Brian Peddie, *Minute: Accommodation aspects of a Scottish Parliament*,
   pts 3–5, 19 May 1997, ibid.

9. Robert Gordon, e-mail, 19 May 1997, ibid.

10. Magnus Linklater, 'Scotland deserves a bonnier House', *The Times*, 17 May 1997.

11. Neil Baxter, 'A cornerstone for the nation's pride', *Herald*, 21 July 1997; Iain Macwhirter, 'Let's build a parliament', *The Scotsman*, 17 July 1997. The issues raised by both journalists were confirmed in a Constitution Group minute of 8 July 1997. 'If we are asked directly whether we intend to site the Parliament in the Old Royal High School, it may be difficult not to give the game away . . . [Edinburgh Council] would probably not welcome a tour around ORHS whilst the Secretary of State pointed out all its defects – indeed they might object altogether so would need careful handling in any event . . . Ministers will want to consider whether they do want to appear completely to kill off ORHS before all the options have been considered – it may seem a little premature. It would also put us at a disadvantage in negotiating with, say, Forth Ports over a site in Leith.' Paul Grice, *Minute: Announcements on Possible Location of Scottish Parliament Building*, pts 4, 7, 9, 8 July 1997, http://www.holyroodinquiry.org

12. Alistair Brown, *Minute: Accommodation Aspects of a Scottish Parliament*, para. 1, 20 May 1997, http://www.holyroodinquiry.org

13. Alistair Brown, *Minute: Accommodation Aspects of a Scottish Parliament*, 6 June 1997, ibid.

14. Alistair Brown, *Minute: Accommodation Aspects of a Scottish Parliament*, para. 2, 12 June 1997, ibid.

15. Alistair Brown, *Minute: Accommodation Aspects of a Scottish Parliament*, para. 4, 16 June 1997, ibid.

16. Isabelle Low, *Minute: Scotland White Paper – Revised Section on Accommodation and Costs*, para. 10.11, 13 June 1997, ibid. According to earlier minutes, sections in parentheses indicated policy matters not yet agreed by DSWR. A minute of 27 June, however, suggested the same method of using parentheses reflected 'the fact that we are still working on details on possible options'. Isabelle Low, *DSWR briefing paper*, p. 2 pt 2, 27 June 1997, ibid.

17. The role of Edinburgh City Council in the site search was uncovered in detail during the Fraser Inquiry.

18. Iain Cane, *Draft Minutes: Scottish Parliament building – Meeting between the Scottish Office and City of Edinburgh Council, Annex B (Sites put forward for consideration but ruled out)*, pt 10, 13 August 1997, http://www.holyroodinquiry.org

19. Evidence given to the Fraser Inquiry suggested that this meeting took place on 25 September 1997, and clarified the identities of all those involved. Anthony Andrew, 'Fraser Inquiry: Letter of Clarification', pt 288, 2003, ibid.

20. John Gibbons, *Minute covering Mr Clement's Letter on Holyrood Road*, annotated by Alistair Brown and Anthony Andrew, 6–8 October

1997, ibid; John Clement to Anthony Andrew, Letter, 16 October 1997, ibid.

21. Andrew Baird, *Draft News Release – Holyrood added to Shortlist*, 8 December 1997, ibid.

22. Archie Rintoul to Alistair Brown, Fax: Scotland's Parliament: Appraisal of Holyrood Site, 6 January 1998, ibid.

23. Quoted in Stewart Mcintosh, 'A chance meeting on the Glasgow–Edinburgh train resulted in the current site being chosen; how to swing a parliament', *Herald*, 23 April 1998.

24. Kenneth Thomson, *Minute: Scottish Parliament Building*, 8 December 1997, http://www.holyroodinquiry.org

25. David Scott, 'Dewar's dark horse may win by a head in the final straight', *The Scotsman*, 9 December 1997; Robbie Dinwoodie, 'Dewar unveils fourth parliament site; late starter is instant favourite', *Herald*, 9 December 1997.

26. *SNP News Release*, 4 October 1997.

27. *Scotland's Parliament: First Report of the SNP Constitutional Affairs Committee on the Location of the Parliament*, 14 October 1997, http://www.holyroodinquiry.org. The material describing Alex Salmond's objections to Holyrood's selection is sourced from his evidence given to the Fraser Inquiry, 13 November 2003.

28. *Scotland's Parliament: First Report of the SNP Constitutional Affairs Committee on the Location of the Parliament*, p. 2, 14 October 1997, ibid.

29. Consultation had been recommended to Dewar by his civil servants two days earlier. Alistair Brown, *Minute: Scottish Parliament Building: Site Selection – Next Steps, Handling and Media Issues*, para. 3, 15 October 1997, ibid.

30. Quoted in Rob Robertson and John McEachran, 'Delay hits choice of Home Rule site', *The Scotsman*, 17 October 1997.

31. Quoted in Rob Robertson and Frances Horsburgh, 'Dewar to brief SNP, Lib Dems and Tories on three options of sites for the Scottish parliament; building on a consensus', *Herald*, 18 October 1997.

32. Quoted in 'Invitation to join parliament site talks dismissed', *Dundee Courier*, 18 October 1997.

33. Paul Grice, *Minute: Meeting with Opposition Parties to Discuss Location*, para. 3, 23 October 1997, http://www.holyroodinquiry.org

34. John Clement to John Gibbons, Letter, 3 October 1997, ibid.

35. John Clement to Anthony Andrew, Letter, 16 October 1997, ibid; Anthony Andrew, *Minute: Scotland's Parliament – Holyrood – Historic Scotland*, 16 October 1997, ibid.

36. John Clement to Gordon Izatt, Letter, 29 October 1997, ibid.

37. Alistair Brown, *Minute: Scottish Parliament Building – Choice of Location*, pt. 6, 3 December 1997, ibid.

38. Pat Kane, 'The mad House; no, it's not a joke. Scotland's new parliament is going to be in a brewery. But it gets worse', *The Guardian*, 14

January 1998; Dorothy-Grace Elder, 'Rattling the cages: Edinburgh has to be Royal Miles better this time', *Scotland on Sunday*, 11 January 1998; Margo MacDonald, 'Parliament's big day out turning into dog's dinner', *Edinburgh Evening News*, 23 March 1999.

39. Jeremy Hodges, 'Touch and glow in the scrum', *Scottish Daily Mail*, 18 September 1998; 'When Dewar's boat comes in', *Edinburgh Evening News*, 6 July 1998; Gerald Warner, 'Hague boxes clever to leave Blair reeling in sleaze row', *Scotland on Sunday*, 12 July 1998; Chris Deerin, 'My design is one hull of an idea', *Daily Record*, 7 July 1998.

40. Brian Meek, 'Undaunted', *Herald*, 15 January 1998.

41. Douglas Fraser, 'Glasgow to house first parliament', *Sunday Times*, 1 March 1998.

42. William Clark, 'Labour brought to book over fears of £200m Holyrood', *Scottish Daily Mail*, 26 October 1998.

43. *Scottish Parliament Official Report*, vol. 1, no. 10, cols 542, 543, 17 June 1999, http://www.scottish.parliament.uk

44. Robbie Dinwoodie, 'Scots firms seen as best bet to win parliament design award', *Herald*, 27 January 1998.

45. Ian Hernon and Stephen McGinty, 'Holyrood site lures world's top architects', *Sunday Times*, 25 January 1998.

46. Elizabeth Quigley, 'The unacceptable price of Holyrood: as contracts for new parliament building are frozen over expense fears, the *Mail* launches a campaign urging politicians to think again', *Scottish Daily Mail*, 10 June 1999; Kenny Farquharson, 'Spare us the Holyrood cringers who don't want Scotland to stand tall', *Sunday Times*, 30 May 1999.

47. Patricia Nicol, 'That Holyrood deadline? Mañana', *Sunday Times*, 30 May 1999.

3

Client and Costs

'We have a unique opportunity to create a new democracy – let's not blow
it now.'
Canon Kenyon Wright, Chair of Executive Committee, Scottish
Constitutional Convention[1]

IN THE SUMMER of 1999, with the handover complete
between Donald Dewar and the SPCB, responsibility for
Holyrood now lay largely in the experienced hands of Sir
David Steel. Joint chair of the Scottish Constitutional
Convention and one of the UK's leading politicians, Steel – like
Dewar – had been one of the few 'big names' at Westminster to
put themselves forward for election to Scotland's new parliament. His pride in the institution's birth and high hopes for the
future were clear when he accepted the historic Claim of Right
on behalf of the Scottish Parliament in June. 'The views of the
people of Scotland have been listened to,' he stated, 'and I hope
that the Parliament will live up to the many aspirations and
expectations placed on it.'[2]

In many ways, Dewar and Steel could not have been more
different. Steel was small and sharp-suited while Dewar was
gangling and scruffy; but both men had come to the Holyrood
parliament project via unexpected routes. Dewar's early
involvement with the parliament building had been prompted
less by an interest in architecture than a passion for Scottish
politics. Indeed, during the initial stages of planning for
Holyrood, he appeared to have displayed little interest in
design and still less awareness of exactly what such a project
might cost. As some of his allies in devolution conceded, it

seemed Dewar's greatest concern was that the new parliament
building should neither be thought too expensive, nor too
flashy. It was an anxiety echoed by David Steel in July 1997,
when he cautioned the new Labour government against 'the
dangers of grandiose extravagance' for the Scottish
Parliament's new premises. While Dewar had initially been
happy with the idea of constructing a simple office block to
house the new democracy, however, Steel's solution to the
problem had been entirely different – and surprisingly lateral.
Although Calton Hill's Royal High School was clearly inadequate for the purposes of a new Scottish Parliament, would it
not be cheaper – he suggested – to bore a tunnel between the
Royal High and St Andrew's House across the road, than start
from scratch with a new building?[3]

Steel's involvement in architecture had been predicted early
by an unexpected source. As a seventeen-year-old schoolboy in
Edinburgh, a family friend had organised an astrological
reading based on his birth chart. The results, he explained to
Holyrood's documentary crew, had been extraordinary. The
age at which he would marry was forecast accurately, as was his
future involvement in public life. But one prediction stood out
from all the others as 'complete nonsense'. The reading predicted that Steel would have an interest in architecture, and it
was the one part of the chart that both he and his wife would
dismiss as utterly ridiculous. But forty-four years later, the
Scottish Parliament's Presiding Officer would receive a massive
surprise. Along with his new role came the chairmanship of
the SPCB, or Scottish Parliamentary Corporate Body, the
board responsible for the financing and running of Scotland's
new parliament. And along with the SPCB's workload came an
extra and unexpected responsibility: the creation of Scotland's
new parliament building at Holyrood.

The SPCB itself was a cross-party body made up of
members from each of the main political parties. All four
members had been surprised by the late addition of Holyrood
to the list of their responsibilities, and few had much idea of
what the stewardship of the new parliament building would

actually entail. Not a single member of the SPCB had professional experience in the construction, building management
or architectural industries. And as Robert Brown – Liberal
Democrat member of the group – confided, he had little
notion of what the SPCB would do once it was in place. As he
explained, 'I had very little idea . . . of what it was and what
its role was. I assumed I was being put on it as some sort of
lawyerly thing from my occupation as a solicitor . . .'[4] With all
the major decisions on the parliament building already made
and the SPCB assigned a huge number of new responsibilities
– not to mention their duties as MSPs – a project as complex
and high profile as the new Scottish Parliament building was
the last thing that should have been entrusted to, effectively, a
bunch of amateurs. Or as Tory SPCB member John Young
rather more forcefully put it, 'we had just come in here as
members of the Scottish Parliament with a pretty full workload . . . plus all these other duties; and then to be landed with
that! Whoever thought that one up needed their minds looked
at, to be quite blunt.'

The failure – or perhaps unwillingness – of some of the
SPCB's members to grasp the key responsibilities of Holyrood
over the coming years would cause the Scottish Parliament
building untold and ongoing damage. But what was equally
worrying was the secrecy in which this client body cloaked the
project. During the years it was in charge of the building
project, the SPCB refused virtually every request for access to
its deliberations by the Holyrood documentary team, and the
crew was allowed just a few minutes' 'privileged access' to
record the group's first meeting with parliament architect
Enric Miralles.[5] Finally, over twelve months after contact was
first attempted, the team was granted admission to film the
SPCB together.[6] As the camera was shadowed round the table
by the parliament's press officers, it was made very clear that
documentary access was *not* welcome. A press officer counted
to sixty, and then the team was shut out.

For a parliament whose watchwords were openness and
accessibility, it seemed the body charged with stewarding the

Holyrood building was determined to keep its deliberations out of the public gaze. Despite this however, SPCB SNP member Andrew Welsh argued in March 2000, 'We believe [the Holyrood project] is a matter that should be independently investigated and openly discussed and questioned.'[7] Quite how this could be fully achieved, when no one was allowed to see them at work and no group member had yet granted an interview to those charting the story of the building, was open to question. For the SPCB, it seemed, its conclusions may well be public, but its deliberations remained fiercely guarded and private. As an interview with Andrew Welsh would suggest once it *was* finally permitted, his stated commitment to openness was perhaps more restrictive than he had implied. 'Can you give us some kind of insight into what goes on [in your meetings]?' asked documentary producer Stuart Greig. Welsh's immediate reaction? 'No!'[8]

The SPCB's chairman Sir David Steel, however, was happy to speak publicly about the Holyrood building, and it was clear from early on that he was keen to take the project forward in what he believed was the best way possible. Despite his own 'uninformed' preference for a Calton Hill parliament, by the time the SPCB took the project over in June 1999 it was his belief that the issue of site selection was water under the bridge. Like Donald Dewar, Steel's own personal vision of what a new Scottish Parliament should be had undergone something of a metamorphosis since the early days of discussion. Now, he believed, 'a new parliament deserves a new building, and I think a make-do arrangement in an old building would not have been satisfactory'. It was this change in perception of what the new parliament's home should be – plus the firming-up of costs associated with it – that would be two of the key factors in the project's enormous rising costs in the public arena. But there were also other crucial and complicating factors at play. And these did not have anything at all to do with progress on the Holyrood building itself.

The public saga of the parliament building's rising costs

effectively began on 9 January 1998, when Donald Dewar unveiled Holyrood as the devolved government's permanent home. The press release accompanying the announcement stated, 'the independent cost consultants advised that a new Parliament building would cost around £50m and that converting St Andrew's House would cost around £65m. VAT and fees would need to be added to these figures to produce final costs as would site acquisition at the new build sites.' The final cost of the parliament at Holyrood, however, was harder to predict. It would, the press release stated, 'depend on the final design, the fees negotiated with the successful architect and the outcome of the competition between developers actually to construct the building'.[9] It was an announcement that would set a train of events in progress which would all but destroy the Holyrood building – and the new parliament – in the public's eyes over the years to come.

Political critics had been following the costs of the proposed project closely. In the devolution White Paper, the government had stated that the cost of Scotland's new parliament building would depend on its eventual site – and on the funding method chosen. The range of figures expressed was between £10 million and £40 million, and few of devolution's opponents believed they would be met. Three days after the Holyrood announcement was made, Old Labour stalwart Tam Dalyell voiced the anger of many, 'Throughout the referendum campaign, some of us asked disbelievingly about the £40 million limit', he stated in the Commons. 'Up it goes.'[10] The Tories' Michael Ancram agreed. For him, the key question was this: had Dewar known that the figures in the White Paper were inaccurate, and if so, why had he not come clean during the referendum campaign? Or was the real truth worse – that the Secretary of State was so badly advised that he had been unaware of a cost rise that had been crystal clear to everybody else. The cost of the new Scottish Parliament had been one of a number of issues on which the Tories had been accused of scaremongering during the referendum campaign. And now, Ancram argued, it looked like all their warnings were turning out to be true.[11]

However, Scotland's newspapers adopted a more sympathetic stance. Although the Glasgow-based *Scottish Daily Mail* had marked the approach of the White Paper with a warning that taxpayers throughout Britain were set to pick up the bill for the new parliament – a bill which it estimated as 'expected to reach at least £50m'[12] – devolution in Scotland was generally producing a buoyant national mood. The day prior to the *Mail*'s warning, *The Scotsman* had reported that a new site – rather than the Royal High – was understood to be the favoured option for the parliament's home, although the higher cost may make it politically unattractive.[13] Within days, a flurry of articles appeared in support of a new building. *The Scotsman*'s Iain Macwhirter argued, 'If devolution is worth doing at all, it is worth doing properly . . . One of our worst characteristics as a nation is our tendency toward penny-pinching pettiness.'[14] In the *Herald*, Ruth Wishart and Neil Baxter also came down on the side of a new build. Baxter, although raising serious questions about a building in the capital and a Europe-wide competition to design it, argued, 'If the Government, and the people, truly believe that they want their own parliament, surely we can find £50m or whatever it might cost to demonstrate to the world that we really mean it.'[15] For Wishart though, the nay-sayers raised a more fundamental question about Scottish small-mindedness. 'Are we so bloody mean,' she wondered, 'that all we can say when faced with our own parliament – our own monument to our own democratic future – is how much?'[16]

As the months passed, however, speculation about the costs of the parliament building began to mount. The bodies promoting both Leith and Calton Hill stressed that their schemes could be brought in for below the £40 million top figure outlined. Yet increasingly, it looked like this total was no longer within aim. 'Informed sources' had told the *Daily Mail* that the high costs of Calton Hill meant it was now out of the question. Leith, at £47 million, looked more likely.[17] The Scottish Liberal Democrats responded by urging Dewar to use cash from the millennium fund if more was needed to build at Calton Hill.

But Dewar argued that the government was looking for value for money from any parliament building, and he remained keen that costs remained within the £40 million budget. Despite this, the Leith and Calton Hill options were, he stated, 'a bit on the low side', and he argued that any costings must be related to what would actually be delivered.[18] The goalposts were clearly beginning to shift, and expectations of what the new parliament building could be were starting to rise among those making the decisions. Alexander Linklater's warning in the *Herald* on 20 September 1997 was already proving prophetic: 'Be afraid, be very afraid . . . when you hear Donald Dewar say that the new Scottish parliament building will . . . cost a mere £30–40m . . .' he argued. 'This is what people say when they've never been an architect's client and haven't given public building more than a passing thought.'[19]

By October 1997, however, the realities of procuring a Scottish parliament building were clearly beginning to dawn. On 17 October, Dewar announced that further information would be needed before moving forward, and less than three weeks later the Commons was told that feasibility studies and costings had been commissioned for each of the three proposed sites.[20] These, it was believed, should produce a more realistic estimate of what the costs of a new parliament building might be. By early December, Holyrood had been added to the list, and the costs were starting to rise. The unveiling of the feasibility studies had coincided with another announcement: the building would have to be bigger. And a bigger building would mean a lot more money.

The parliament feasibility studies had indicated that Haymarket, Holyrood and Leith would all cost around £50 million to construct, before VAT, fees, fit out and the cost of the site were added. St Andrew's House, the Calton Hill location, was put at £65 million before extras.[21] These figures were publicly announced on 23 December, but the total, the Scottish Office 'let slip', could be as much as £95 million.[22] According to the *Daily Record*, a Scottish Office news release placing the total cost as 'in the range of £70m–95m' had been swiftly withdrawn and replaced by an assertion that 'the question of costs varies from site to site'.[23] The new 'all-in' total – many newspapers pointed out – now seemed to be more than double the top figure announced in the White Paper five months earlier. While some of Scotland's journalists concentrated on the 'spiral', 'soar' or 'balloon' of the cost rises, others were more pragmatic. *Scotland on Sunday* declared, 'The fact that the estimates are rising . . . should not be a matter of concern. The figure of £40m always seemed too low, whereas £100m has the ring of realism about it.'[24] But a *Scotsman* leader piece took a more cynical view. 'Isn't it amazing,' it asked, 'how wrong you can be about the costs of meeting the requirements of a Scottish parliament . . . [and] how a new, expanded sense of those requirements can mysteriously materialise once the public has been persuaded of the principle?' The government was 'right to think big', it argued, 'But it should also talk straight.'[25]

However, as 1998 dawned, it became clear that the government was not the only one apparently not talking straight – or accurately. In January, confusion about costs was rife in the newspapers, with £50 million, £80 million and £100 million all being quoted as figures for the proposed building. Some journalists stated – correctly – that the total figure released for Holyrood was £50 million plus VAT, fees and site costs. But others referred to a '£50m parliament building', to an £80 million cost that was double the White Paper's top figure, and to a total expected to approach £100 million. Input from political opponents did not help clarify the situation. Dewar himself refused to confirm the £100 million figure, arguing that 'a lot of the costs are open to negotiation. It would be very unwise of me to accept some sort of global figure.'[26] And although his stance could certainly be called politically useful, it was also very true; there is no better way to ensure a cost escalation than to advertise that more money is available. However, a manipulation of the new parliament's costs was beginning to take place – and not just by the government. Its clearest expression would be seen in *The Scotsman* on 28 March. An article by

Graeme Stewart claimed, 'it emerged yesterday that the £50m quoted by the Government for the construction of the building did not take into account VAT and fees. Once these factors are added the bill could rise to £69m.'[27] Stewart was reporting – inaccurately – the story of a hidden price rise. It was a story that the Scottish Office had broken itself with a press release nearly three months earlier.

As the year continued, so did the erroneous and confusing press reports, with £60 million and £200 million now emerging as figures to join the rest. Yet £50 million was now clearly the figure established in the public imagination, and what was becoming very obvious was that this referred to two entirely different things depending on who was using it. For those in the know – or who understood building – it referred to construction costs alone, to which extras would inevitably be added. But to others, it was the parliament building's total budget. With this figure firmly planted in the public imagination, opposition politicians, and some newspapers, now had a potent political weapon to be used in the coming years. As David Steel would confide to the Holyrood film crew in August 1999, Dewar and his team had made a fundamental mistake in underestimating the costs of the new building. 'I think they were determined, understandably, to keep the cost figures down in terms of public presentation . . .' he pondered, '[but] in my view we should never have talked about the construction costs of the building because you can't construct the building without buying the site and paying the architects and all the rest of it. So it was a totally meaningless figure the £50 million that was originally talked about.'

In January 1999, however, Holyrood's costs would be dealt their most shattering blow yet. News of Project Manager Bill Armstrong's departure hit the headlines; and his most damaging reported claim was that the building's true price would be – according to the *Mail* – 'nearer £100m than the £50m originally promised'.[28] Another report put the new costs more conservatively, at nearer £70 million.[29] Despite these various raised figures, the official line remained that the building was still on target for completion to the '£50 million plus' budget, and by the second half of 2001. However, there was now a caveat. John Gibbons publicly stated, 'We can still deliver a building for £50m, but that may not be the best for Scotland.'[30] Privately, he would be more forthcoming. £50 million, £55 million, £60 million, £70 million and £100 million were all possible figures – but each would produce a very different building. What would be needed from the new parliament was political direction and guidance for the level of building they were aspiring to create. 'I would be surprised,' he told the film crew, 'if we were not looking at ultimately a building of £60 million.' For others within Holyrood, however, their 'gut feel' about the project had already led them to more worrying conclusions. One had flagged up concerns that construction costs alone could take Holyrood as high as £95 million, whereas another reasoned that the overall total for everything was unlikely to leave change out of £135 million. Holyrood's costs were about to be publicly revised. But not yet.[31]

With Scotland's new MSPs in place from 6 May, attention was now fully focused on the parliament building's costs. And with public confusion and misinformation rife – and £27 million 'managed out' of the official total – the figures being publicly debated by politicians were increasingly conflated, inaccurate, or downright mischievous. With Scotland's politicians beginning to mutter that they'd rather stay in their temporary accommodation than move to the new building planned at the other end of the road, *Scotland on Sunday*'s William Paul identified exactly what was now going on on all sides. Listing a selection of figures recently quoted in the political and public arenas, his conclusion was the following. 'Select a figure,' he wrote, 'according to your prejudices.'[32]

However, in spite of the enormous difficulties press misrepresentation and political sleight of hand were causing the Holyrood building by June 1999, the handover of such a complex project to a new client body was already raising its own problems. David Steel was clearly keen to see Holyrood's new parliament completed as a building of great national and international eminence, but what was immediately apparent as the SPCB took Holyrood over was that a project as complicated as the Scottish Parliament building was far too difficult a task to be dealt with by politicians, whatever their reputation. Steel maintained that although the current costs of £109 million were still within target, quality – ultimately – should take precedence in any balance between public expenditure and excellence. It was, after all, a building that needed to last for two hundred years. Inevitably, this could lead to increased costs, although none, he claimed in August 1999, were currently foreseen.

But what *was* worrying was that there seemed to be no real understanding that cost and timescale on the project were inextricably linked. Any delay on a building project means money; costs for standing contractors down, costs for prolongation, costs for redesign and even costs simply for keeping the site ticking over. But when asked if the autumn 2001 timescale was realistic, David Steel's response was this: 'I would not worry about being ready to kick off the autumn session of 2001 in the new building. I'd far rather get it right that have people going into a thing that's been rushed at the last minute and find things are not quite right. I would even go so far as to say that if we had to put off moving in till January 2002 I wouldn't cry about that. I mean, what's a month or two difference in a building that's going to last a couple of hundred years?' While his sentiment may have been admirable and was certainly in tune with the criticisms over timescale coming from both the architectural world and certain sections of the parliament, the answer to his question was this: a month or two's difference could cost millions.

Yet client responsibility for Holyrood did not rest entirely with the inexperienced SPCB. Alongside the 'political' client for Holyrood was the 'professional' client, the Holyrood Project Team, headed by Project Sponsor Barbara Doig. Immaculately manicured, swathed in silk scarves and hugely loyal, this civil servant was the 'client representative' with ulti-

mate responsibility for translating the parliament's requirements to the architects, surveyors and the engineers who
would be working on the Holyrood job. It was a complex and
delicate balancing act. In addition to representing MSPs'
needs, Doig was also responsible for ensuring that the new
building would work efficiently for the parliament's clerks, IT
staff, broadcasters and – ultimately – the visiting general
public. On top of all of this, she was the woman charged with
ensuring that Holyrood would be delivered on time, on budget
and to the required standard of quality. It was a Herculean task
with multiple competing pressures. Moreover, as Doig confided, it was a task where all those involved – despite their
differing professional imperatives – had the same ultimate
objective, to get Scotland's first parliament building in 300
years successfully delivered. There would be daily squabbles,
but there was also a great bond of enthusiasm and passion for
getting the building done. As she explained, 'You *have* to be
enthusiastic or you won't deliver a complex project like this,
because it will take every ounce of strength you've got . . .'

However, if the debate on the Holyrood building had highlighted anything, it was the uniquely contradictory demands of
Barbara Doig's role. Part of her job was to supply information
on Holyrood to those politicians who requested it. But any
information she gave out could – and would – ultimately be
used politically against the project she was meant to be stewarding. Doig was caught in a professional Catch-22. And in a highly
political environment, that was a very dangerous place to be.

In August 1999, though, Barbara Doig was upbeat. She was
reassured by the first signs of how the new SPCB would
operate, and it had proved, she said, 'extremely good' in supporting the Project Team's initiatives to improve future communication with Scotland's new MSPs. Another debate on
Holyrood, at this stage, seemed extremely unlikely, and if the
last debate had been anything to go by, it was certainly something to be avoided at all costs. Yet what Doig couldn't possibly
have anticipated in August 1999 was that over the next two
years alone Holyrood would prompt not one more debate, but

four, each more wearying and depressing than the one before. And what she certainly couldn't have foreseen was that within a year, she would become Holyrood's first major casualty. She would not be the last. And by the time she left the project in May 2000, her opinion of the SPCB would have changed beyond all recognition.

Notes

1. Canon Kenyon Wright, Letter to *Sunday Herald*, 7 March 1999.
2. *Parliamentary News Release* no. 0023/1999, 'Sir David accepts "Claim of Right for Scotland" on behalf of the Parliament', 29 June 1999, http://www.scottish.parliament.uk
3. *Lords Hansard*, col. 1536, 24 July 1997, http://www.parliament.the-stationery-office.co.uk/pa/ld/ldhansard.htm
4. Brown suggested that this assumption was probably correct, given the issues that the SPCB had to deal with.
5. At this stage, the film team was unaware of the pattern of restricted access that would emerge, and wrote to thank the Press Office for the additional minutes allowed. It was hoped that this would foster good relations and encourage greater access in the future. This did not transpire. Susan Bain to Andrew Slorance, Letter, 11 June 1999.
6. This footage would be of the SPCB and new Progress Group together. A number of concessions had been made by the film crew to achieve even this limited access. Rather than request to film an entire meeting – which was clearly getting the team nowhere – it asked permission to record archive shots only, in the hope that diplomacy and a foot in the door could lead to greater access. It didn't work. Susan Bain to David Steel, Letter, 6 June, 2000.
7. Quoted in Katrina Tweedie, David Scott and Gary Duncan, 'Miralles warns of greater cost if "interfering" continues', *The Scotsman*, 3 March 2000. Welsh had asked for Scotland's Auditor-General to look into Holyrood.
8. Following gentle prompting, Welsh would give a general description of how the SPCB operated. Individual interviews with the SPCB's Labour, Liberal Democrat and SNP members took place on 11 April 2000, and with Tory member John Young on 8 June.
9. *Scottish Office Press Release* no. 0029/98, 'Scottish Parliament to be built at Holyrood: Dewar opts for new building in historic heart of Edinburgh', 9 January 1998, http://www.scotland.gov.uk, http://www.holyroodinquiry.org
10. *Commons Hansard*, col. 81, 12 January 1998, http://www.parliament.the-stationery-office.co.uk/pa/cm/cmhansrd.htm

11. *Commons Hansard*, cols 37, 38, 12 January 1998, ibid.
12. 'All Britain to pick up the tab for new Scottish parliament building', *Scottish Daily Mail*, 17 July 1997.
13. John Penman, 'Scottish Office to pick up the tab for a new parliament', *The Scotsman*, 16 July 1997.
14. Iain Macwhirter, 'Let's build a parliament', *The Scotsman*, 17 July 1997.
15. Neil Baxter, 'A cornerstone for the nation's pride', *Herald*, 21 July 1997.
16. Ruth Wishart, 'Let's all get out there and grab it', *Herald*, 21 July 1997.
17. William Clark, 'Parliament next door: Ministers come under pressure to back Leith as seat of government', *Scottish Daily Mail*, 23 September 1997.
18. Quoted in Rob Robertson and Frances Horsburgh, 'Dewar to brief SNP, Lib Dems and Tories on three options of sites for the Scottish parliament; building on a consensus', *Herald*, 18 October 1997.
19. Alexander Linklater, *Herald*, 20 September 1997.
20. *Scottish Office Information Directorate*, 'Donald Dewar orders further work on parliament site selection', 17 October 1997, http://www.holy roodinquiry.org; *Commons Hansard*, col. 107, 4 November 1997.
21. *Scottish Office News Release* no. 2110/97, 'Dewar takes parliament information to the people', 23 December 1997, http://www.scotland.gov; DLE's feasibility report revealed that, 'A very rapid and broad assessment of cost' has been undertaken for [Holyrood],' resulting in a figure of £49.5 million. Hugh Fisher, *Executive Summary: Feasibility Report*, 12 December 1997, http://www.holyroodinquiry.org
22. Tom Brown, 'Holyrood is model for future; Shock as build bill hits £95m', *Daily Record*, 24 December 1997.
23. Tom Brown, 'Model ideas for our parliament', *Daily Record*, 24 December 1997.
24. '£100m could well be cheap at the price', *Scotland on Sunday*, 21 December 1997.
25. 'Facing the costs of the parliament', *The Scotsman*, 22 December 1997.
26. Quoted in Peter Macmahon, 'Holyrood? We were just very taken with it', *The Scotsman*, 15 January 1998.
27. Graeme Stewart, 'Dewar's Holyrood dream teams', *The Scotsman*, 28 March 1998.
28. Paul Riddell and Elizabeth Quigley, 'I quit as Holyrood bill soared towards £100m; Donald Dewar faces storm over rising costs of the new parliament', *Scottish Daily Mail*, 16 January 1999.
29. Shirley English, 'Builder alleges £20m overspend', *The Times*, 16 January 1999.
30. Quoted in ibid.
31. Project sponsor Barbara Doig explained to the Fraser Inquiry, 'I and my colleagues judged that we could not translate risk allowances into estimated costs, which were additional to a total estimated cost which already contained a reasonable estimate for contingencies. We did not

feel able to request a budget increase for risks which might not happen. An agreement by Ministers for an additional budget for risk allowances would have . . . encouraged the Design Team and contractors to over-run.' Barbara Doig, 'Precognition', 2003, http://www.holyrood inquiry.org

32. William Paul, 'Cheap option for parliament misses whole point of the history lesson', *Scotland on Sunday*, 30 May 1999.

4

The Architect

Thy sons, Edina, social, kind,
With open arms the Stranger hail;
Their views enlarg'd, their lib'ral mind,
Above the narrow rural vale.
Robert Burns, 'Address to Edinburgh'

WHEN THE NEW Scottish Parliament voted – narrowly – to proceed with Holyrood in June 1999, Enric Miralles greeted the news with a characteristically obscure simile. It was, he told John Gibbons on the phone from Barcelona, like having 'a flower in your arse'. Scotland was giving birth to something beautiful; but the process of doing so was not only unusual, but – for its architect – increasingly painful.

Miralles was a man of inherent contradictions. Highly intelligent with an impish sense of humour, he exuded both enormous intellectual creativity and tremendous naughtiness. He was, in the words of more than one colleague, 'a rascal'. If Miralles could be typified by anything, however, it was his unusual and eclectic offices in Barcelona. Accessed via a claustrophobic, dingy side-street edged with barred windows and corrugated-iron shop fronts, EMBT's enormous wood double doors and tree-lined balconies were an unexpected surprise. The high-ceilinged offices and expensive finishes inside spoke of wealth and success, the paper-strewn desks and jumbled library of enormous industry and curiosity, while the entire feel of the place was pure Miralles. Bathed in warm Spanish sunshine, and flanked by huge wood-shuttered windows, the offices were welcoming, full of mysterious corners, and slightly overwhelming.

For those who loved and admired Miralles, he was an immensely talented conundrum. 'Some of these aspects of his personality you'll never discover why they're there,' confided Holyrood colleague Mick Duncan, 'but they're intriguing.' For others, the architect was quite simply a nightmare, as Holyrood's ex-Project Manager Bill Armstrong would explain. 'In the short time I dealt with him he was either away doing another job somewhere else or he was in Barcelona . . . He was an impossible man to deal with really; and the Scottish Office were not prepared to get a hold of the situation and deal with it.' Miralles was complex, he was simple, he was enormously likeable and he was immensely frustrating. If anywhere helped in understanding him, it was here.

Enric Miralles' involvement with Holyrood began in early 1998, when Secretary of State Donald Dewar announced details of a competition to find the new parliament building's designer. 'We will be looking, in the first instance, for architects with a proven ability in producing buildings of the quality, complexity and sensitivity we are looking for on the Holyrood site,' he stated. 'This is a unique opportunity to create an exciting building . . . of which we and generations to come can be proud. We intend to get it right.'[1]

Whatever Dewar's enthusiasm, however, the prospect of a competition to design the new parliament was met with an extremely mixed response. While some believed that the nation deserved 'a spanking new building for a new political era and a new millennium',[2] others worried that the method chosen meant that this iconic symbol of Scotland was unlikely to be designed by a Scot; and fears were growing that small Scottish practices were being actively excluded. Initially, it had seemed, the method of moving forward had been uncertain. The first announcement of intentions had stated that a *design* competition for the new building was to be held, and the Royal Incorporation of Architects in Scotland had welcomed the news with their own press statement. 'The [RIAS] welcomes the Secretary of State['s] . . . ongoing support for architectural excellence in Scotland . . .' it declared enthusiastically. 'Hopefully, this should be yet another opportunity for Scottish architects to demonstrate their superb abilities.'[3]

Six months later, it would be a very different story. Throughout the early decisions on the project, initial assumptions had turned out to be different to what was eventually wanted, and with a site for the parliament chosen, the form of the contest was now being given detailed thought. 'Design competition', it appeared, had been a catch-all term, and it swiftly became clear that instead the job would be to choose a *designer*.[4] For Donald Dewar, the route offered powerful attractions. A bold statement now would be a firm gesture of political confidence, and by opting for this format he could ensure that Holyrood would get a big-name architect to do the job. With the timescale tight, the benefit of speed was appealing, and it was hoped both architect and client could work together to develop the building. 'There was clear conscious thought given to using a procurement route that would demonstrate to the world that Scotland was re-emerging as a nation,' John Gibbons would later explain to the film team, 'and there was no better way than through attracting the world's greatest designers, if you like, to the competition; and in the process of doing that, you drew attention to the fact that Scotland was re-emerging. And that was the intent.'

On 26 January 1998, the competition to find a designer got underway. 'We expect to receive hundreds of applications from throughout Europe,'[5] Dewar confidently predicted, but, in fact, the competition received just seventy. 'I think the use of competition was not one that most architects would recognise,' RIAS Secretary and Treasurer Sebastian Tombs would argue in April 2000, 'it was not a design competition per se, it was a method of selecting a designer and a design team . . . [and] there were . . . considerable impediments to modest size practices putting their names forward.' For another critic, opinions were couched less diplomatically. 'The competition was a shambles, quite honestly,' he stated, 'it *wasn't* a competition . . . When [the shortlisted] schemes were produced and shown at the Royal Museum . . . what was very clear was none had worked on identical set[s] of conditions. All the sets of drawings were done in a different form. They were incomparable . . . so you weren't comparing like for like.' If the choice of the parliament's site had been controversial, the selection of its designer was about to prove even worse.

On 23 March 1998, the Holyrood selection panel gathered for their first formal meeting. Already, John Gibbons had held discussions with individual members,[6] and as with all major decisions on the parliament building, the process of what was intended had quickly evolved. Three weeks earlier, selection panel member Kirsty Wark had been told that a sift of entries would be done before the session.[7] By 23 March, all that seemed to have changed. 'When I discussed it with the panel members, they were all quite clear that they were not prepared to have somebody else's sifting of the full field of 70,' John Gibbons would later remember, '. . . So in essence I took the 70 [entries] . . . to the panel members, and in a variety of ways all of them saw the 70 . . .'[8]

The change would result in a long and damaging controversy. Miralles had been taken off the list of entries by Bill Armstrong, who had placed him forty-fourth of the seventy firms applying.[9] In the panel's list, Miralles would be in the top twelve. 'I didn't think he had the capacity to do the job,' Armstrong would confide in the film team frankly. 'He didn't have the experience to do the job. He met very little of the criteria that had been set out in the brief for the architect.' By late spring, John Gibbons had visited Barcelona, and returned advising that the practice was busy, and was likely to need help to deliver. 'I think when [John] came back from Enric's practice, he didn't have any doubts that he should be on the shortlist and that indeed he could deliver the Parliament,' one panel member remembered later, 'but I think he thought that perhaps just [as an aid] to working well . . . there might be some help needed. And in the end, every single one of the architects on the shortlist was married to a Scottish architectural practice in some way and I think that gave people the comfort of knowing that there was someone close to home, as well as the lead architect.'[10] In Miralles' case, that office would be RMJM Scotland.

The partnership between Miralles and RMJM would provoke enormous speculation in the public domain, and result in recurring friction between the company's Catalan and Edinburgh directors. RMJM was one of Scotland's largest architectural firms, and had been knocked out of the competition as the numbers were cut from seventeen to twelve. 'It was a marriage made in Hell as far as I would have thought,' Bill Armstrong would explain to the Holyrood film team. 'I mean, these things don't work. I've never come across [a situation] where two sets of architects try to work together where they work reasonably well.' For Sebastian Tombs, however, the arrangement was not that unusual. 'I think . . . the more successful practices internationally achieve competition wins . . . in different locations, different nations, and have then to deliver a project under completely different practising requirements . . .' he would publicly explain. 'So, they would normally form a liaison or link or work with an executive team to deliver a project on the ground, and this is quite a regular occurrence.'[11]

Whatever the protocol of the link-up, RMJM's re-emergence in the competition would provoke years of allegation, claim and rumour, resulting in immense professional damage and personal hurt. Managing Director Brian Stewart was an ex-neighbour of John Gibbons, the company had already designed the Scottish Office headquarters at Victoria Quay, and they appeared to have won the parliament job through the back door. 'I'm quite sure that the selection committee had their own reasons for appointing the architects they did,' one source would tell the documentary team, 'but RMJM were on the case from day one.'

In fact, the formation of the joint venture had been considerably more straightforward. By spring 1998, Miralles' office boasted a large file of letters from Scottish architects, all of them offering help on the Holyrood job. RMJM Scotland was not among them. But Miralles was both shrewd and very determined, and he was passionate about the chance to build Scotland's parliament. He'd been impressed by RMJM's Scottish Office building at Victoria Quay, and recognised that the company would offer him a delivery mechanism in Scotland. RMJM also had a proven track record in government building, and it was Enric Miralles who would make the first approach. For some within the company, the initial reaction to his overtures had been surprisingly muted.

As project architect John Kinsley would tell the film team, there had been a 'kind of ambivalence at that stage about whether we should be playing second string to somebody else'. But Miralles' reputation had gone before him, and as Kinsley explained, 'the opportunities to work with somebody like that don't come around very often'. Brian Stewart and colleague Mick Duncan felt things should be taken further, and Duncan had flown to Barcelona to discuss the job. 'I found that the concept [for the building] was immensely powerful,' he later recalled. 'I found him as a man [an] immensely inspirational, human and communicative person, and I believe that at that time I . . . sensed a good chemistry there, which I believe was an essential prerequisite for setting out on what was a potentially [a] very challenging and professionally demanding project . . . The other important aspect, I believe, was that he believed that in us he detected a very compassionate ally.'[12]

For John Gibbons though, the benefit of hindsight would prove highly instructive. 'I think with all of the partnerships that came forward at the competition stage, there was a sort of interesting perspective on how they would work together,' he would tell the film team in 2001. 'I think at that stage, one tended to really believe that the very positive characteristics of both partnerships would be what would drive them . . . that those strong points would be what would weld the team together. In terms of the arrangements that we supervised and entered in[to] with them, we insisted on there being a joint arrangement – and I don't think even with hindsight we would want to change that . . . But I mean with hindsight, one would say we would . . . certainly not be facing the same problems now had we been more proactive with their organisation.'

In spring 1998, however, with Miralles still entered without RMJM and the designer for the new building undecided, speculation about who would design Scotland's parliament was beginning to mount in the press. Miralles was repeatedly identified as the most avant-garde on the shortlist, and some observers were describing him as a strong contender. In the early stages though, few seemed to believe that he would win. For architectural writer Hugh Pearman, it was 'good to see him getting through to the second round'.[13] To Penny Lewis at the *Sunday Times*, two emerging favourites were Benson Forsyth and RMJM.[14] And even John Gibbons seemed uncertain about who would come out triumphant. 'There is an amazing range of talent,' he observed at the press conference to announce the final five on the shortlist. 'Richard Meier alone has an incredible track record of prizes and awards. Rafael Vinoly is considered to be perhaps the leading architect in the world in terms of design track record.'[15] Miralles, who would prove the clear winner by a significant margin, at this stage seemed to be far from a foregone conclusion.

Yet by June, Miralles was beginning to be widely and publicly rumoured as the contest's front-runner. Perhaps the most 'conceptual' of the design approaches put forward, his drawings were almost impossible to categorise – and the public clearly found them hard to understand. 'I don't like it, I don't like it at all . . .' complained one visitor to the public exhibition. 'But to be fair, it looks like he had to rush to get his idea in.'[16] The short timescale for the competition was certainly raising problems, but there was a familiar issue already compounding the task. On 9 January, the competition's announcement had stressed public involvement.[17] Just five days later, private discussions seemed to qualify its scope. '[The Secretary of State] said he, of course, wanted the public to be informed,' a minute recorded on 14 January, 'but did not want the debate that generated to slow the process down.'[18] Political opponents,

Scottish architects and now the general public could argue with some justification that they were feeling excluded. And the resentment that this was breeding was laying fertile ground for the problems about to unfold.

On 6 July 1998, Enric Miralles – in close partnership with RMJM – was announced as the parliament's winning architect.[19] It was, the selection panel declared, a unanimous decision. 'A lot of people came with kind of landmark buildings,' Donald Dewar would tell the documentary team, 'great monuments to the power, the authority, the mystery of parliamentary government. I don't think – at least I speak personally – that I ever wanted that.' For a parliament that was intended to be 'of the people', the ideal design would need to be non-monumental – just as the site had to fit in among the population, not be elevated above them on a hill. And as panel member Joan O'Connor explained, 'Enric Miralles won that competition not only for his leaves in the landscape [idea], but he won it because he said one thing to Donald Dewar. He said, "After all, parliament is just a different way of sitting together." And that captured my imagination.'

The statement had summed up completely the new form of consensual, accessible politics that the panel had been hoping to achieve. But there were other reasons Miralles had been so successful. Highly charismatic, he had begun one interview by rearranging all the seating to demonstrate the impact that 'sitting together' could have. It was an essential understanding of a political forum where discussion would be paramount. His 'upturned boats' design was reminiscent of Leith, Dewar's original favoured site. And for panel member and broadcaster Kirsty Wark, Miralles' character was itself a bonus. 'People were very empathetic to Miralles,' she remembered, 'in a sense that was a bit of a surprise. It was also a surprise that Donald Dewar really took to [him].' Dewar, famed in part for his brusque no-nonsense Calvinism, was certainly an unusual advocate for the architect. 'I'd have thought perhaps for Donald he'd have been a bit fey,' mused Wark, 'but he kind of appealed to Donald's romantic side as well, I think. But also because he'd done his homework. And Donald appreciated that, and he appreciated what he had to say.'

For one insider, however, the competition had proved a considerable disappointment. On 11 June, just weeks before Miralles' win was decided, Bill Armstrong had sent an unhappy minute to John Gibbons. 'I find it hard to believe that such an allegedly massive architectural talent cannot produce one "approach" which is convincing and acceptable,' he stated. 'If this had been an architectural competition they would all be disqualified for ignoring the brief.'[20] For Gibbons, the worries highlighted a series of misunderstandings. 'I think some of the comments here are only valid in relation to a classical design competition . . .' he would later argue. 'I mean, "ignoring the brief", I do not think the information that was being provided in such a conceptual form was necessarily going to be 100% accurate in translating the brief in terms of precise fit between the brief and the proposals that were being put forward.'[21] For Bill Armstrong, though, it looked like the form of competition had suddenly changed. 'I knew it was a designer competition,' he would explain years later. 'It had now become an architectural competition, in the sense that it was the picture that was going to be selected, in my view.'[22]

In early July 1998, almost everything within Holyrood seemed rosy. Dewar had his signature architect, the parliament's location was settled – if not popular – and the selection panel was certain it had got the right man. However, despite the panel's conviction that Miralles could deliver something spectacular, a series of critical problems was beginning to brew.

The brief for the competition had been based on what were then considered to be appropriate standards of construction; and when the designs put forward had been costed, Miralles' had proved the most economical. However, *none* of the costed designs had come within the £50 million range.[23] As one insider would confide in 2003, the initial price tag for the building had been something of a concern. 'I think Donald was too timid,' they remembered. 'Basically I think he was worried about the Parliament seeming to be too expensive, I think he was worried about the reaction. I also think Donald personally didn't actually have a huge grasp on money.'

Over the coming years, the 'naivety' of the political client – in the initial form of Dewar, but more markedly in the SPCB and wider parliament itself – would prove to be an enormous hurdle for the Holyrood parliament building. The chosen 'designer' route had been intended to allow architect and client to work together closely, to create the most visionary – and practical – parliament possible. However, for that to work successfully, an experienced and competent client was essential – and the Scottish Parliament would consistently prove to be neither. As the years passed, it would be increasingly obvious that the Holyrood building was ruled not by considerations about cost and timescale, but almost entirely by political game-playing. 'The politics of bricks and mortar are very important . . .' Joan O'Connor would later confirm, 'because bricks and mortar are used as the weapons.'

With Miralles and his partners chosen, Bill Armstrong unhappy, a shifting brief, confused public, and speed and politics dictating everything, Holyrood was not off to an auspicious start. The fact that the designer chosen was both cutting edge and unpredictable only made an already complicated situation even more so. More importantly, it would turn out, Miralles would provide a very easy – and conveniently foreign – scapegoat. Yet whatever the problems already stacking up before Holyrood, what no one could have anticipated in July 1998 was the tragedy which would unfold over the coming years. As Enric Miralles' wife, Benedetta Tagliabue, would confide to the Holyrood film crew a year later, '[Architecture] is a profession which is very hard. I hope everything goes well with the Scottish Parliament, but you have to be always very prepared for suddenly having nothing.' Within twelve months, her husband would be dead.

Notes

1. *Scottish Office News Release*, no. 0127/98, 'Secretary of State gets design for Scottish Parliament building underway', 26 January 1998, http://www.scotland.gov.uk, http://www.holyroodinquiry.org

2. 'Dewar did his homework: there are good reasons for choosing Holyrood', *Herald*, 10 January 1998.

3. Draft *Scottish Office Press Release* no. 0916/97, 'Design Competition for new Parliament', 16 July 1997, http://www.holyroodinquiry.org; *RIAS Press Release*, 'Design competition for new parliament', 16 July 1997, ibid.

4. *Minutes: Holyrood Parliament Building*, 14 January 1998 http://www.holyroodinquiry.org; *Minutes: Scottish Parliament Building Steering Group*, 15 January 1998, ibid; *Minutes: Scottish Parliament Building – Site Selection*, paras 11, 12, 23 January 1998, ibid.

5. *Scottish Office News Release*, no. 0127/98, Secretary of State gets desig for Scottish Parliament building underway', 26 January 1998, http://www.scotland.gov.uk, http://www.holyroodinquiry.org

6. *Minute: Scottish Parliament Building – Design Team Selection Panel Meeting on 23 March, Meridian Court*, para. 3, 20 March 1998, http://www.holyroodinquiry.org

7. Paul Grice to Kirsty Wark, Letter, 3 March 1998, ibid.

8. John Gibbons, Fraser Inquiry, pt. 425, 24 November 2003, ibid.

9. William Armstrong, 'Precognition', para. 4.6, 2003, ibid.

10. The Scottish Office press release detailing the shortlisted teams would detail their differing Scottish credentials at this stage. Miralles and Vinoly were still entered singly. The press release announcing the display of the design concepts would clarify that by this point it was the non-UK entrants who had formed alliances with Scottish firms. *Scottish Office News Release* no. 0929/98, 'Final five design teams for Holyrood Parliament named', 7 May 1998 http://www.scotland.gov.uk, http://www.holyroodinquiry.org; *Scottish Office News Release* no. 11/69/98, 'Visions for Holyrood Parliament go on show', 5 June 1998, ibid.

11. Sebastian Tombs, evidence session, pt 205, 2 December 2003, http://www.holyroodinquiry.org

12. Mick Duncan, evidence session, pts 224, 226, 3 December 2003, ibid.

13. Hugh Pearman, 'Designs on a poisoned chalice', *The Scotsman*, 28 March 1998.

14. Penny Lewis, 'The £60m design to die for', *Sunday Times*, 15 March 1998.

15. Quoted in Robert Dawson Scott and Penny Lewis, 'Famous Five with grand designs on new parliament', *The Scotsman*, 8 May 1998.

16. David McIntosh, 'Public look for that vital spark', *Edinburgh Evening News*, 6 June 1998.

17. 'We are determined to make use of the best architectural expertise and also to involve the general public in working up the final design . . . We will . . . be running a competition to find the best architectural talent . . . But the winner will be chosen on merit. The public will then be invited to see a range of options for the site before the final design is chosen.' *Scottish Office News Release* no. 0029/98, 'Scottish Parliament to be built at Holyrood: Dewar opts for new building in historic heart of Edinburgh', 9 January 1998, http://www.scotland.gov.uk, http://www.holyroodinquiry.org

18. *Minute: Scottish Parliament Building – Design Competition – Meeting with RFACS and RIAS*, 14 January 1998, http://www.holyrood inquiry.org

19. *Scottish Office News Release* no. 1389/98, 'Architect chosen to design Scottish Parliament', 6 July 1998, http://www.scotland.gov.uk, http://www.holyroodinquiry.org

20. Bill Armstrong, *Minute: Selection of Design Team*, 11 June 1998, http://www.holyroodinquiry.org

21. John Gibbons, evidence session, pt 353, 25 November 2003, ibid.

22. Bill Armstrong, evidence session, pt 757, 2 December 2003, ibid. The roots of this confusion perhaps lies in a minute of 22 January. 'Ministers have agreed that the competition should be to find a designer for the Parliament building though with a form of design competition built in for the three or four shortlisted design teams.' Paul Grice, *Minute: Scottish Parliament Building: Announcement of Procedure to Select an Architectural Design Team*, para.3, 22 January 1998, ibid.

23. Documentation provided to the Fraser Inquiry would explain, 'The variety of approach taken by the individual teams is confirmation of the vital necessity for the selected design team . . . to establish a meaningful financial framework within which design development can proceed. This must be achieved very early in the process. The Brief must be understood and adhered to in order that the risks inherent in undertaking such a project within an extremely tight timescale and a finite budget can be properly managed . . . [A] detailed and like-for-like comparative statement on the cost implications of the five submissions is not possible.' DL&E (Davis Langdon and Everest, cost consultants), *The Scottish Parliament Building: Architectural Selection Process Cost Commentary*, 10 June 1998, ibid.

5

I'm so Sorry, he's from Barcelona

'Enric Miralles was always getting this prize. And anybody who follows politics can understand why: because of course he was a Catalan. If only he'd been a Hottentot we'd never have been near him.'
Margo MacDonald, MSP[1]

WITH ENRIC MIRALLES selected as the new parliament's lead designer, Scotland finally had a focus for all the frustrations that the entire Holyrood process had generated so far. Within hours of EMBT/RMJM's appointment, the backlash against him had begun.

On 8 July, just two days after the architect's selection, the first serious 'anti-Miralles' story broke. The Catalan designer would be cast as 'El Collapso', after it emerged that the roof of a sports stadium he had designed in northern Spain had given way.[2] A day later, it was confirmed that Miralles had actually not been guilty of the fault at all. Building contractors were to blame, and reports of a multi-million pound lawsuit against him were untrue.[3] In the *Herald*, Neil Baxter argued that Miralles could never be the right choice for the parliament's architect; his nationality was 'simply wrong'. This view, Baxter argued, was not xenophobic or nationalistic: it was common sense. A nation which desired a measure of self-governance should surely be capable of designing its own parliament building. And anyway, Miralles' metaphor of upturned boats was both 'singularly inappropriate and . . . the design fits neither its physical nor its historical location.'[4] In both the *Mail* and the *Telegraph*, architectural academic Gavin Stamp was simply outraged at the entire process so far. 'Mr Miralles' design may or may not be a worthy winner,' he argued, 'that is not the point.' For him, the real problems lay at a far more fundamental level. 'Good architecture requires a good brief,' Stamp declared, 'and there cannot possibly be a satisfactory brief when the Scottish parliament has yet to be elected – let alone debate what its evolving needs might be.'[5] Despite support for Miralles from some of the UK's most distinguished architectural critics, it was Allan Brown in the *Sunday Times* who most accurately summed up the reception Holyrood's lead designer was now facing. With the architect looking for a Scottish home from which to base his activities, the solution to his housing needs now seemed obvious. 'His avant-garde "upturned boats" design . . . has made Enric Miralles the focus of some derision since its unveiling . . .' Brown pondered. 'The Spanish architect might well respond accordingly: by living on the site of a former leper colony.'[6]

However, whatever the disquiet surrounding the Holyrood project in the outside world, within the parliament enterprise it was already becoming apparent that things were not unfolding according to plan. Veteran project manager Bill Armstrong had been called in at the start to help set up the historic building venture. But it now seemed that the job he had been employed to do and the job that Holyrood was becoming were two entirely different things.

According to Armstrong's own account, Enric Miralles spent the first eight weeks after EMBT/RMJM's win on holiday, and on his return '[he] went on to spend money on all sorts of peripheral things that were not in the brief . . . They all had to come out of the budget, and . . . he never accepted that there wasn't going to be extra money available.' For Armstrong, this was the first sign that he was about to part company with the Scottish Office on the way forward. Systems available to control the architects, he argued, had not been put in place, and 'they didn't have the guts to tackle the man and make him do what he was supposed to do'. Between August and November, Armstrong's project reports repeatedly recounted delay, knock-on effects and little progress, warning of serious disruption to the programme if the position did not improve.[7] And by late November, his conclusion was unequivocal. The timescale was now in jeopardy – and it was 'entirely the fault of EMBT/RMJM'.[8]

For Armstrong, there was an obvious solution. 'I mean, I went through an exercise of saying, "Alright . . . take Miralles to a certain stage, take his design and . . . pay him off – and let RMJM finish the job,"' he remembered. The idea had been rejected. For the Project Manager, the problems were the start of an evolving culture clash between client and architect that would ultimately lead to enormous cost implications. 'I think [it comes down to] this attitude to what you would call the "signature architect" . . .' he mused, 'if they want to go down a route they will push that route, and unless the client is strong enough to withstand it [there will be problems].' With Miralles appointed against his wishes, the Project Manager resolved to give the job six months, and then resign if the situation wasn't working. In December 1998, that was exactly what he would do.

Yet while Bill Armstrong struggled to hold Miralles to the job first planned for, others within Holyrood saw the situation entirely differently. Scotland now had a world-class architect to design its headquarters. And while Dewar's criterion of speedy delivery remained essential, a more flexible and creative environment was needed to deliver the vision. Miralles himself already had fears for the future. He worried that Armstrong was trying to play both project manager and architect, and that the programme – and the brief – were unrealistically tight.[9] As Holyrood's main driving force, John Gibbons explained his role to the documentary crew, the gulf between Armstrong's view and his own was all too clear. 'The role that I've had in the Scottish Office for the last twenty years has been essentially as an "enabler", to make sure the conditions are right for creative architects like Enric to deliver their skills in that context,' Gibbons explained. 'I'm the interface between a complex, large bureaucratic client . . . which may not always have the highest respect for architecture or artistic activities . . . I can make sure that [problems are] presented to [Enric] in a way which he can understand and resolve, and . . . I can present to lay clients what his proposals are in a way that they can understand.'

A clash between the two approaches was now inevitable, as relationships within the project began to unfold. While the RMJM end had rapidly mobilised, in Barcelona things were taking more time. And it seemed the situation was starting to lead to some friction. 'Particularly, what Miralles appeared to be taking from the way things were developing,' Gibbons would later remember, 'was that he was being eased out of the lead role because of the proximity that we had to the Edinburgh office and the way we were able to deal with the Edinburgh office . . .'[10] To ease communication, RMJM had taken a flat in Barcelona. 'It even got to the stage where RMJM did a sort of re-draft of his proposal, and it was acceptable,' Bill Armstrong remembered. 'It went out to Barcelona, and Miralles blew his top. He said, "I was the appointed architect: I will do everything on this job. You will take no decisions whatsoever."'

With feelings high, diplomacy and firm handling were imperative. Yet it seemed Armstrong's skills – while important – were not bearing fruit. '[H]e was taking a pretty firm line with EMBT/RMJM and was sending them increasingly strong letters,' one key figure remembered. 'Now I think that has a significant part to play in robust project management, but I was a bit concerned that he did not seem to have a back-up strategy and that the proposition he was making was that we would have to go for the nuclear option of sacking the design team, or at least sacking the EMBT part of it if we did not get responses.'[11] For Barbara Doig, the situation was critical. '[A]t that particular stage, it did not seem to me to be the best approach of making progress,' she would explain later. 'We were still at [the] very early stages of the design, and the Project Manager was pushing it down a particular management style, which . . . Well, I do not think Señor Miralles was going to respond to that kind of management of the relationship.'[12] In

November, she was asked to arrange Armstrong's replacement, bringing his intended departure forward by nine months.[13] In the event, however, Armstrong would beat her to it. On 1 December 1998, he resigned.

For those still at Holyrood, what the project most needed was being achieved by John Gibbons. 'I think it needed [matter of fact communications] to some extent,' explained one key figure, 'but it also needed something that would help if we got complete standoffs with the parties very far apart and just megaphoning at one another . . . [T]he role of John Gibbons was invaluable through this period because he spent a considerable amount of his time and devoted a great deal of his energy to working with EMBT/RMJM to find ways of helping them to work effectively together to deliver material of the right quality and so on.'[14] For Armstrong though, his position was simply untenable. 'John Gibbons . . . became so influential on the job that there was no role for the project manager at the end of the day,' he told the film team, 'in my terms, anyway.'

Yet it was not John Gibbons' role alone – nor the growing warmth and friendship between Gibbons and Miralles – which had underpinned Armstrong's departure. As 1998 unfolded, a far more serious problem had emerged. With the brief for the building still developing, requests were coming in for extra space. Extra space would clearly mean extra costs, and with the architects already struggling to meet the restrictive circulation requirements, it was quite clear that the current budget was not going to withstand the pressure. A request for more money, however, had been met with a deeply worrying response. 'I was told that it wasn't available . . .' Armstrong recalled. '[I was told], "We've got an election coming up early next year. We can't go back; we've said it's going to be £50 million. We can't go back now and say the building cost is going to be more. It's politically not acceptable."'[15]

Within less than a month, Armstrong's departure had hit the mainstream press. For the first time, disquiet with Enric Miralles' appointment had crystallised into explicit criticism from the inside track. And far more damningly, a key source from within the project was now confirming what had been suspected for months: the costs being given publicly did not match the figures on the inside. The impact of the story was immediate, and as the months progressed, public perception of the project got steadily worse as more and more news about Holyrood was uncovered. Miralles, having promised to move to Scotland, had not done so, and the public was having to pick up the bill.[16] EMBT/RMJM itself was being 'ripped apart by huge rows' as Miralles '[threw] a Spaniard in [the] works'.[17] The designer's involvement in other architectural competitions raised questions about whether he was being 'distracted' from the job at Holyrood.[18] And, increasingly, Scotland's new MSPs were beginning to mutter that they would rather stay in their temporary home than move to the new building. 'Personally,' wrote Rob Brown of the *Sunday Herald*, 'I'd have sent Señor Miralles packing from Leith Docks on an upturned boat back to Barcelona.'[19]

But whatever the validity of these stories – and there was no doubt that many of them were true – a worrying feature was soon to emerge in some of the Holyrood press coverage. '"Upturned boats," Miralles' original image for the building, has become a term of derision in the hands of the rubbishers,' bemoaned Magnus Linklater in late May. 'There is even the none-too-subtle implication that the chap is foreign, probably unreliable, and is never around when you want him. I expect to see the word "mañana" in a *Sun* headline any day now.'[20] Miralles, an unconventional Catalan, was about to fall prey to a deeply unpleasant form of public criticism. Opposition to his complicated and unusual design was understandable, as was deep-seated unhappiness about the process by which Scotland's parliament was being procured. But some of the criticism of the architect would become rooted in something far less forgivable. It would be symptomatic of the legendary 'Scottish cringe'. But far more disturbingly, it would be racist.

With Holyrood having narrowly survived the June 1999 vote, work began to rebuild the shattered morale of all those on the building's inside track. After what Miralles laughingly described as a 'personal revenge' of stopping work on Holyrood for three or four days, now he was back designing, his enthusiasm for the parliament project was utterly undimmed. The political process had been – he conceded privately – far more difficult than he could ever have imagined, but chance meetings with supportive Scottish strangers in Edinburgh shops and hotels had obviously delighted him and provided a welcome source of strength in the face of sustained press and political attack. With John Gibbons now providing close support and friendship – not to mention 24-hour personal availability by mobile phone – it looked like the parliament building was finally back on course.

However, while the public storms over Holyrood abated – briefly – one serious problem was refusing to go away. Brian Stewart and Mick Duncan, Miralles' co-directors at the Edinburgh end of EMBT/RMJM, had a deep professional regard for their Catalan colleague, and the three shared an irreverent sense of humour which cut through many barriers of culture, personality and ambition. But in terms of working methods, the two companies were extremely different. '[Enric] thinks of buildings as works of art, basically . . .' explained Mick Duncan. 'He's very interested in form, light, colour; all these sort of tactile issues. And that's exceptional. I've never met anybody who's so interested in that.' As part of the selection process, the team had been asked if a clash of egos between signature architect and RMJM's large international business might cause problems for the future. Miralles' response had been firm, Brian Stewart remembered, 'He said "I'm a basketball player, not a snooker player." Now, what he was trying to convey to everybody was he's a team player.' Less than a year later, it was already looking like this was far from being the case.

By late summer 1999, relations within EMBT/RMJM were in crisis. Miralles – often away from Edinburgh – had launched himself into a lone crusade, and was refusing to make use of his architectural partners. Repeated reminders that the project had been won by a joint company – not Miralles alone – had provoked fury, upset, and Barcelonan insult-flinging, typical discussions of RMJM's crucial role often concluding, 'Brian, if you say that once more I'll scream!' The Edinburgh end of the operation felt jaded and let down. Miralles – who liked to be liked, and certainly liked to be seen as efficient – was distraught, and the clash between the type of client and process he was used to in Spain, and what was confronting him now in Scotland was causing the architect, and the project, huge difficulties. Both artist and perfectionist, Miralles was locked into a fast-track delivery process where cost and programme were paramount. More time would certainly produce a better building – a point which the designer argued vigorously. But on a political timetable, under a public spotlight, where taxpayers' money was being spent, more time was simply not a possibility. 'It was interesting this morning, actually,' Brian Stewart explained to the film crew in mid-September. 'He said, "You're very good at managing, and I'm very good at drawing." And the problem is . . . he fails to see that the drawing has to be managed . . . [the] drawing process has to have some structure and it has to have some logic; and it can't be "I'll do a bit of that this week and I'll do a bit of that [next week]."'

Holyrood's designer – it was now becoming obvious – was demanding the freedom to do everything; and the impact that this was having on the project, and on internal relations, was profound. For the process to work efficiently and targets to be hit, decisions would have to be made swiftly – not easy in an intensely political process where party pressure seemed as crucial as practicality. And once decisions *were* made, it was essential that they were not revisited; almost impossible with a signature architect of Miralles' type. 'We'll probably have a referendum on door handles later on, you know,' laughed Alan Mack, Holyrood's Operations Director for Bovis, a bearded, sharply dressed, no-bullshit Londoner, who had a wry and incisive take on the whole proceedings. 'I mean, how silly is it gonna get . . . you start to wonder. [And] once they've decided then Enric'll change it . . . 'cause he'll want to design the door

handle personally! . . . But I mean that's what you're paying for
. . . I thought that's why they employed this architect in the first
place.' For Brian Stewart at EMBT/RMJM, however, frustration was now turning to serious worry. 'It's not an open cheque
book,' he confided to the film team, 'and it's got to have some
sort of rigour and control . . . [because] the longer it takes the
more it's going to cost.' To Stewart, it seemed, there were now
only two ways forward. The client must either decide to discipline everything far more rigorously, or the building would be
ready when it was ready, and would cost what it would cost.
'Now that may be,' he explained, 'don't misunderstand, that
actually might not be a bad way to go.'

By early autumn 1999, with the programme slipping, Armstrong's replacement feeling excluded, future options under
discussion, the architects diverted by changes demanded post-
debate and Miralles' alternative designs deemed unacceptable,
the need was agreed for urgent remedial action.[21] A review
would be carried out, and out of the back of that, the current
position on plans, programme and cost investigated. For Enric
Miralles, it was yet more bad news. The perfection he was
seeking was unable to be accommodated. And now – to make
things worse – he was also experiencing serious problems with
his new client body, the SPCB.

From the point of EMBT/RMJM's win to the May 1999 elections, Miralles had enjoyed a direct and friendly working relationship with those making the decisions at Holyrood, be it the
selection panel which originally chose him, Chief Architect
John Gibbons, or Scotland's eventual – and inaugural – First
Minister, Donald Dewar. Communication between both sides
had been fluent, seamless and straightforward; essential,
Miralles believed, because '[it] needs to be a friendly, nice building, and this is only done if all the direct communication
happens fluid without problems, no?' Yet with project handover
to the Scottish Parliament in June 1999, all that had begun to
change. Now, the architect believed, the SPCB's political imperatives were causing them to affect 'pretending detachment' to

the process, and the project was lacking the personal energy and commitment on the client side that he believed all buildings desperately required. 'You need to have a clear client, not a committee to whom you could communicate . . .' he confided in the film crew, obviously unhappy and concerned. 'Until now we felt very much at home and doing the things with a lot of . . . understanding and support around us. I would say now it is the same, but [it] is lacking this quality of . . . direct communication that for me is very important.'

However, while the client side at Holyrood certainly had its problems, as yet only gradually emerging, for some at the heart of decision-making, the dilemma the architect found himself in was completely different. 'He hasn't got a good rapport with the SPCB because he hasn't been here . . .' John Gibbons declared, shrugging. 'We have learnt how to deal with Enric in Barcelona, communicate with him in Barcelona. We have been used to having meetings in Barcelona. I don't think he can expect the client . . . to get up and go and meet him Barcelona. And just by the fact he's operating at that distance he's bound not to be able to build up the rapport that people can build up who are just down the road.' Miralles may have been demoralised and unhappy throughout the summer of 1999 as the project began to evolve along a route with which he was not familiar. But what was clear to many on the inside track was that whatever the problems surrounding the parliament building itself, its signature architect – however passionate – was not entirely exempt from blame.

By the end of September 1999, after three days of meetings, a presentation to the SPCB, and serious deliberations about how the project should now push forward, a resolution was finally on the way. On 4 October – after an abortive start – a letter was received from EMBT/RMJM, laying out the proposed joint working arrangements for the future. Miralles, essentially, would continue with overall design responsibility, and Brian Stewart's role was management of design and implementation.[22] At last, it was believed, Miralles' creativity could be given a firmer structure, and the problems of the past put aside. Yet despite the feeling of relief, it was clear that some worrying central issues remained outstanding. At the height of the recent crisis, Brian Stewart had confided in the documentary team that the client would need to be clearer in the instructions it gave the architects, and in particular in those that it gave to Enric Miralles. However, three days *after* the SPCB meeting, none of the key players had yet seen the crucial missive that David Steel was said to be writing, and no one even seemed certain of what the document would contain. 'How did you know? I didn't know he was – how can you – who told you there was a letter?' laughed Brian Stewart, incredulous, when asked by the film team about the letter's expected contents. 'I believe he's writing to us . . . I have no idea what he's going to say.' Miralles' response to the same question was similar. 'These things start feeling a bit like in the 1001 [*Arabian Nights*],' he laughed, sleeves rolled up in Bovis' site offices. 'Everybody talks about this letter, and three days that I'm here and I have not seen it. So the letter, it may be flying from one room to the next; but I'm very happy to read the famous letter.'

For an architect who was challenging to control, and who thrived on direct and close communication with his client, such a complex process of decision-making and instruction was bound to have disruptive consequences. And, in a building process in which speedy and effective communication was paramount, a three-day wait for direction was undoubtedly hardly ideal. With architects EMBT/RMJM back on track, and an easy humour returning, the problems facing the project were now beginning to shift fundamentally. 'I mean, one tends to think at this stage that the key to the project being successful is in the hands of the design team,' John Gibbons confided, back in his book-lined office at Victoria Quay, 'but we never do that. We know full well it's actually the client is going to be the key issue. If the client decides it wants to re-examine the issue of MSP rooms, if the client wants to make other decisions about Queensbury House or any more decisions about the debating chamber or the landscaping, these are all likely to have more dramatic impact on the programme than really anything the design team can do.'

His words, spoken in autumn 1999, would prove remarkably prescient. The client was about to make a series of conflicting requests that would again deflect the Holyrood team from the key objective of getting the building built. Yet just as prophetic as Gibbons' judgement had been the words of former Project Manager Bill Armstrong, some months before he left the parliament in December 1998. 'I mean, we did say when the brief was done, you know . . . if you change this, you are opening a Pandora's Box,' Armstrong explained to the Holyrood film team, relaxing on a sofa as he recalled the project's early events, 'and that's exactly what's happened.'

Notes

1. Interview, 22 January 2002.
2. The original collapsing roof story seems to have broken in the *Edinburgh Evening News* and *Daily Record*: Nick Morrison, 'Roof falls in as Holyrood designer faces lawsuit', *Edinburgh Evening News*, 8 July 1998; 'Parly architect is sued over roof collapse', *Daily Record*, 8 July 1998.
3. Raymond Duncan, 'Miralles in the clear on lawsuit claim', *Herald*, 9 July 1998; Lindsay McGarvie, 'The day the roof caved in; I wasn't at fault says Holyrood architect', *Scottish Daily Mail*, 9 July 1998; Tony Ellin, 'Day the roof caved in on Enric's new building', *Daily Record*, 9 July 1998.
4. Neil Baxter, 'Greening the Green', *Herald*, 13 July 1998.
5. Gavin Stamp, 'Donald Dewar, design dictator', *Daily Telegraph*, 7 July 1998; 'Design ruling that denies the principle of parliament,' *Scottish Daily Mail*, 8 July 1998.
6. Allan Brown, 'Architect has designs on leper colony site', *Sunday Times*, 19 July 1998.
7. Available on http:www.holyroodinquiry.org
8. William Armstrong, *Project Team Report to Project Sponsor*, pt 7.6, 30 November 1998, http://www.holyroodinquiry.org
9. John Gibbons, 'Precognition 2', pts 9, 6, ibid.
10. John Gibbons, evidence session, pt 148, 3 February 2004, ibid.
11. Robert Gordon, evidence session, pt 262, 16 December 2003, ibid.
12. Barbara Doig, evidence session, pt 304, 4 December, 2003, ibid.
13. Statement by Barbara Doig, *Fraser Inquiry*, p. 13, ibid.
14. Robert Gordon, evidence session, pt 266, 16 December 2003, ibid.

15. Project Sponsor Barbara Doig would take a different view. 'As the design became firmer, and indeed as the client's additional requirements for more briefed space in October came through, there were continual attempts to improve the cost estimate and to make sure that the design was meeting requirements . . . We were all trying to achieve a very great deal in that time, and in retrospect to be exercising that discipline, absolutely making it clear that this client was serious about its budget, we simply could not, as the client's side, have done anything else. We did not have the information on estimated costs to be able to go and seriously ask for a budget increase.' Barbara Doig, evidence session, pt 253, 4 December 2003, ibid.

16. Quoted in Paul Riddell and Elizabeth Quigley, 'I quit as Holyrood bill soared towards £100m: Donald Dewar faces storm over rising cost of the new parliament', *Scottish Daily Mail*, 16 January 1999.

17. Ron Mackenna, 'Miralles throws a Spaniard in works: Parly row over architect', *Scottish Mirror*, 25 January 1999.

18. Martin Hannan, 'Concern grows over Miralles and Holyrood', *Scotland on Sunday*, 14 March 1999.

19. Rob Brown, 'Counterblast', *Sunday Herald*, 30 May 1999.

20. Magnus Linklater, 'Gloomy parochialism set in stone', *Scotland on Sunday*, 30 May 1999.

21. Mustard Mustard, 'Health of the project report', pt 14, 26 August 1999, http:www.holyroodinquiry.org; Martin Mustard, 'project review', para 3.0, 6 September 1999, ibid.

22. Enric Miralles and Brian Stewart to David Steel, Letter, 4 October 1999, ibid.

6

Mixed Messages

'*It is beginning to be hinted that we are a nation of amateurs.*'
Earl of Rosebery, Rectorial Address, Glasgow, 16 November 1900

BY LATE SEPTEMBER 1999, with the immediate critical problems within Holyrood resolving and a form of regular presentation to the SPCB decided, attention turned to an issue that had been troubling the project from its earliest days. The brief for the parliament building was still too restrictive, and with the building bigger than the brief – and being designed for a far more complicated site than envisaged – the costs of the project were again getting higher too.

In August, Holyrood's cost consultants DL&E had predicted a construction cost figure of £115 million for the parliament complex,[1] one of the key factors that had triggered September's internal review. The rise had been caused – in part – by the addition of 4,000m^2 to the building, and with no one able to clearly identify where the extra space had come from, a report had been called to find out.[2] With the cost of the building causing worry, Paul Grice, the parliament's Chief Executive, had instructed that the SPCB would not be told of the price rise until the review of the problem had been completed. On 14 September, the SPCB was told that 4,000m^2 seemed to have been added to the building. Appended to their report was an 'end of August' estimated total of £109 million.[3]

Yet by mid-September 1999 – allowing for everything that had happened post-debate – it was already becoming apparent that the timescale for the building was also in serious trouble. The 'Stage D' report was delayed by five months, the project was facing a revised completion date of January 2002, which was already known to be unachievable, and suggestions that summer 2002 should be considered for the chamber were now being raised on the inside.[4] 'I don't think September 2001 is possible,' a worried Brian Stewart confided in the autumn. '[I] think it was possible in January, February, March. I don't think it's possible now – and I actually feel that we would probably be foolish to try and do that. I think if we can start to manage ourselves better, collectively, I think certainly opening of parliament on September 2002 is possible. But I still think that we have got to work hard to achieve that. I really do.'

With reviews of the project complete, however, and confirmation given that the latest budget forecasts were unacceptable, all key players at Holyrood now embarked on a massive cost-cutting exercise. The client had targeted up to 25 per cent worth of cuts, and for Alan Mack at Bovis, this task had one huge snag – more delays. Time taken out to reassess the debating chamber and surrounding area had meant time standing still with the meter ticking. And now *more* time was being spent re-examining where the project stood in budget terms, ensuring that the programme – again – was going to be stretched. As ever, more time meant more money. But for a designer building where quality was central, taking time out now was crucial as it could also guard against serious problems further down the line. 'At the end of the day, this job is all about quality,' Mack explained to the film crew. 'It's not a bloody supermarket . . . And if you take the time out now . . . we get it right now, it saves a lot of money, a lot of time later on.'

What those now engaged in radical thinking at Holyrood could not have expected, however, was a completely contradictory instruction about to come in from the client. At a crisis meeting on 30 August, Brian Stewart and cost consultant Hugh Fisher had warned that the £62 million budget was now unachievable.[5] Both Barbara Doig – aware of the £115 million figure – and David Steel, who apparently was not, had insisted the budget stood.[6] Yet by 20 October, Brian Stewart was writing to Doig personally, worried that the architects had only now been given a cost estimate for the building, and that the project had never borne any relation to the £62 million they were now being told was inviolate. 'You and your colleagues are fully aware of my views in relation to costs,' he had argued, frustrated. 'The budget . . . does not remotely reflect the project as submitted at the competition stage and as developed over the last 15 months. The current total [of £115m] . . . apparently underpins my view . . . [I]t is quite impossible to adapt the current project to achieve a reduction of £53 million.'[7] If Stewart was worried by this though, things were about to get worse. On 17 November, the architects were sent the SPCB's decisions on the cost-cutting options, which were to be incorporated into the next stage of value engineering. Attached to it was a request for extra space, which was bound to cost more money.[8]

With the SPCB's approval, the design team had now been instructed to instigate a feasibility study, to see how the extra room that was needed could be incorporated on the site. Achieving any of this without costing money – or time – was completely impossible. And for those charged with managing it, the dilemma the request threw up was enormous. 'If we were to go back and say, "Right, to do what you want us to do now we will have to freeze everything, and it may take us three months to carry out that review . . ."' a frustrated Alan Mack argued, in heated discussion with EMBT/RMJM's Brian Stewart, 'Anyone within reason would say, "Well, don't do it. Just don't do it. We're too late."' For John Gibbons though, the instruction highlighted a more fundamental worry. 'I mean, I wish I knew how [the client doesn't] understand the relationship . . .' he worried quietly. 'It seems very obvious to me, but probably I'm too close to it. If you want a bigger thing it's gonna usually cost you more. It's just one [of] those things.'

For those in the world outside the project, the story of Holyrood's problems just seemed to get worse and worse. Despite the intensive cost struggles being fought on the inside, for both press and political opponents the building was an open goal. By October, the *Scottish Daily Mail* was reporting that the cost of devolution itself was 'spiralling', while the suspected price of road alterations around Holyrood meant the total had 'mushroomed again, beyond the outrageous £109m already admitted'.[9] David McLetchie, leader of the Scottish Tories, responded that each penny spent on maintaining the situation meant less money spent on health and education.[10] In November, David Steel announced that almost £1 million had been trimmed from Holyrood. The *Mail* reported that the savings were 'modest', and quoted both a Scottish Tory spokesman calling the cutback 'peanuts', and an SNP source who described them as a 'gesture' by 'defensive' David Steel. '[A]ny trimming in costs must be welcomed,' stated the Tory, 'and hopefully this £1m will be the start of serious cost cutting.'[11] In December, Steel announced that the cost was going to go up, due to additional space requirements and work needed on Queensberry House. For Tory David Davidson, the rising price was another 'last minute fire-fighting operation' which showed that Dewar had not thought the plans through.[12] And in February, Margo MacDonald called for Miralles to report to MSPs and answer questions, 'I want to ask the man himself to confirm or deny that the plans are constantly changing . . .' she explained. The *Evening News* called her demands 'hardly surprising . . . [Miralles] cannot be allowed to presume that he and the builders have carte blanche to proceed at their own pace without any regard to the cost'.[13]

Yet while some of these political concerns were apparently rooted in frustration, for Alan Mack at Bovis one thing was becoming increasingly clear. 'I naively thought that perhaps politically they'd try and use this as a way of demonstrating that politics can work effectively,' he argued. 'What we're seeing here is the downside of it, is the negative stuff . . . And it's very, very apparent people are just standing around waiting to see what's gonna happen, and then utilising that in some personal way . . . I use that expression, the soft underbelly of the politics. By God it's come into play because all you've got is the party politics, which, if it's just left alone and runs its own course, could actually destroy the thing.' His assessment of Scotland's new political system, of which Holyrood was to be the icon, was utterly damning: 'Party politics?' he sneered, 'Tremendous! It's a destructive force.'

On 1 February 2000, after months of cost assessment, re-evaluation, redesign and radical thinking, the design team at Holyrood had achieved what in September had seemed near impossible. Money to be saved had been identified, and with contradictory demands coming in from the client – not to mention a U-turn from Historic Scotland over the treatment of A-listed Queensberry House – the entire project had been re-evaluated, and a completely new approach to the organisation of the building determined.

Yet the entire fraught period had had an unexpected outcome. Miralles – always surprising – was clearly delighted that his design was now more 'strong and clear' than it had been previously, and, for Brian Stewart, the enforced reorganisation of site had ultimately meant a chance to tackle the long running problem of excess circulation space. The impact of the client's request for extra room on top of an up-front cost cut had reduced the potential savings found from £20 million to only six or seven.[14] But overall, EMBT/RMJM was pleased. 'If you're going to add 3,000m² on to a building – that's about 10 per cent of its area – you can only do that in a sensitive location, in a sensitive building volume like that by doing something radical,' explained Mick Duncan, showing the film team through the revised drawings that the exercise had produced. 'That takes quite a lot of intellectual and mental effort at this stage in a project. And sometimes – as Enric says – you know, you welcome that because it does enable you to bring a different meaning to the project . . . It's ironical it's been brought about by desire for more space – [but] I think that is all very positive.'

While the impact on the parliament's design had been beneficial though, what was now emerging was that relations between the Barcelona and the Edinburgh ends of EMBT/RMJM had become friendly and were professionally working very well. On a site visit to show the SPCB a mock-up of MSPs' radical sail-shaped office windows, Miralles had been plainly delighted to spot Brian Stewart in the car park, and the two had exchanged relaxed and affectionate banter while Miralles listened with surprising warmth and fondness to the teasing of his Edinburgh friend. The two offices' staff were working closely and productively together, and – most tellingly – the RMJM end of the consortium had played a large part in the recent radical rethink, something that would have been unheard of during Miralles' tussle for ownership only a few months before. The festive period too had consolidated the company's internal relations, and for Christmas Brian Stewart had bought Miralles a Scottish 'Jimmy hat', which the Catalan designer had proudly donned as he settled to watch *Braveheart* on TV. With the SPCB approving the revised designs, money saved, the complex better, and EMBT/RMJM working effectively, the project was now finally set to take its first major step forward. Or was it?

On 24 February 2000, just days after the SPCB had enthusiastically endorsed the revised project and asked Enric Miralles to proceed with all haste, Presiding Officer David Steel made an announcement to Scotland's new parliament. Although 'substantial progress' had been made in taking the Holyrood scheme forward, the SPCB believed that available details on cost and timescale did not allow it to provide 'sufficiently robust' information. In response, it had commissioned an independent review to scrutinise the project and give parliament an objective assessment of where things stood.[15] The news had been announced to both the press and to the parliament. The problem was that no one had thought to inform the design team. The first they had heard about it was when they read about it in the Sunday papers. 'I'm just very upset and disturbed that something of this scale and potential impact should be handled in a very bad way,' worried Brian Stewart, scanning through a copy of the press release in his office. 'It's sort of leaked, you know. It's like John Barnes reading in the paper that he's been sacked. I mean, it's just the wrong way to manage such an important thing as this.'

For EMBT/RMJM, the news of the review – to be headed by architect John Spencely – had come as a seismic shock. Months had been spent weathering the problems arising from client handover, and finally everything seemed to be back on track. This assessment, and the accusations accompanying it in the public arena, were regarded as a direct attack on its competence. The appointment of an architect to head the review appeared to suggest that any problems must lie with the designers, and Brian Stewart had been 'particularly insult[ed]' by the implication that the SPCB relied on the architects' team to provide information on cost and programme – something which was not part of its job. But if this new review was demoralising, even more disturbing was the way that it appeared to be evolving from the client end.

In the run-up to the review's announcement, EMBT/RMJM seemed to have been given no indication that the project had any new fundamental problems. And even on the day that the press release had been issued, RMJM had received only 'some indication that there might be another committee established, to look at what's been done and assess where we [are]'. All signs had suggested that the plan was to concentrate on the project's management, and in particular on the role of the professional client, the Holyrood project team. But with the issue of a formal press statement, all that seemed to have changed. 'The Client's attempts to explain . . . away how . . . it move[d] from that to what is now appearing in the press release – which is really a very strong focus on the design team – was that the terms of reference were set by others over which they have no control,' explained Mick Duncan quietly, 'and that's our immediate client. But that's quite a different animal from what we originally were led to believe was going to be let loose on us.' The confusion that all this client-side manoeuvering would generate plunged the project into yet another round of damaging and demoralising criticism. And yet again, both Enric Miralles and the design team would be in the front line.

With a press release about Spencely's appointment now issued, the impact of the announcement was almost immediate. Despite both David Steel and – unexpectedly – Donald Gorrie coming out in support of Miralles,[16] many of Scotland's newspapers now targeted the Catalan architect as a key focus of their reports. The *Evening News* stated that independent auditors had been called in 'to check figures produced by Mr Miralles' design team . . . alleged to have overestimated the final bill to give themselves room to manoeuvre', a charge also run in the *Daily Record*, which claimed that Miralles was now facing the sack.[17] *Scotland on Sunday* accused Dewar of picking 'Catalan architect Enric Miralles to construct the new building on the basis of a back-of-a-fag-packet "concept" inspired by upturned boats rather than a properly considered and costed design.' '[T]he terms of the contract mean that the more expensive the proposed parliament becomes, the more Miralles will receive in fees,' it argued. 'Thus the leap from an original plucked-from-the air £40m to a truly frightening £230m is no particular cause for concern over in Spain.'[18] Speculation about the level of Miralles' fee – based on a percentage of a £230 million building – varied between £10 million, £19.5 million, and £20 million. Whether the £230 million sum referred to basic construction costs or an all-in total remained unclear, as comparisons continued to be made with a variety of figures from the past. The only winner in the entire debacle was Miralles himself, concluded *The Scotsman*, who 'must smile every time there is a squabble over the minutiae of interior fixtures or office space which leads to yet another redesign'. A cap, it suggested, should have been put on the architect's fee at the outset: 'There should be no incentive for change or delay.'[19]

More worryingly, however, attacks on Miralles now seemed to have as much to do with his race as his professional proficiency. In the 'Scotsman Diary', it was joked, 'Enric "Miracle Man" Miralles' had 'choked on his paella' upon hearing suggestions that the Holyrood building might be behind schedule.[20] In *Scotland on Sunday*, he was 'Señor Costas Afortune'.[21] The

Evening News published a cartoon with Miralles as Fawlty Towers' Manuel.[22] And in the *Scottish Sun,* under the headline 'Why the El does our £230m Parly need a big bullring, Señor?' the option suggested to keep costs down was this: 'They'll take one look at Spanish architect Enric Miralles' plan and ask the question: Do we really need a 20,000 seater bullring, matadors' dressing rooms, tapas bars, flamenco dance halls, the bell tower to chuck a live donkey from, or the Julio Iglesias Solarium and Sauna Wing?'[23] 'This is xenophobia in Scotland,' confided a disgusted Mick Duncan, '[a] picture of Miralles looking sweaty . . . right? Find the worst picture . . . And the thing is, that once a newspaper gets in a frame of mind like that . . . you just can't read it . . . because it's so way off the target. And I find all of that disturbing, because you don't know if [what] you're reading in a newspaper is correct ever again.' For Duncan, as for many within Holyrood, it was now clear how some of Scotland's newspapers had chosen to operate. 'One of the things that really gets me is . . . the distortion of the truth for political purposes within a newspaper,' he explained with quiet anger. 'I think it quite unbearable in a democracy, and they're actually abusing it in my view. I mean, some of the things that are being said are utterly scandalous. And the thing is, you can't pause to think about it before something even worse is said.'

Fortunately, however, some of Scotland's journalists had picked up that it was the relationship between the two-part client, not the architect, which was at the root of Holyrood's current problem. Most of these commentators focused their criticisms on the SPCB, who – from within the project – was now clearly perceived as being out of its depth. The *Sunday Herald*'s political editor, Douglas Fraser, came closest to the prevailing internal mood when he described the group as 'five MSPs whose main role is to ensure the parliament is provided with enough stationery and paper clips, but [who] inadvertently [seem] to have stumbled into a political hard hat area.' He summarised SNP SPCB member Andrew Welsh's decision to call for an audit report into Holyrood, as well as Spencely's investigation, as follows: 'Andrew Welsh . . . [has asked] the auditor-general for Scotland to have a good nose around whatever Welsh and his colleagues have been up to – because, it would seem, Welsh isn't too sure himself.'[24] However, the SPCB was not about to sit back and take what was being flung at it. Within a week of Spencely's appointment being made public, Tory SPCB member John Young responded by launching a stinging attack on Donald Dewar. Describing the SPCB's predicament as the result of being handed 'a succession of poisoned chalices', he criticised the site, the costs and Dewar's reported intent to place a £109 million spending limit on the building. Whoever had thought that Holyrood could be built for £50 million, he claimed, had been 'crackers'.[25]

However, the SPCB was certainly not the end of the problem. That there were difficulties in communication between this political client body and the professional client, the Holyrood project team, was utterly beyond doubt. In spite of the savings identified in the autumn 1999 review, the cost consultants had continued to predict a construction figure of £115 million; and by February the most likely estimate had gone up again, by another £10 million – excluding all the usual add-ons.[26] But as early as September 1999, Brian Stewart had expressed concerns to the film crew about the way this information was being conveyed to the SPCB, and alarm bells were ringing that some information was only getting as far as the project team before it stalled. At a meeting with the HPT that July, the architects had expressed their concerns about costs not fitting the design now being instructed. But their worries '[were] not minuted in the way that we felt that [they] should have been minuted', explained Stewart, '. . . [so] I asked Mick if he – in an independent way – could . . . record and submit to the parliament team what I was saying as a matter of record, which he did.'[27]

Yet even this situation was not as clear-cut as it at first appeared. By both Stewart and Duncan's own admissions, communication between the project team and SPCB was – for the designers – a 'closed book' to which they were not privy.

And as Barbara Doig explained to the film team, she had been submitting increasingly regular briefings to the SPCB, with indications suggesting that this dialogue was building up empathy and trust. 'It's just about communication, isn't it?' declared Alan Mack at Bovis. 'That's the problem here . . . we get back to things moving down through the line . . . You address things that you think people are understanding in English . . . maybe you'd be better speaking Esperanto and get the message across or find some other format of understanding. Maybe we do everything in pictures from now on, I don't know . . . We've got a 27-page report going out this afternoon about cladding, and you can bet your bottom dollar nobody'll read it. They might read the first page. So now we have to do an idiot's guide on everything . . . you know do a picture on the front and maybe people'll look at the pictures. You're getting me into a real cynical mood here!' The real problem seemed to be that the SPCB was now not emerging as a typical client. It was a cross-party body, and at the debate in June 1999, only one of the four political members – Labour's Des McNulty – had actually voted for Holyrood to push ahead. The building project, effectively, had a split political client, over half of whom had not supported the building they were supposed to be stewarding. And this left Barbara Doig in an impossible position.

With the SPCB's behaviour over Holyrood apparently being driven neither by political nor building considerations at any given time, it was never possible to gauge what its *real* views on the project actually were. Doig described her role as being 'the meat in the middle of a very unpleasant sandwich', and it was believed by many that the SPCB's call for a review had been prompted as much by politics as by genuine concern about where Holyrood was now heading. 'I think the independent review was put in place because the [SPCB] . . . took a look at some of the information that was being presented to them, and at the meeting itself . . . appeared to be understanding . . .' explained Barbara Doig. '[They] then left the meeting and began to think with their political hats on rather than perhaps [their] building committee hat[s] . . . And there was a lot of work to be done on the information that I had given them . . . But that routine process was totally interrupted by political considerations.'

To John Gibbons, still at the helm of Holyrood, the process now unfolding was both frustrating and saddening. Exercises were already in place to ensure that value for money was being tested, and moves were also underway to gain more precision about costs. If the client wanted a cheaper building, there were only two ways to do it, and yet more costly prolongation was not one of them. 'If we try to reduce the amount of money that's being spent on the project, then we've either got to reduce the standard of the building or we've got to reduce the size of the building,' he explained bluntly. 'Both [are] possible, but both need a degree of collaboration from the client to accept those things. I mean at the moment we're hearing, "We want the best building in the world, but it has to be the cheapest building in the world." And that isn't possible.' Brave decisions would have to be taken, and – crucially – these decisions would have to be upheld. Perhaps, it was hoped, John Spencely's review would provide advice from someone not 'tainted' by the entire process so far, as those on the inside track were clearly seen to be. For a man given a month to deliver 'the facts' on the Holyrood project, it would be an enormous responsibility. And although it certainly would be difficult, John Spencely couldn't possibly have anticipated how the project was about to unfold.

Notes

1. Ian McAndie to Barbara Doig, *Feasibility Estimate (Cost Check Issue 9) at 30 August 1999*, 1 September 1999, http://www.holyroodinquiry.org
2. A letter from Paul Grice to Brian Stewart would record the following: 'The origin of and reasons for the additional space were not . . . clear to me at the time the DL&E cost check was produced and, for that reason the cost check was not regarded as reliable. It did become clear, once the Holyrood Project Team and Design Team considered the matter in detail, that the additional 4,000m² could largely be attributed to the natural evolution of the design, for example, in accommodating

plant room, etc.', Paul Grice to Brian Stewart, Letter, 16 November 2000, ibid.

3. *Holyrood Building, Progress Report and Update to Papers, SPCB (HB)(99)1–5, Annex B* (circulated under cover of memo to PS/Presiding Officer on 26 July 1999), ibid. Paul Grice's instruction came to light as part of evidence submitted to the Fraser Inquiry, Paul Grice, 'Precognition 2', pts 23–4, 2003, ibid.

4. Martin Mustard, *Project Review*, paras 1.0, 1.1, 6 September 1999, ibid.

5. *Minutes: Client Project Team Meeting/Principals*, paras. 3, 5, 30 August 1999, ibid.

6. David Steel to Enric Miralles and Brian Stewart, Letter, 8 September 1999, ibid; Barbara Doig to Enric Miralles, Letter, 9 September 1999, ibid.

7. Brian Stewart, Enric Miralles and Mick Duncan to Barbara Doig, Letter, 20 October 1999, ibid.

8. Barbara Doig to Enric Miralles and Brian Stewart, *Value Management Exercise – SPCB Client Decisions*, 17 November 1999, ibid.

9. 'End this costly spiral', *Scottish Daily Mail*, 4 October 1999.

10. Elizabeth Quigley, 'Crisis as cost of Holyrood escalates', *Scottish Daily Mail*, 4 October 1999.

11. Quoted in William Clark, 'Parliament trims £1m off cost of Holyrood building', *Scottish Daily Mail*, 13 November, 1999.

12. Quoted in 'Queensberry work to send parliament cost soaring', *Edinburgh Evening News*, 1 December 1999.

13. Ian Swanson, 'Miralles "must explain new Parliament delay"', *Edinburgh Evening News*, 8 February 2000; 'Called to account', *Edinburgh Evening News*, 8 February 2000. The latter comment appears to be a response to Miralles' comments that the building should not be rushed.

14. Auditor General for Scotland, *The New Scottish Parliament Building: An Examination of the Management of the Holyrood Project*, pt 1.20, September 2000, http://www.scottish.parliament.uk, http://www.holyroodinquiry.org

15. *Scottish Parliament Official Report*, vol. 5, no. 2, col. 139, 24 February 2000, http://www.scottish.parliament.uk. Evidence submitted to the Fraser Inquiry revealed that the SPCB had held a crisis meeting on the evening of 23 February following cost information given for the revised design on the 22nd. The new reported construction cost estimate was £125 million, and a final total remained impossible to quantify. The evidence given to the Fraser Inquiry by the SPCB would confirm and supplement what the group had told the film team in interview.

16. Ian Smith, 'Put Holyrood on hold for the sake of us all', *Scottish Daily Mail*, 29 February 2000; Ian Swanson, 'Cabinet in call for Holyrood price cut', *Edinburgh Evening News*, 29 February 2000.

17. Karen Rice and Ian Swanson, 'Holyrood bill "to go up £20m a month"',

Edinburgh Evening News, 25 February 2000; Carlos Alba, 'Parly architect faces sack as costs spiral; £40m bill soars to £250m', *Daily Record*, 25 February 2000.

18. 'Putting a lid on Holyrood costs', *Scotland on Sunday*, 27 February 2000.

19. 'Bringing the Holyrood headache under control', *The Scotsman*, 28 February 2000.

20. Ritchie Mclaren, 'Scotsman Diary', *The Scotsman*, 2 March 2000.

21. The Trials of Mungo Mckay, 'When you're in a hole, best to stop digging', *Scotland on Sunday*, 12 March 2000.

22. Boyling Point, *Evening News*, 28 February 2000.

23. Rikki Brown, 'Why the El does our £230m Parly need a big bullring, Señor?', *Scottish Sun*, 2 March 2000.

24. Douglas Fraser, 'Tortured Chamber', *Sunday Herald*, 5 March 2000.

25. Quoted in Andrew Nicoll, 'You handed us the poisoned chalice Donald', *Scottish Sun*, 3 March 2000.

26. Auditor General for Scotland, *The New Scottish Parliament Building: An Examination of the Management of the Holyrood Project*, pts 1.20, 1.27, September 2000, http://www.scottish.parliament.uk, http://www. holyrood inquiry.org

27. Mick Duncan to Brian McGarry, Letter, 1 September 1999, http://www.holyroodinquiry.org

7

An Independent Review?

*'I think that they would like to see my report before I've written it . . .
There is a lesson that I have learned in life having worked for the
government before, that there is tendency for "independent reports" to the
government not to be independent at all, because you get your steer or
would-be politics. And that's for me to handle.'*
John Spencely[1]

FOR CHARTERED ARCHITECT John Spencely, the period since his appointment to review the Holyrood project had been a mixture of responsibility and fear. Spencely was sixty years old, a past president of the Royal Incorporation of Architects in Scotland, and retired chairman of architects Reiach and Hall, who had joined the Holyrood shortlist themselves, in partnership with Rafael Vinoly, after being knocked out of the competition at an early stage. Bespectacled, bow-tied and fiercely honourable, he cut a foppish dash in a parliament environment largely populated by bureaucrats and suits. And despite his initial euphoria at being offered the job of Holyrood assessor, the enormity of his task had quickly begun to sink in. As he confided privately to the documentary team, 'This all started [as] a phone call on a Thursday . . . I had a meeting on the Friday . . . I went to my club for dinner and I drove home with a glass of wine inside me and I stopped outside my door and I thought, "Oh shit, what have I taken on? . . . This is terrifying."'

Spencely's awareness of the intensely political environment he now found himself in was clearly apparent. Shortly after the election, he had met one of Scotland's opposition leaders by chance at lunch, and had been told – in no uncertain terms – that this man viewed his job as establishing his party as the official opposition. '[He said] he would do *anything* in order to get himself into the position as being recognised as the leader of the opposition,' Spencely confided to the film crew. 'Now if that is the game you are playing then anything else is grist to your mill.' One of the key problems that Holyrood now faced – Spencely assessed correctly – was the political environment into which it was emerging. And with the building project now ammunition with which to attack First Minister Donald Dewar, Spencely believed that 'what the politicians – what the parliamentarians – have got to do for the nation is to rise above this with this debate, and see this in non-political terms.' Judging by what was appearing in the newspapers and in the parliament, this admirable outcome now seemed very unlikely indeed.

Political reaction to the news of Spencely's appointment had been entirely predictable, as opposition MSPs launched a variety of attacks aimed to sink Donald Dewar himself and the Holyrood parliament building. SNP chief Alex Salmond demanded that the First Minister accept personal responsibility for the current situation rather than shuffling it on to the SPCB, and called for additional expenditure to be met by the Treasury.[2] Tory leader David McLetchie accused Dewar of having conned the public about the building's costs in the devolution referendum, then stuck to the well-worn Tory line of listing what else Holyrood's outlay could be spent on.[3] This view was echoed – surprisingly – by leading members of the SNP, a move away from the party's more familiar 'why not Calton Hill?' stance.[4] For the Executive's part, a spokesman for Donald Dewar made it clear that MSPs from all parties had demanded more office space for the building, thereby jacking up costs. The Tories and SNP were singled out for particular criticism as being most vociferous in their demands.[5] Embarrassingly, within days *The Scotsman* ran an article claiming to have seen confidential documents which revealed just the opposite. The greatest demands for space had come not from the opposition, but from ministers and special advisors of the Executive.[6]

Amid all this political infighting however, two determined voices remained louder than all the rest. For Donald Gorrie and Margo MacDonald, news of Holyrood's latest controversy was merely proof of what they had been warning of from the beginning. Both welcomed comments made by David Steel which seemed to suggest that alternatives to Holyrood may not be ruled out. And – in line with Gorrie's long-term stance – the *Herald* quoted him as saying that if Spencely's conclusions showed the Holyrood situation to be disastrous, the Calton Hill option should be revisited again.[7] But while Gorrie's heart still clearly lay with Calton Hill, the realities of the situation seemed to be tempering his position. As he admitted to the film crew late one evening in his temporary parliament office, much as he disliked the Holyrood site and believed it to be a mistake, he now believed that the best option was to press ahead with creating a good building at the current location, if Spencely believed it could be done. 'I would infinitely prefer that we could go back to the beginning and have, I think, a much better selection of buildings up on Calton Hill or Regent Road,' he explained, sitting at his desk as the dusk gathered behind him. 'But it's quite difficult to move from where we are now to that . . . I think, much as I dislike the site, if we could make a runner of . . . Holyrood . . . we should try and do that.'

However, for SNP firebrand Margo MacDonald, the current Holyrood crisis called for more probing of a situation which she described as a 'potential catastrophe'.[8] Encouraged by party leader Alex Salmond to pursue the Holyrood issue, Margo had become a relentless campaigner on everything she believed was wrong with the project. And as one of the parliament's most vocal, charismatic and skilled public speakers, she was certainly succeeding in getting the topic exhaustively aired.

When the film team had first met her in August 1999, Margo's concerns about the Holyrood building were clear. She was worried about the siting, the competition model had only shown a proportion of its volume, and local comment had raised issues that the traffic impact on the city would be adverse. 'And those were the simple reasons: straightforward,' she stated. But it had also seemed that, for her, the process had raised additional fears. 'I didn't want to believe that Calton Hill had been knocked out for political reasons,' she confided. 'I have since learned that it almost certainly *was* knocked out for political reasons . . . Think brown sauce bottles, think logo, design, symbolism of the House of Commons. Everybody recognises it . . . it's an icon.'[9]

For Margo, the motivations behind the Holyrood decision – at that time – had seemed obvious. But her views also appeared to be partly rooted in the inaccurate public and political opinions of why key decisions had been made. 'It is said,' she told the film crew, 'and I'm told it's true – actually, I *do* believe it, *it is true* – that Donald Dewar and his crowd in the Labour Party . . . began to question whether or not it was altogether politically wise to throw in this symbolic building into the mix. And it is alleged, and I believe it to be true, that Donald said, "Anywhere But Calton Hill," because it was some sort of nationalist icon . . . And for those really cheapskate, narrow, horribly parochial reasons, I think . . . we've ended up with really rather a nice building – and certainly I think rather a nice concept – in the wrong place.'

While Margo may have been wrong on this fundamental issue, however, her frustration on the subject of the Holyrood project did not seem in doubt. By the time the film team met her again in March 2000, her attitude to the building had become noticeably more angry and concerned. Through official parliamentary channels, her newspaper column in the *Evening News*, and a canny ability to engage with the public with accessible – and eminently quotable – opinions, she had become *the* voice that raised a number of public questions about where the project appeared to be failing. Yet for others observing the process, it appeared there may be other – very different – motivations behind her attacks.

As early as June 1999, Iain Macwhirter had written in the *Sunday Herald* that 'There are serious questions to be asked about the way the Holyrood building was commissioned, and there must be adequate controls over costs.' However, 'Unable to resist making populist headlines over the cost of the new parliament,' he had argued, 'Margo MacDonald and Donald Gorrie have put the skids under the Miralles building . . .'[10] It was an opinion echoed consistently by many within the project itself. 'Day to day she changes her tune – and she's not properly informed, she's not properly briefed,' one Holyrood insider confided, again in June 1999, when it was already clear the situation was causing the project problems. Another key player – nine months later – viewed Margo's opposition with far more scorn. 'She's obviously got a degree in building and construction expertise,' he argued, sarcastically. 'I mean . . . what she knows [about] building you could write on the back of a stamp; what I know about politics I guess is the same. But I don't stand and make my mouth go about things I don't know anything about . . . So we just don't take any notice of her.'[11]

For Margo though, her determination to pursue the Holyrood issue needed only one justification; and it was one that appeared to make considerable sense. 'In Scotland, there still is not an approval in general, or an understanding, or an acceptance of this project on this site,' she explained, dressed in hard hat and luminous tabard, looking out across the muddy excavation, 'and so therefore I think that it's my job to ask questions and to find out as much as I can about this site in comparison to others . . . I don't know until I've got the facts. And it's really a bit galling to be told that you're stirring up trouble when all you're trying to do is answer the questions that you're asked as an MSP . . .' Whatever Margo claimed, however, the impact that her opposition was having on the project was causing increasingly damaging effects. In a public and political environment where negative comment would have massive and cumulative influence, and with a lack of any credible champion backing the job, Margo was *the* most quotable voice of the Holyrood project. The problem was, she was both an opponent and an outsider, and some of her legitimate observations would be coloured by this relation to the building. And if there remained – as she argued – a lack of public acceptance of the parliament project, it was certainly fair to suggest that at least some of it was due to her own ability to keep the Holyrood building in the news.

However, with John Spencely now appointed, Margo MacDonald was to raise a key and pertinent question. 'I asked for an independent assessment to be made of the project,' she confided, 'and to be honest I was surprised that someone outwith the architectural circle in Scotland wasn't selected . . . I don't want to impugn the man's expertise, ability, experience, objectivity . . . but I now know enough about the project I think to be able to judge how objective the assessment might be.' With Holyrood as politically pressurised a project as it was architecturally, one question now loomed large. Would John Spencely's independent review be as independent as everybody hoped?

John Spencely was absolutely adamant that he would not be leaned on, and – determined that both his report and the building project should be recorded independently – he had been willing to meet the film team for a chat. His initial impressions of the building project had proved enlightened. 'As usual it's a problem of communication I think,' Spencely pondered, 'and people perhaps not always understanding what they're being told . . . And I've no doubt that . . . part of our recommendation will be to change the way [the management is] done.' The real issue however, he believed, lay somewhere else. The unusual complication of a client-change midstream had led to size increases – 'for good reasons'. And this in turn had had effects which caused worry for Scotland's political elite. 'I mean, the point about this project is that everybody is doing their best with the best of intentions,' he argued astutely, 'but it has consequences which people don't like. It's getting more expensive, and the politicians are very nervous about the attitude of the public.' So what might his review offer that could maybe set the record straight?

John Spencely's gut instinct about Holyrood was that the decision to press ahead or quit was a test of the nation's will – and for that reason, it was important that the project kept going. Although he said he was 'neutral' on the choice of site, he believed that moving the parliament now would simply replace one set of problems with another – and he was convinced that those calling for a change of location were motivated by one thing: 'They want to kill the project. That's really what it is.' 'The majesty of the state is reflected in its building,' he argued with obvious sincerity, 'and you can see this in France and Germany and Australia; civilised societies have always spent money on their buildings as a sign of [their] prosperity and . . . confidence.' For Spencely, it was essential that a nation with a devolved parliament should have a physical symbol of it. And if Edinburgh city centre was the chosen location, Holyrood, next to a royal palace, was hard to beat. 'I do support the project,' he stated firmly. 'I'm looking into some difficulties with it, and I'm . . . making no comment about whether it is the right or the wrong scheme. But as a project, we have to get behind it.' The big question was, how much was Scotland prepared to spend? Although Spencely was utterly determined that his review would not be leaned on and his conclusions would be autonomous, he clearly had all the credentials to provide what the Holyrood project needed – a justification for moving forwards. As a fundamentally decent and straightforward man stepping into a political arena, he simply didn't know that he did.

For all within the building project, however, Spencely's Holyrood review now meant one thing: more delay. And just as worryingly, there was also now the chance that MSPs might take the opportunity to introduce more changes. 'We've been working since Christmas with the design team on a series of drawing revisions,' explained Alan Mack, frustrated. 'Now this incorporates all of the most recent changes in the desires of the

Client . . . and the culmination of all this is that we would get
. . . sign off and start getting cracking with detailed drawings
by the end of April. Now, if the client at the end of April then
turns round and says, "No, I don't want that; I want something
smaller," or, "I want to change it," we are back into the cycle
again and there is no way you can cut that.'

An interview the film team conducted with David Steel in
early March hinted this scenario was already perilously close.
'I had a very, very constructive dinner last night with Enric
Miralles and Brian Stewart,' he explained to them, 'to go
through what we might do to try and reduce the space
requirement, reduce some of the specification without tam-
pering with the quality of the building and in particular focus
on other ways of reducing the cost of the fitting out . . .' Not
only were demands being revisited to see whether space could
be cut down on, but the architects were now being asked if
areas could be left unbuilt 'which our successors could then
fill in in later years'. While superficially attractive in the short
term, the impact of these revisits, along with the disruption of
a review, could ultimately result in a devastating outcome.
Time spent slowing down or re-instructing people meant the
timescale of the project would be lengthened, and this in turn
would incur extra costs. In short, Scotland could end up with
a parliament that was smaller – or inferior – to what was currently planned. But it could cost exactly the same – or even
slightly more.[12]

On 8 March 2000, Enric Miralles – away from the eyes of the
press – was secretly smuggled into Scotland and whisked to the
Scottish Executive headquarters to meet John Spencely. He was
greyer, thinner and more weary than usual, but his enthusiasm
and ebullient good humour remained intact. Despite his laid-
back demeanour, however, the problems at Holyrood were
beginning to take their toll. Miralles was perplexed at the decision to call in an 'independent reviewer' to examine the
project, although he was clearly hopeful that the outcome of
the assessment would be good. 'There is no fear at all because

it's a perfectly transparent process,' he told the film team firmly. 'Maybe, on the contrary, I think he could be positive, because he will have the time and the energy to explain the things better, to summarise the things, to put clarity in it – because again we are busy with other things.'

If Spencely's review was looked on positively though, the prospect of a debate on his conclusions certainly was not. Miralles described the continuing lack of public information as 'a disaster', and he was obviously worried that another political debate would simply be a re-run of the previous – misinformed – one a year before. 'What I'm always asking the Holyrood representatives is that they should explain to people better,' he stated to the documentary crew with passion. 'At this moment [there] should be a small booklet or a small pamphlet, full of . . . thousands of pages, and thousands of information, thousands of beautiful images, and there should be a booklet when everybody goes into a meeting . . . [that gets handed over].'

For Brian Stewart at EMBT/RMJM, the reluctance of the client to bring the full facts into the open was perplexing. 'I mean, we don't normally go into this level of detail on every project [because] it's not necessary,' he explained to the film team, showing them through 3-D computerised animations of how the Holyrood building would eventually look, 'but this is such an important project. And we want to take people along with us.' The architects were prepared to present all available information to all MSPs, if it proved to be necessary. But ultimately, the decision of how to convey it to the parliament was up to the SPCB. And here – it seemed – the information had reached an immovable log-jam.

In early March 2000, David Steel had made a surprising comment in an interview with the Holyrood film team. 'Well, we have been in the difficulty that until we have completed and approved the design there's nothing to show the public,' he argued. 'I mean, I'm hoping that the report that we will be presenting next month to the parliament should be a report with a lot of illustrations in it so that people will see for the first time what it's going to look like.' Yet over six months earlier, he had told exactly the same film team this: 'I'm amazed by the use of computer technology. I mean we sit and we look at visual presentations of the chamber from different angles. We look at it as though we're sitting in a back seat, then we look at it from the Presiding Officer's view, and it gives you an amazingly realistic feel of what it's going to be like. And that's helped us a lot.' For Steel, the difference between what the film team had seen with their own eyes and what he was now describing was that previous available illustrations of the building had only depicted the parliament 'in the vaguest sense'. And now that design work had been carried forward, the new and revised parliament design could engage the public in the concept once again. For one close observer, watching the situation – and its destructive impact – from the inside, neither the decision to keep the information private nor Steel's explanation of why it was happening made the slightest sense at all.

For Enric Miralles though, it now seemed that any attempt by his team to inform Scotland's politicians was largely wasted effort, as '[What] the parliament debates are about is everything except the thing they debate . . . It's always like a secret agenda.' 'At this moment the project is completely built . . . conceptually . . .' he stated, shrugging. 'The project is done. And the thing is that really nobody seems too interested in knowing it.' While in the outside world the architect was viewed largely as the parliament's guilty party, from inside the project the situation was almost completely the reverse. 'There's no doubt in my mind,' John Gibbons confided, frankly, '[that] there is a limit to the number of times he will want to start again or amend his designs. I think we have to be very careful . . . now about how we change course if we don't want to lose Enric Miralles.' As it would turn out, the now serious likelihood of Miralles walking away from the building would never come to fruition. Within four months – shortly after the parliament had voted on Spencely's conclusions – Holyrood's signature architect would be dead.

*

By 22 March 2000, John Spencely's report was complete. It was, he joked to the film team, 'five days ahead of our deadline and within budget!' And its findings were 'very damning. It is damning of the whole management of the process. And I think people should lose their jobs – I really do . . . I think there are some people who should be severely criticised for what they have done.' For some people – whom he had been careful not to name – Spencely's conclusions would undoubtedly result in an uncomfortable ride. Figures – although not inaccurate – had not always been put together coherently, nor had they always been reported up the line. And on one issue, John Spencely was unequivocal. 'The design and cost have been operating on two parallel tracks: I mean, it's fundamentally stupid . . . that's the biggest single management error that's been made – to allow cost to be detached from design. Pointless. And that's really why we've lost a year, I think. That and the change in the brief.'

Holyrood, he believed, had developed the three classic characteristics of a badly managed project: the design and budget were out of kilter; there were no approvals in place; and the programme wasn't being adhered to. And, it seemed, there was another problem. The project was bedevilled by an 'obsession with secrecy, and they're all spinning. And it just gets out of control you know, and it actually blows back on them in the end.' The publicly stated completion date, he believed, was 'quite deliberate fudging', as although the building may be *completed* in 2002, it certainly would not be occupied. And that message – publicly – was not being made clear. Despite this, however, Spencely was convinced that the project would go ahead, because if it didn't, devolution was 'a dead duck'. 'I hope that this will be the one and only review,' he confided firmly, 'because if you keep pulling up plants by the roots, you know, they die. And people will just walk away . . . Why should people be crucified? Why should they expose themselves to this? I mean Miralles has been given a terrible time, a really terrible time . . . The things that are being done to search out dirt on people . . . to see whether they can be tarnished, that is not fair.' With Spencely's review complete, it only remained to see how Scotland's politicians would respond to it. Whether they would decide on the facts, however – or on the basis of their prejudices – would still remain to be seen.

Notes

1. Interview, 8 March 2000.
2. *Scottish Parliament Official Report*, vol. 5, no 2, cols 158–9, 24 February 2000, http://www.scottish.parliament.uk
3. Ibid, col. 160.
4. Alex Salmond to Donald Dewar, Letter, 25 February 2000, http://www.holyroodinquiry.org; Eben Black and Kenny Farquharson, 'Steel in firing line as cost of new Scots parliament soars', *Sunday Times*, 27 February 2000; Frances Horsburgh, 'Soaring costs put Holyrood at risk', *Herald*, 28 February 2000; Dave King, 'Steel: the new Parly could be scrapped', *Daily Record*, 28 February, 2000.
5. Murray Ritchie, 'MSPs handed Holyrood blame', *Herald*, 1 March 2000.
6. Dean Nelson, 'Holyrood bill "inflated by demands from ministers"', *The Scotsman*, 2 March 2000.
7. Frances Horsburgh, 'Soaring costs put Holyrood at risk', *Herald*, 28 February 2000.
8. *Scottish Parliament Official Report*, vol. 5, no. 2, col. 139, 24 February 2000, http://www.scottish.parliament.uk
9. Margo was also concerned about the lack of development area for the parliament. 'Remember that I'm a Nationalist,' she stated. 'I want to see this parliament become a real parliament, and not as Billy Connolly so memorably – and I think probably so accurately put it – a pretendy parliament.' Interview, 25 August 1999.
10. Iain Macwhirter, 'Don't let our parliament become Strathclyde region writ small', *Sunday Herald*, 13 June 1999.
11. This was only one view of Margo's position, and her main criticisms of the Holyrood project remained consistent throughout.
12. During the Fraser Inquiry, it emerged that this approach had apparently originated with Parliament Chief Executive Paul Grice. According to his evidence, the SPCB ultimately decided not to pursue this course of action. Paul Grice, 'Precognition 2', paras 56–8, 2003, http://www.holyroodinquiry.org; Paul Grice, *Minute: Holyrood Project*, 6 March 2000, ibid; *Extract from Minutes of SPCB Meeting*, 7 March 2000, ibid.

8

The Spencely Debate

'*Self-interest stifles all compassion, just as in children; but bureaucrats add hypocrisy to boot.*'
Honoré de Balzac, *The Bureaucrats*

O N 4 APRIL 2000, twenty-four hours before the crucial debate on Holyrood's future was due, a presentation and question and answer session was laid on at the parliament site for Scotland's MSPs. Its intention – in the light of continuing media speculation about the building – was to ensure that politicians of all parties had the information they needed to make an informed contribution to the proceedings. Buses were laid on to ferry them from Parliament HQ to Holyrood, sandwiches were provided, and the design team had worked overtime to ensure that as much information as possible could be shared before the crucial vote. Hopes were high that finally the design and project teams could demonstrate an accurate state of play. But as the MSPs began to arrive, determination turned to despair. Only sixteen had bothered to turn up.

For EMBT/RMJM's Brian Stewart, the turnout from Scotland's new politicians was both an intense disappointment and deeply angering. His experience of the last debate had been that MSPs didn't want raw information on the project lest it interfere with how they had decided to vote. And already, it looked like this debate was going to be the same. If, he reasoned, Holyrood was to be ditched, starting again elsewhere couldn't be better, nor could it be cheaper. A new brief would be needed, months of work would be wasted, and the accumulated knowledge of the teams involved would be

94

thrown away. More significantly, if any new building was going to be the same size as the planned one, it would cost almost exactly the same. For Stewart, scrapping Holyrood due to MSPs' failure to accept available information merited only one description. 'It's highly irresponsible,' he stormed. 'That is really profligate with public money; I mean it really is. And it's for all the wrong reasons.' In such a political environment – all were sure – leaving Holyrood now would simply replace one set of terrible problems with another. 'If it's another site,' Stewart laughed dryly, 'watch out! I mean whoever is promoting that, if they think they're going to have a smooth run at it then they're sadly wrong.'

For Bovis' Alan Mack, however, the behaviour of Scotland's MSPs provoked cynicism, bafflement and outright disgust. Over the last few weeks, it had become increasingly clear to him that the effort he and the design team were putting in at Holyrood was almost irrelevant. Politicians had made up their minds how they were voting, and they had made them up according to the 'frenzy of newspapers and media and God knows what else just feeding on non-fact – on tissues of lies.' It was, he stated, 'a bloody damning indictment of our amazing democracy', and it should raise one key question for the missing members' constituents: why didn't you go and find out the facts? The answer, he believed, was clear. In his view, Holyrood did not have a competent or responsible client. What it seemed to have was 129 individuals who were not interested in the parliament building except where it provided a political weapon. Or as Mack rather more forcefully put it, 'We're just very useful to be used. And I just feel used, because it's very, very apparent that it's just a series of pissing contests going on between these various groups, and it's all about who can score points off who, and who can get rid of someone else and put somebody else down. And the project is irrelevant.' To Mick Duncan at EMBT/RMJM, however, the situation offered a profoundly depressing insight into Scotland itself. 'It's really unfair to treat a project like this for political motivation,' he pondered sadly, 'and nobody will thank them for that – ever – doesn't matter which way it goes. I think they'll just be laughed at. Of course nobody will [though], because the papers will think it's good fun.'

For Margo MacDonald – one of the few MSPs who had turned up to the briefing session – the absence of Scotland's representatives was rooted in a very different reason: their attitude mirrored the feelings of the country. 'Lots of them are so terribly confused,' she explained to the film crew. 'There has been so much confusion about this project. There's also a feeling that it has become so complicated that folk are just gonna wait till the debate tomorrow before they make up their mind.' While there was little doubting Margo's sincerity, nor her commitment to addressing her constituents' concerns over Holyrood, her analysis did beg one fundamental question. With millions of taxpayers' pounds riding on the result of the forthcoming debate, was choosing to remain confused until the very last minute *really* a legitimate excuse for public representatives?

Whatever the motivations behind the behaviour of Scotland's new politicians, there was no doubt they were making the job of getting Holyrood built very difficult indeed. In a climate where MSPs were publicly stating that the building might not go ahead, the potential was there for a devastating cost impact. If contractors were pricing for a building they knew might not be built, either a series of jacked-up prices could be quoted so that a cancellation fee could be collected, or the project would receive no interest in the marketplace at all. 'You'd like to think it is a team game,' Alan Mack argued, frustrated, 'you would like to think that the client is actually interested in getting his job, and you'd like to think that he would want to create an environment that would make it easier for his team to get the best job. But it's almost becoming the other way here because [you've] so many different sets of agendas running.'

For one man, these agendas had been thrown into stark relief over the last few weeks. A few days before the design-team presentation, independent expert John Spencely had given his own briefing to MSPs. By his own estimation, roughly two-thirds of Scotland's politicians had been missing. Yet it had been his meeting with the four main party leaders that had proved most instructive. All of them had asked questions designed to assist their political positions, and their behaviour at the session had been, he explained smiling, 'very entertaining'. Lib Dem leader and deputy First Minister Jim Wallace had sat behind Donald Dewar, asked only one question and 'really kept his mouth shut – which I thought was kind of odd for a party leader'. Tory leader David McLetchie 'was banging on about private finance' – something Spencely had not been asked to look into – 'which of course was absolutely irrelevant'. And it had been SNP chief Alex Salmond who had been 'the most lawyer-like. He had an agenda and he was aiming to get information out of me,' Spencely explained. 'He was cross-examining me, and I didn't find that an entirely enjoyable experience. He was the only person who turned up with an assistant . . . who sat and wrote down every answer. I didn't take to Mr Salmond, I have to say.'

What was clear – once again – was that Holyrood's future hung on a vote that was largely political. And with that the case, no one on the design or construction teams had any way of predicting which way either it or their futures would go. It was a scenario summed up simply by EMBT/RMJM co-director Mick Duncan as 'totally disabling'. 'If it *is* a free vote,' Alan Mack confided in the film team, 'and hopefully the people of Scotland have appointed 129 people there to represent them . . . then you would like to think that they will make the right decision . . . But if it's purely a political contest that's gonna go on then God knows what'll happen.' The fact that such an important vote was going ahead with most of Scotland's MSPs choosing to remain uninformed was for him so unbelievable that it almost defied articulation. However, as always, he did his best. 'It is pathetic, isn't it?' he spluttered. 'It's absolutely pathetic . . . They're standing in judgement. They can't even be bothered to get off their arse and come along and have the information spoon-fed to them. I mean, how do you think it makes . . . I mean, . . . it's just nuts, absolutely nuts. It just defies . . . it's surreal, it really is. It's not reality. I mean, maybe these guys will get a proper job next time, I don't know. But it just defies description. It's crazy.'

At the other end of Edinburgh, however, a very different information session about the Holyrood building was already taking place. Former *Sunday Times* journalist and conservationist David Black, who would emerge as Holyrood's most vocal press critic, had organised a public meeting in the Museum of Scotland to air matters in advance of the debate. It would prove a very different – and very illuminating – illustration of the immense difficulties Holyrood now faced.

Black had spent much of the 1970s trying to prevent demolition by the University and Corporation in south-central Edinburgh. His activism had led him into journalism, and – he believed – Holyrood had several motivations at its root. The building was part of New Labour's Cool Britannia strategy, and with the party determined to ensure that Calton Hill was not selected, Scotland was now paying for a building in which it had had no say. The spectre of the Cunningham amendment loomed large,[1] and 'rebranding' seemed at the root of everything. It was a powerful emotional argument, effectively stating that Holyrood was a symbol of centralised rather than devolved decision-making. However, it had one – very serious – problem.

David Black was entirely peripheral to everything that was going on at Holyrood, and had only spoken to John Gibbons, *the* key figure, since day one, briefly. It had been a fleeting encounter that Gibbons clearly recalled 'The only time he's consulted me was following the debate . . . on the architecture policy, when he asked whether he could come and see me to talk about the Holyrood project . . . We were putting forward diametrically opposed views about some of the background, and he said, "All very interesting, can I come and talk to you about it?" . . . And I said, "Yes, any time." Well, I haven't heard from him since.' Despite this, however, Black's position was passionately held, and as the years went by his vocal criticisms – both in Scotland's letters pages and a self-penned book – would make him an increasingly quoted Holyrood commentator. His pointed attacks would both reflect, and inform, a significant proportion of Scotland's Holyrood coverage. David Black may not have been on the project's inside track, and as a result much of what he stated would be wrong, but, to some of the Scottish media, he would become the parliament building's leading 'expert'.

The mood of Black's public meeting was a mixture of genuine concern, suspicion and outrage. Those attending, panel included, were clearly disappointed and alarmed at some of the decisions and approaches taken so far, and the feeling of many seemed to be that the building – if it went ahead at all – should certainly be paused for re-evaluation. What was equally clear, however, was that among the serious legitimate concerns being raised at the forum, there was some information – circulated as fact – which was anything but accurate.

One audience member – in a wheelchair – had heard that there were no specifications for the disabled in the new building. It was completely untrue, but she was not corrected. There was clear concern over continuing speculation that Queensberry House might be bulldozed. But EMBT/RMJM was adamant that the building was crucial to its design, and Brian Stewart had even disagreed publicly with Spencely's suggestion that it should be demolished and built anew.[2] 'It would,' he argued to the film crew, 'be quite wrong to demolish that house . . . I will not be a party to demolishing Queensberry House, and Enric Miralles will not, and [Mick] will not.' Despite this, another spectator at Black's meeting declared with authority that Miralles 'doesn't like [Queensberry House], I mean, he's not happy with old buildings'. The chair of the meeting, journalist Lesley Riddoch, confessed her ignorance of the issue, and the point was allowed to pass unchallenged.

But most disturbing of all, one 'expert' panel member – speaking as a voice of 'authority' – informed the meeting that although the SPCB reported that piles and flooring had been laid in the underground car park, 'I defy you to show me where it is. I live across the road from the site. I pass it every day. I watch it every day.' He was wrong. When asked privately by the film team whether he could substantiate his allegation, the 'expert's' reply was this: 'Well, I can't substantiate it in terms that I don't have access to the site . . . I said this to the public in terms that unless the car park is underneath the MSP block then it is very difficult to see [it] anywhere on the site . . . You have to say, "Where is it on the site?" It's not visible.' So what was his evidence? 'All I said was that it's not visible, so in that sense my eyesight is my evidence. My eyesight's my evidence in terms of the amount of delivery lorries of concrete that go through the place each day – that doesn't seem to happen very much.' It was hardly an incisive, or an informed, perspective.

The confusion arising at this public meeting was indicative of a growing problem Holyrood was now facing. With suspicion about the process rife, and no credible voice of support from within the project, numerous 'experts' were cropping up to comment on Holyrood's problems. However, few were well informed, and most were actively hostile. The misinformation that this resulted in would have a serious and lasting impact. The public arena was so full of political and 'expert' truths, half-truths and nonsense about the parliament building that it was almost impossible for anyone to negotiate through it to discover what was really going on. And the secrecy surrounding Holyrood served only to perpetuate growing suspicions and antagonism. The documentary team itself – supposed to have 'privileged access' – was locked in an ongoing battle to gain press passes, which had been repeatedly refused on the peculiar basis that a documentary team was not a news crew. And on the morning of the MSP question and answer session, the behaviour displayed by some members of the parliament's press office had reached extraordinary new heights. Stopped by a press officer and told it couldn't film the meeting because, he claimed, the design team didn't want them there, the crew was almost simultaneously greeted by Brian Stewart, declaring that it must come in to record what was going on. 'Parliament first, Holyrood second: that's how it's always been,' one of the parliament's more officious press officers would later state over lunch. It was an attitude that completely failed to recognise the parliament building's vital iconic significance. And it was not only failing to disperse attacks on the project; it was, albeit unintentionally, practically inviting them.

At half past two on 5 April 2000, MSPs began to arrive for the crucial debate on Holyrood's future. In the weeks since Spencely's appointment, the project had scarcely been out of the news. PFI had been suggested as an option for funding the building – and ruled out.[3] The Public Accounts Committee at Westminster had been urged to investigate the project, in a move welcomed by Donald Gorrie but branded 'insulting' by Margo MacDonald.[4] And SNP leader Alex Salmond had argued that newly released feasibility studies on possible parliament sites showed that the costs of Holyrood had been pinned low, and Calton Hill inflated. He accused Dewar of operating an 'ABC' principle – 'Anywhere but Calton Hill.'[5]

But the biggest scandal now breaking was that Spencely's report had revealed the 'hidden cost' that many had so long suspected. At the June 1999 debate, MSPs had been told the construction cost estimate of the building was £62 million. According to Spencely's review, £27 million more had been excluded.[6] With Donald Dewar defending his officials and Salmond on the attack, for one journalist enough was finally enough. 'That [Dewar] didn't know about hidden extras . . . is a disgrace,' Lorraine Davidson argued in the *Sunday Mirror*. 'That the First Minister seems to think the situation is OK is even worse.' But while Salmond might be ahead on political points, she argued, 'the job of a good opposition party must also be to take a hard look at the consequences of its actions . . . A botched parliament building won't benefit any of the political parties. But a Parliament we can be proud of may help restore the public's faith in the new Scottish govern-ment.'[7] Whether the public were about to get it was quite a different matter.

However, whatever the allegations circulating, what none of Scotland's politicians yet realised was that something far worse was already unfolding. Enric Miralles had not attended the MSPs' presentation the day before, and – when questioned on his whereabouts by the documentary crew – it was clear from the reactions of his colleagues that a serious problem was emerging. Unable to articulate it, they had left it to John Gibbons to explain the situation in the site car park the follow-ing morning. With tears streaming down his face, he confided that Miralles had been diagnosed with a brain tumour and had been flown to Houston for emergency surgery. It was the worst possible news, both personally and politically. Miralles had become a close friend of John Gibbons, and had developed a strong professional friendship with his partners at RMJM. Holyrood itself was on a knife-edge, but Miralles' illness, for his colleagues, was infinitely worse.

As the debate began, Miralles' absence was high on the agenda. An article had appeared that morning in the *Evening News* reporting that Enric, '"hurt and disillusioned" by criti-cism of his scheme' was to take a back seat on the parliament project in future. The piece seemed based largely on a mis-understanding of the EMBT/RMJM spread of responsibility, and even managed to contradict its own main thesis by quoting Brian Stewart's words, 'He has not taken a back seat, it's just that no-one has wanted to speak to me in the past.'[8] However, the article had clearly found an audience with some of Scotland's politicians. Miralles was not available, and, understandably, MSPs wanted to know why. 'I . . . requested that Enric Miralles should be asked to keep the promise that he made to MSPs when he spoke to us last year,' declared a scarlet-clad Margo MacDonald. 'He said that he would be willing to come back and to discuss with us the progress of the project. Where is he? I would certainly like to discuss the progress with him.'[9]

EMBT/RMJM co-director Mick Duncan had predicted twenty-four hours earlier that the debate would cherry-pick Spencely's report for political motives. As the session unfolded, it was certainly clear things hadn't improved. However, while the now familiar posturing of Scotland's politicians was both depressing and disturbing, what the debate did offer the documentary team was a rare opportunity to see the SPCB in action. 'I've been to look at the Flemish parliament and The Hague with them,' Brian Stewart had explained nearly seven months earlier, 'and they're very rational and very clear thinking people . . . They're all reasonable . . . but what the political process is going to do to these MSPs when it comes to decision-making . . .' With only one of the political members having voted to back Holyrood at the debate in June 1999, the client's performance in April 2000, after nearly a year at the helm, would be a very illuminating experience.

As Liberal Democrat SPCB member Robert Brown rose to speak, he exhorted all colleagues to vote not by party line but individually. Holyrood, he argued, had been 'bedevilled by a variety of conflicting agendas – political, professional and media', but the overriding consideration must be that all should act as trustees for the real client; the people of Scotland. Backing the £195 million budget and 2002 end date proposed by Labour's Gordon Jackson,[10] he declared that parliament should reaffirm the project on the basis of the information now before them, and push ahead. For Labour's Des McNulty, the conclusion was the same. However, the conclusions – and the behaviour – of the SPCB's two opposition members were to come as a profound shock.

As Andrew Welsh and John Young stood to argue, one thing became strikingly clear. Both appeared to focus on the mistakes of the past – and while this was alarming enough, both men also seemed keen to exonerate the SPCB from responsibility. Their contributions to the debate would earn them criticism. 'Members today have picked up the fact that the [SPCB] is a parliamentary body,' declared Liberal Democrat Tavish Scott, 'and that means that Andrew Welsh and John

Young cannot be semi-detached members of the SPCB. Those gentlemen were appointed by Parliament, and they should accept that.'[11] Labour's Mike Watson was equally damning. 'I have not . . .' he argued, 'been impressed by the defence put forward by members of the [SPCB] . . . [W]e as a Parliament put its members in charge . . . [t]herefore, if there is responsibility, we members share it . . . If [the SPCB] were not exactly asleep at the wheel, they were certainly gazing out of the side windows for quite a bit of the journey.'[12] Holyrood, it was now clear, was stewarded by a body that was split as to its future direction. And as John Spencely would later confide, the divided vote was something he felt was 'absolutely scandalous. There has to be a corporate responsibility. I mean, the idea of having on a committee people who don't believe in the project is just nonsense. You can't run a business like that; you can't run a project like that. Everybody's got to be behind it.'

With the votes counted, Holyrood was through, and by a larger – though not much larger – margin than last time. For the design team and John Gibbons, however, who had watched from the public gallery, there was little cause for celebration. The vote had, again, divided broadly along party lines, and there had been little improvement in the SPCB's position. But what had really upset those within Holyrood had been comments made by Margo MacDonald. In her closing speech, she had declared, 'If Señor Miralles is ill, that gives us another week or two to play with.'[13] And although she could not have been expected to appreciate the gravity of the situation – particularly following David Steel's all too brief explanation of Miralles' absence – the tone of her comments had caused enormous distress. They had been, confided one insider, both 'cheap' and 'awful'.

However, on one key issue, Margo had been right. Spencely's review had succeeded in upping the official budget to £195 million, but the project now had a cost 'ceiling'.[14] It was, she confided firmly to the film crew, 'the worst possible outcome . . . We've virtually got a fixed term contract of £195 million. Now what happens if we find that to make the place look decent we need to spend £199 million? Do we not spend that money? Do we end up with something really cheap?' Under the construction management contract by which Holyrood was proceeding, a cost cap, essentially, was unworkable. The project was continually evolving in a changing market, and a final price could never be known till the end.

As John Gibbons would later explain, Spencely's report *had* been independent, but it had also been a means to an end. 'I've always seen this process [as] a sort of war with a series of battles in it if you like,' he explained in his office, 'and . . . the ultimate end goal is to get this building finished and occupied within a certain timescale . . . We've had to take strategic decisions from time to time [and] . . . from that point of view, the independent review was a very useful tool to help us progress . . . Coming from [Spencely], it's valid and it's conclusive and it's obviously the right thing to do. It would not have been accepted coming from us.' Holyrood – again – was through to the next stage. But as ever, the scrutiny was not over. Although Spencely's review was complete, a request had also been made for Scotland's Auditor General to investigate the project, and a report to the parliament's Finance Committee was also now underway. Yet before either of these would be delivered, Spencely's accepted suggestions had to be put in place. And as always with the Holyrood project, party politics – yet again – would get in the way.

Notes

1. Labour MP George Cunningham's amendment required the Secretary of State to lay an order before parliament repealing the Scotland Act unless at least 40 per cent of the eligible electorate voted 'yes'. In the devolution referendum of 1979, Scotland voted in favour of devolution by 52 per cent to 48 per cent, but only 32.9 per cent of the total electorate had joined the majority.
2. Karen Rice, 'Demolishing house will delay Holyrood', *Edinburgh Evening News*, 1 April 2000.
3. Valerie Darroch, 'PFI should fill the Holyrood hole', *Scotland on Sunday*, 12 March 2000; Ian Swanson, 'Private funding for Holyrood ruled out', *Edinburgh Evening News*, 13 March 2000.

4. Ian Swanson, 'Westminster set to join Holyrood probe', *Edinburgh Evening News*, 20 March 2000; Sarah Schaefer, 'Parliament: devolution – row over MSPs' expensive new home', *The Independent*, 21 March 2000.

5. Quoted in Ian Swanson, 'Parliament building "too big for Holyrood"', *Edinburgh Evening News*, 29 March 2000.

6. John D. Spencely, *Report on the Holyrood Project to the Scottish Parliamentary Corporate Body*, pt 4.3.4, March 2000, http://www.scottish.parliament.uk, http://www.holyroodinquiry.org

7. Lorraine Davidson, 'The Queen of spin: Forget price wars, we don't want a bargain basement', *Sunday Mirror*, 2 April 2000.

8. Quoted in Karen Rice and Ian Swanson, 'Hurt Enric steps back', *Edinburgh Evening News*, 5 April 2000.

9. *Scottish Parliament Official Report*, vol 5, no 13, col. 1344, 5 April 2000, http://www.scottish.parliament.uk. Quote corrected by reference to taped footage.

10. Cols 1346–7, Amendment S1M-720.2, ibid.

11. *Scottish Parliament Official Report*, vol 5, no 13, col. 1343, 5 April 2000, ibid.

12. Ibid, cols 1320–1.

13. Ibid, col. 1346.

14. The background to how this figure was arrived at was provided to the Fraser Inquiry by Paul Grice: Paul Grice, 'Precognition 2', paras 64–6, 2003, http://www.holyroodinquiry.org

9

All Change

'Buildings are like football teams: they need supporters.'
Enric Miralles[1]

IN THE IMMEDIATE aftermath of the Spencely debate, it soon
became clear that the fallout from it would be anything but
brief and damage free. Margo, it was said, had written to David
Steel and Donald Dewar, demanding answers about Enric
Miralles' illness.[2] 'A source' had stated that Spencely's recommendations 'had reinforced the preference of people working
on the project for getting rid of [Queensberry House]'.[3] And
within the project itself, there was concern that the tight deadline for the report's delivery had resulted in some problems.
EMBT/RMJM – already battered from enormous and
extended public pressure – had reacted to some of Spencely's
findings with both 'outrage and a bit of disbelief', while at
Bovis great exception had been taken to the estimated completion date of late 2003. 'That's just patently untrue', a frustrated
Alan Mack had argued. 'By the level of the information ... that
has been gleaned in the last fourteen, fifteen months, we are
obviously far, far more aware of the ... nature of the programming outputs that we can achieve ... We are ... confident that
... 2002 – end of – is achievable.'

John Gibbons, however, was unusually downbeat. 'I knew
from speaking with John Spencely where the gist of the criticism was and where the substance of the problem as he saw it
was,' he explained to the film team frankly, 'I mean, that had
been quite reassuring and interesting. But I can see it would
always be difficult to translate that into a short lucid document

that was not open to misinterpretation.' Whatever the complications thrown up by Spencely's review and its interpretations,
however, far worse – for everyone – had been the experience of
the Holyrood debate that followed.

For those who had witnessed Scotland's politicians in operation a year ago, even the first 'examination' of Holyrood had
not prepared them for the behaviour now aimed not only at the
project but at Brian Stewart. And for Stewart, the entire experience had left him sickened, disgusted and shaking with rage.
'I thought it was awful,' he confided furiously to the documentary team. 'I thought . . . the behaviour of some people was a
disgrace, it really was a disgrace . . . [And] if you said to me,
"Wow . . . you must have thought that was fantastic [that you
won]" . . . no I wasn't, I wasn't happy at all . . . I felt personally
insulted, I felt the business was insulted, and I felt that the
behaviour of some of the people there . . . was, I just can't find
words to express it . . . If it's just abuse you can heap on people
who are trying really very hard, then I'm afraid you've just lost
your way.' For one senior Bovis member who had attended the
debate in Alan Mack's absence, his first insight into Scotland's
new democracy had provoked a profound reaction. '[He] said,
"What a shambles!"' recalled Alan Mack. 'Quote: "They were
rude . . . they're downright liars, and they make it up as they go
along. I'm not sure whether I want to vote again; what a nightmare. What an eye-opener – an eye-opener" – I think that was
the classic. And that was literally just fresh out the chamber.'

Yet despite the effect that another Holyrood debate was having
on all those in Edinburgh, from Enric Miralles in Houston
there was extremely encouraging news. While lack of public
information in Scotland about his condition was causing
understandable frustrations, privately – it was clear – the
architect was on the mend. Within twenty-four hours of the
debate's result, a jubilant Miralles had sent his colleagues a fax.
'Good news! Best!' he wrote, 'Thanks for your kindness. Enric
Miralles.'[4] For all within Holyrood who had grown immensely
fond of the designer the news of his recovery had come as a

huge relief. 'He's described as comfortable,' a clearly emotional John Gibbons explained to the film team, 'and he's writing again – which is a good thing. And that seems to be the critical period. And in overall terms . . . they are happier; they are "more hopeful" I think was the actual word that the hospital used. That really is about the extent of what we know.'

By 28 April, word had come in that Miralles would be in hospital for another four weeks, and although passionately interested in the project again, the long-term seriousness of his condition remained unclear. Gibbons was making plans to visit him in America, and procedures were already being drawn up to find new ways of working between Edinburgh and the States. Finally, it seemed, an extremely difficult, worrying and emotional period was over. For Gibbons, sitting tearfully in his office, it was clear that the time since Enric's illness had been upsetting, draining and worrying. 'Yeah, absolutely,' he confided quietly, 'made more difficult really by not being able to share it, I think. But anyway, it could have been worse,' he faltered, 'in the sense – you know – we didn't think he'd make it, basically.'[5]

With the pressures of the debate finally over, Miralles recovering, and Holyrood yet again pressing forward, one issue within the project now dominated. Following suggestions in John Spencely's report, the Scottish Parliament had instructed the SPCB to establish a 'progressing committee' to work alongside it at Holyrood. The group's remit was to finalise the building's design, complete the project by the end of 2002 within a £195 million total, and report regularly – or as required – to the SPCB and other members. For those within the project, it was something of a relief. '[Being the client for a building project] needs . . . intense concentration week in week out, and time and space for it . . .' Project Sponsor Barbara Doig confided, seated in her on-site office in May. '[And] right at the beginning . . . I couldn't believe that . . . [the SPCB was going to be] the formal client, because I said last June to various colleagues . . . "This won't work . . . is there not another way? Can they not co-opt other people on to it?"'

Doig had been so concerned about the political client's set-up that she had visited the director of Legal Services to see if there was any way around the situation. The answer had come back 'No.' But with Spencely's review complete and tactfully suggesting that it would be 'prudent' for the SPCB to consider if it had the time or expertise to fulfil the day-to-day client function,[6] the prospect of a more focused 'Progress Group' now offered exactly what Holyrood had been missing – a client body that could concentrate on the parliament building alone. Yet as the weeks, then months continued, the creation of the Progress Group began to display just one notable and consistent feature: a complete failure to make any progress at all. The question was, why?

Exactly a month after the Spencely debate, *Herald* journalist Robbie Dinwoodie ran a story that revealed the depth of political infighting in which Holyrood – and the still to be formed Progress Group – was now mired. The SNP had vetoed George Reid, one of their most senior politicians and the parliament's joint deputy Presiding Officer, from becoming chairman of the new committee. And the reasons quoted seemed to typify the party's approach to Holyrood all along. 'We saw no reason on earth why we should end up in the position of defending this whole project by having one of our members chair this committee,' one SNP member was quoted as saying, while a party spokesman argued, 'it was the Executive parties who brought us to this position and it was their responsibility to deliver the new Parliament complex on time and on budget. It would have been wrong for one of our MSPs to have been forced into a position of justifying their position.'[7]

It was an act denounced by the *Sunday Herald*'s Iain Macwhirter as 'as crass a demonstration of mindless party political sectarianism as we're likely to see for many years'.[8] And he wasn't the only one disgusted by the SNP's behaviour. For independent assessor John Spencely, who had already met George Reid to discuss how the Progress Group would operate under his stewardship, the act of sabotage provoked an uncharacteristically outspoken response. It was, he told the film team in disgust, 'deplorable', 'contemptible', and 'pathetic'. But if the SNP's behaviour was appalling, the behaviour of Scotland's other political parties was certainly not much better. The Labour–Lib Dem Executive was resisting pressure to put a minister on the new Holyrood committee, while the Tories were responding with a refusal to put any of their members on the Progress Group at all. It was – to say the very least – an inauspicious beginning. But despite the enormous problems already facing the Progress Group in the wider political arena, what was becoming progressively clearer was that the creation of the committee was facing one, virtually insurmountable obstacle. And that obstacle was the SPCB.

By early April 2000, nearly a year after the SPCB had taken over at Holyrood, the group's deliberations – for the documentary team – still remained a completely closed book. Despite multiple requests for admittance into meetings, the film crew was still being denied any access to decision-making whatsoever, and had even been forced to request brief archive shots rather than documentary footage in order to gather material of the SPCB together at all. On this occasion, after being removed from the meeting before serious discussion formally started, the team had to resort to filming through a glass panel in the door in an attempt to gain footage of the SPCB 'in action'. And – with a parliament press officer helping them carry their tripod out of the room before shutting the door in their faces – the frustrations that this was raising were beginning to take their toll. The SPCB were public figures discussing a publicly funded project. The films were commissioned by the BBC and Scottish Screen, and supposed to be telling Holyrood's inside story. And it was proving virtually impossible to find out what was going on. Angry and disillusioned by the lack of transparency the SPCB was exercising, producer/director Stuart Greig was on the verge of giving up. 'Oh fuck it; it's not worth it,' he sighed depressed, peering through a window into the meeting. 'I'm sure it's easier making a film about the building of the Treblinka.'

However, from within the project, worried voices were now

beginning to mutter about what really went on behind the SPCB's closed doors. While Labour's Des McNulty appeared to be largely exempt from criticism,[9] frustration at the group's other three political members was – by spring 2000 – becoming worryingly and increasingly apparent. 'It's become more political, which is something they can't help,' John Gibbons confided tactfully to the film team. 'I mean they are political animals and they are connected to other political activities, so certainly . . . we became increasingly aware that the members of the [SPCB] appeared to be being manipulated by their political parties. That they were not really . . . the ideal that we'd been hoping [for].'[10]

While most were reluctant to criticise the SPCB on camera, off-screen the frustrations with the group were becoming abundantly clear.[11] At meetings and presentations with the group, it was confided, sectoral interests had emerged between the members, and a sense of competitiveness – and even hostility – was also becoming apparent. For one insider, the group was the 'three monkeys'. For another, they were not used to applying their minds to building projects 'if they have minds at all'. One attendee described them as 'a precious bunch', to whom 'even the simple things in life are difficult', while another was sick of being treated rudely, and had refused to attend any more meetings until the SPCB learned to behave.[12] As ever, though, it was left to Alan Mack to state these feelings on record. 'My own personal view,' he argued to the film team, '[is that the SPCB have] all got a totally personal agenda. It's got absolutely bollocks to do with any constituents. If I were a constituent I'd be wanting to know why they aren't asking particular questions, why they aren't doing their job properly . . . I'd love to be a politician, by God, you don't have to work for a living, that's for sure.'

Yet the real problem the SPCB seemed to be presenting was with the formation of the new Progress Group. When the documentary team had finally secured interviews with the SPCB's four political members, when each had been asked about the make-up of the new committee it appeared that lessons of the past had now been learned. What Holyrood really needed was the right expert advice, clear management and effective reporting mechanisms that could ensure that problems were spotted quickly and remedied. However, as the weeks passed by, it began to become clear that the progression of the new Progress Group was doing anything but progressing. And from within the project, it was beginning to become apparent why.

Inside Holyrood, word was now suggesting that the SPCB had decided not to co-operate in appointing a body that – effectively – would take over from them. Donald Dewar, it was said, was furious at the lack of the Progress Group's progress, and it seemed the next move might be a motion of no confidence. The worst of all worlds would be a political shadow committee, but by 28 April it looked like the group was moving towards this option. By 3 May, a technical, professional Progress Group had been endorsed by Holyrood's main players, but by the 11th – with George Reid out of the picture – it seemed an unwieldy mix of four to five politicians, plus three to four professional members, would be the most likely format of the group. Parliament Chief Executive Paul Grice was trying to create a committee that looked democratic on paper and – as the four members of the body apparently couldn't agree on a solution – the decision had been referred to party managers. For John Spencely, the emerging format of the Progress Group was worrying. 'I mean, one doesn't want to be Dr Doom,' he told the film crew frankly, 'but it's certainly not what I had expected or intended; and it really seems to me actually all it is is a mirror image of the [SPCB]. And that's just silly, I think. But maybe they'll make it work. I mean, I *hope* they make it work.'[13]

Spencely was now in a tricky dilemma. Before he had submitted his report, Paul Grice had asked him to remove his recommendations for who should serve on the new Progress Group. 'He said it would make life difficult for him,' explained Spencely, and I said, "Alright; well, in that case, I will take it out." I regret that now; I should have stuck to my guns.' His original hope had been that one member of the SPCB would take on the role of liaising with the project team, with the setting up of a Progress Group a 'second best' option. The intended body would be small, tight and cohesive; a deputy Presiding Officer, the Project Director, Paul Grice, and John Gibbons. And some technical people? 'No!' Spencely argued with conviction. 'John Gibbons . . . and the Project Sponsor if he or she's an inexperienced person . . . I mean . . . they're employing a project team and a design team who are extremely highly qualified people. They don't *need* any other advisors. God . . . advice is coming out their ears . . . that's not the point.'

Before its membership had even been finalised, it looked like the Progress Group was already headed for disaster. And however effective its eventual make-up, the length of time it was taking to reach a conclusion was threatening the usual knock-on effects. Holyrood was locked into a tight programme of delivery in which everyone had to play his or her part – at the right time – if the building was to be completed to timescale and budget. And yet more procrastination meant, as ever, yet more potential delays. 'What we're frustrated about generally is the fact that we seem to be working for a client that is a vacuum,' explained Alan Mack, 'that doesn't seem to realise that he is a client and that he has responsibilities as the other half of the contract . . . You know . . . if they can't make a decision on [the Progress Group], how are they going to make a decision on construction, or issues affecting construction? It's frustrating.'

Yet while the Progress Group's non-progression continued to bubble and hinder, Holyrood was preparing for still another change at the top. On 31 May 2000, the SPCB issued a press release, stating, 'The members of the Parliamentary Corporation wish to place on record our appreciation of all Barbara Doig's hard work . . . Contrary to some recent press articles, the Spencely Report into the Holyrood Building Project did not criticise Mrs Doig. We wish to make clear our support for her and we wish her well on her return to the Scottish Executive.'[14] It was a statement that endorsed a stand made roughly two months earlier, as Barbara Doig explained. 'I'd been to see the Executive at the end of March,' she confided in the film team, 'but . . . within a few days of that, the Clerk sat down with me and said that the [SPCB] had given me a vote of confidence and . . . quick as a flash . . . I realised – no, that didn't mean any-thing to me, that I could see the problems that were there. And I just responded, "Well, that's very nice thank you. But you should know that I am thinking that perhaps I'm not confident that the arrangements are right".' For Barbara Doig, one of the parliament's most loyal defenders, the previous year had been one of enormous change.[15]

On 8 March 2000, the documentary team had been inter-viewing Barbara Doig at her offices when she made a striking statement that had taken them completely by surprise. Loyal, discreet and supportive, she had always negotiated her way around difficult areas of discussion, and presented a picture of Holyrood which was both diplomatic and often – for the film crew – frustratingly circumspect. On this occasion, it was clear, both Doig and her team had suffered badly. 'It is an abrasive, harsh, violent environment,' she had stated, 'but it's not going to help anybody, or help the Holyrood building project, if we behave in that way.' Individual MSPs had phoned her and been 'quite abusive down the phone at me – and that's not particu-larly pleasant', while personal attacks played out in the papers were to have a devastating effect. By her last day in charge of the parliament project, her disbelief at the behaviour of some of Scotland's MSPs would be all too apparent.

On 30 May 2000, twenty-four hours before her departure, a story had hit the media that reported serious questions about project sponsor Barbara Doig. Quoting Margo MacDonald's intention to question the process by which she had been offered another senior government post, a *Scotsman* article argued that Doig had been 'forced out' of her role after Holyrood's costs had 'spiralled from £50 million to nearly £200 million'. 'I feel resentful,' MacDonald had stated, 'that, as an MSP, I am making fairly detailed criticism of someone who is not able to give a public account of her actions. But it would be wrong if I did not ask questions as this lady has been in charge of a big, big project which involved relationships between different government departments and she did not make a success of it.'[16] In the days following, Doig would tell the film team, 'I think actually if I hadn't gone, I might have saved myself some of the media grief, because, in fact, the worst of the media coverage has actually come . . . once it became public knowledge that I was going. And I just *cannot* understand that. I cannot understand an elected representative naming an official . . . and who can make allegations without any back-up. I've no right of reply and it just sits there on the record.'

Over the preceding weeks, the pressures of Holyrood had begun to tell on everyone. Miralles was recovering from a brain tumour, Brian Stewart had been taken into hospital, John Gibbons – now seriously considering his position – was suffering severe leg pain, and Doig – who had taken only two days' sick leave over an eighteen-year period – had become bedridden with stress-related arthritis. 'And I had toothache yesterday,' Alan Mack wryly joked. Even Donald Dewar, incensed by what was going on and constantly apologising for the impact the 'vendetta' against him was having on the project, had been taken into hospital for tests. For Doig, the situation she had found herself in – she now saw – was impossible. 'It was a dawning realisation earlier in the year . . .' she remembered, 'and, of course, by that time, I was . . . very well aware of the client and the kind of client behaviour that was going to go on through the project . . . And basically I had the feeling that it was going to paralyse the model of project sponsorship, I just [would] not be able to do my job.'

With between half to three-quarters of the SPCB's membership seemingly politically or personally opposed to Holyrood at various stages, Doig's role of representing their interests had been utterly unworkable. 'I can't represent their interests because . . . obviously I've always been for the project,' she argued. 'I've believed in it. It's my job to do the project. Not to represent the interests of somebody who's against the project.

So there's a basic incompatibility there.' When Holyrood had hit rough seas, however, the behaviour of individual members of the body had provoked dismay. 'Well, what can I say?' Barbara Doig queried. 'Gobsmacked that every paper I wrote at that time was clearly leaked. Not by the [SPCB as a group], by individuals. And I find that incomprehensible. But then that's politics.' In autumn 1999, she had been instructed by the Clerk of the parliament not to speak to the SPCB individually when she had wanted to get it up the learning curve. And similarly, she argued, David Steel had told her not to speak to party groups about the Holyrood building itself. 'So I find it a little bit ironic then when I'm accused of not communicating with MSPs when I've actually been operating under instructions of the [SPCB],' she laughed wryly. 'I think the client's representative has to be true and believe in the client until the very end. And my end comes later today.'

With Barbara Doig's departure, Holyrood was now in flux. Scotland appeared not to want a new parliament building, a significant proportion of the SPCB was opposed to the project, and politicians – and certain sections of the press – appeared to remain largely hostile. There was no project director in place, no Progress Group, and – within weeks – there would be no architect. So what was the future for Holyrood? Barbara Doig was utterly candid. 'I would be very surprised if it came in on the present programme and on budget,' she explained to the film team. 'I've left it in a state that I'm confident that if things went straightforwardly . . . it could be done . . . But there's been nothing straightforward or ordinary about this project so far. It's been a bit like a soap opera. I mean, if anybody had started scripting it at the beginning I don't think they'd have had this outcome at all.' At Bovis, Alan Mack was even blunter. 'If you look at history and what's already proceeded,' he argued, 'then you'd say we're in for a real long time and we're in for a lot of money . . . My gut feel tells me that there'll be issues with the design team. I think there'll be further issues with the client . . . And that inevitably will mean delays – and inevitably those delays will cost money . . . So I suggest you go out and buy a lot of film at real cheap rates, cheap knock-down prices – you're gonna need it!'

On 28 June 2000, nearly three months after parliament had instructed the creation of a Progress Group, the final line-up of the new client body was announced.[17] Robert Gordon – a key figure since the beginning and head of the Executive Secretariat – was to be the Executive's nomination, while John Gibbons – now acting as project director until a successor for Doig was appointed – was a member too. On the professional side, David Manson, a distinguished quantity surveyor, and Andrew Wright, past President of the Royal Incorporation of Architects in Scotland, would provide technical support. Both had been previously involved in the project, then moved aside, at the very earliest stages. And there were three politicians: Labour's Lewis Macdonald, the Liberal Democrats' Tavish Scott and Linda Fabiani from the SNP.

In terms of Spencely's ideal membership, the make-up of the group was not encouraging, and his opinion that the project sponsor's responsibilities should remain unchanged had been dismissed.[18] Holyrood now had an unwieldy mix of politicians, professionals and bureaucrats to aid the SPCB, and Barbara Doig's role had been broken into parts. For Doig, though, although the new approach to her job may prove less efficient, ultimately, it may be for the best. 'The model that's been adopted of project sponsorship, I think, may suit the political circumstances better,' she confided on her final day at Holyrood. 'There will be a more diffuse set of responsibilities across three or four people. And I think that may make it more bearable for the individuals concerned.' For Alan Mack though, another project director meant one thing: more complications. 'It's gonna be difficult,' he told the film team, 'because a new person will take time to come in and learn the rules. God forbid, if there are any.'

In the event, however – despite its inauspicious beginnings – the final line-up of the Progress Group would prove a significant improvement on the client problems faced with the SPCB.

Despite the intensely political nature of Holyrood, the group would develop a generally successful camaraderie, avoid party divisions and make genuine attempts to grapple with the project in the years ahead. The body would not be without its problems, though. There would be difficulties of understanding, and the relationship between this new client body and the project team would suggest that problems in communication still remained.[19] Secretary to the new Progress Group would be Sarah Davidson – a tall, striking 28-year-old civil servant who, just a year later, would become Holyrood's Project Director number four. The Progress Group now had a daunting task to deliver: Scotland's new parliament must be finished by December 2002, and within a budget of £195 million. Its first full business meeting was scheduled for 4 July 2000. Although nobody yet knew it, it would be the day of Enric Miralles' funeral.

Notes

1. Interview, 10 June 1999.
2. 'MacDonald pushes for answers on health on Miralles', *Edinburgh Evening News*, 24 April 2000.
3. Ian Swanson and Karen Rice, 'New fears over threat to Queensberry House', *Edinburgh Evening News*, 26 April 2000.
4. Enric Miralles to Brian Stewart, Mick Duncan and John Gibbons, Fax, 5 April 2000.
5. Interview with John Gibbons, 6 April 2000.
6. *Report on the Holyrood Project to the Scottish Parliamentary Corporate Body by John D. Spencely*, pt 9.4.2, March 2000, http://www.scottish. parliament.uk, http://www.holyroodinquiry.org
7. Quoted in Robbie Dinwoodie, 'Party vetoes Reid for project post', *Herald*, 5 May 2000.
8. Iain Macwhirter, 'Danger: politicians at work saving their backsides', *Sunday Herald*, 28 May 2000.
9. This exemption seems to have been based on ability rather than party politics. In the film team's interviews with the SPCB members, Liberal Democrat member Robert Brown also seemed to have a similar approach.
10. While not all members had been subjected to such party political string-pulling, admissions from within the group – when the film team finally did interview them – confirmed that individual party pressure

certainly did exist. 'I took the view myself,' explained Lib Dem member Robert Brown, 'that the [SPCB] should have been in a position . . . to arrive at a united view as to what we should be advising parliament to do [about Holyrood].' But the SPCB's own resolution had required changes at one member's insistence after he'd consulted with his party leadership. 'I think it was a paragraph at the end of the day which didn't have the significance, I think, attached to it by the member concerned. But . . . there was obviously anxiety about how it was going to read with his party colleagues,' Brown explained.

11. During the Fraser Inquiry, the following comments from Barbara Doig would come to light: 'Following careful reflection on the SPCB meeting on 1 February I have concluded that it is important to set out for you . . . my analysis . . . of the SPCB's performance as the client for the Holyrood building . . . I am unconvinced that the Body understands the importance and elements of its role, the complexity of procuring under considerable media pressure a building with so many external interests, and the implications of its decisions. For the most part members appear unwilling to devote the time required to read the material provided, discuss the subject matter in depth, receive advice and give an appropriate amount of instruction . . . Individual members' attendance is patchy across meetings and in any single meeting there is a variety of starting and finishing times. Members change their views between meetings and have difficulty recalling factual information and previous presentations and decisions accurately.' Barbara Doig to Paul Grice, Letter, 7 February 2000, http://www.holyroodinquiry.org

12. In the film team's interviews with the SPCB in 2000, a more harmonious and consensual view of proceedings would be described, although Robert Brown indicated that party influences had been exerted, and Des McNulty revealed a personality clash.

13. During the Fraser Inquiry, an additional reason for the delay emerged. It appeared there were obstacles in formulating a mechanism of delegation from the SPCB to the Progress Group while maintaining the SPCB's role as legal client. The draft Memorandum of Understanding went through several revisions at the SPCB's instruction. Paul Grice, 'Precognition 2', paras 73–7, http://www.holyroodinquiry.org

14. *Parliamentary News Release* no. 025/2000, 'Parliament bosses thank Holyrood Project Director', 31 May 2000, http://www.scottish.parliament.uk. John Spencely, however, told the film team that he believed a project sponsor had been employed who was the wrong person for the job, and who, he believed, was *known* to be the wrong person for the job. Interview, 7 April 2000.

15. The Fraser Inquiry revealed that despite this affirmation, Barbara Doig's loss of confidence in the SPCB seemed to have been mirrored by its loss of confidence in her. 'There was a strained relationship, and so much depends on confidence at a senior level in an organisation . . . I

would not go so far as to say that they had no confidence; that would not be true, but I detected that there was strain on that. They were not as confident as they had been, and that has obviously got to be an important point for me to consider, because if you are fighting against a lack of confidence in you, you are always in a sense on the back foot . . .' Paul Grice, evidence session, para. 223, 10 February 2004, http://www. holyroodinquiry.org. This information supplemented what the film team had heard from the SPCB itself.

16. Quoted in Alison Hardie, 'MSP raises questions on role for manager criticised over Holyrood', *The Scotsman*, 30 May 2000.

17. *Parliamentary News Release* no. 032/2000, 'Professional edge to Holyrood Progress Group', 28 June 2000, http://www.scottish.parliament.uk

18. *Report on the Holyrood Project to the Scottish Parliamentary Corporate Body by John D. Spencely*, 9.4.2, March 2000, ibid., http://www.holyroodinquiryorg

19. It is impossible to establish exactly where on the line of communication between HPT and HPG the problems existed. It seems, though, that the information flow between professional and political client had significantly improved.

10

Farewell, Enric

'He was a monumental man . . . And the way he was treated
was absolutely disgraceful.'
Mick Duncan, co-director EMBT/RMJM[1]

IN LATE MARCH 2000, the Holyrood documentary team was
filming routine shots at RMJM's riverside offices in
Edinburgh. Suddenly, completely without warning, Brian
Stewart leant back against a filing cabinet, put his hands over
his eyes and began to cry.

Enric Miralles had recently rung Stewart at home. He and
his wife Benedetta had been distraught, incoherent and very,
very emotional. 'Intuitively I felt that he wasn't absolutely
certain what was wrong,' Stewart confided. 'I just felt that he
knew it was serious, and, you know, something would have to
be done.' Stewart rang John Gibbons to see if he could shed any
light on the matter. Gibbons couldn't; perhaps this was a
marital crisis. But as the next two days came and went it
became clear that a far more serious picture was emerging.
Miralles' office didn't know where he was and he had stopped
answering his phone at home. What was going on?

By the beginning of the following week, Miralles was on
the phone to Stewart again. The message was worrying, but
still unclear. It appeared the architect had some sort of
tumour that was affecting one side of his body, but its symp-
toms were devastatingly mundane. Miralles had fallen off his
bike and injured his knee, and he and John Gibbons – who
had a sore leg – had hobbled round the office together, joking
that they were clearly past the age for cycling. Nobody

thought Miralles might be losing his balance. The architect had also complained in passing of pins and needles in his arm while leaving a meeting with David Steel. No one had given it a second thought. And Miralles' own wife, Benedetta Tagliabue, had laughingly dismissed her husband's recent complaints of tiredness. 'He was saying, "I don't know why I'm tired,"' she remembered, 'and I was teasing him saying, "Why do you say you don't know? You're taking the plane twice a week, you're working all day long. It's the most normal thing that could happen."'

But over a two-day period, Tagliabue had been proved tragically wrong. Miralles had suddenly lost feeling in his right arm and had gone to see his GP. He was referred directly to the hospital, given tests and scans, and sent home. Almost immediately, the architect was called back in. The scans had revealed a massive and inoperable tumour in a very inaccessible part of his brain. He had weeks, maybe days, to live.

For Miralles, Tagliabue and their young family, the sudden news was shattering. 'From then on our life changed,' Tagliabue recalled, sitting thin and pale faced at their offices in Barcelona, 'the perspective of life changed . . . he felt immediately that death was very next to him, even if I didn't want to believe it.' The next few days were torturous. Miralles knew he was going to die, but his wife refused to accept it. 'I didn't want him to discuss anything at all because I didn't want to hear this possibility . . .' she explained, 'we were just going to make him better. This was the truth.' Miralles' illness was both unbelievable and horribly real. And while despair, disbelief and desperate hope engulfed the family in Barcelona, in Edinburgh a deeply worried Brian Stewart was left unclear about what to do. The full facts of Miralles' illness remained uncertain, and such was his friend's despair that Stewart had been unable to push him on facts he clearly wasn't able to volunteer. Miralles' studio was equally unsure about what was going on: they seemed to think he was lecturing in America. Information was coming in sporadically, and being gradually pieced together via a series of deductions. Just how serious was the situation?

Within days, news came in that Miralles was in Houston. After several days of utter desolation, a bullish aggression had emerged: he was not going to die without a fight. He had set about finding the best place in the world for treatment, and within twenty-four hours he and his wife were there. 'We've flown . . . without thinking to [the] United States,' Tagliabue remembered, 'without even knowing if we had any possibility there. And I think we had a lot of luck there, because we found a good surgeon and we found big help from some friends . . . They really supported us and made life as easy as it could be in such a difficult moment'. On 28 March, Miralles sent RMJM a fax. Although desperately ill and facing imminent life-saving surgery, his characteristic humour was still in place. 'A picturesque doctor will operate . . . on Wednesday,' he wrote. 'I hope to be able to see you at the debate, and open the building together, if God allows.' If he couldn't make the debate, the architect would send a message he wanted read out to Scotland's MSPs. His writing, normally fluid and accompanied by cheeky doodles, was so shaky it was almost illegible, and it took some work to decipher all of the words. Praising the team who had worked on Holyrood so far, his message to them was heartfelt and deeply touching. 'The project is ready,' he wrote to his colleagues. '(Could be cheaper, a bit smaller . . .) but the project is ready. Do not be afraid. Scots never are . . .'[2]

Miralles' fax was the first confirmation that the tumour was on his brain, and was very serious. But it was still unclear in Edinburgh what the prognosis was, and no one was sure if the tumour was even malignant. With the debate approaching, the burden of the situation was weighing increasingly heavily on Brian Stewart. In such a hostile press and political situation and with the real extent of Miralles' illness still far from clear, the proper course of action remained uncertain. For the film team, the reasons for his caution would be obvious. As Tagliabue would later confide, on the day of his operation Miralles had received telegrams from some of Scotland's press along with well-wishing messages from his friends. In them were statements telling him he ought to give an interview to clarify the situation at Holyrood. 'I mean . . . what do you want to clarify?' she asked, horrified. 'He was fighting for life and he didn't have any wish to sell his image of a person fighting for life to the press. And also they were calling to the Spanish consulate. It was really terrible.'

Twenty-four hours before the debate, Brian Stewart decided he had to speak to John Gibbons. 'I'm not trying to understand politics because I think that's pretty difficult unless you're in it,' he confessed. 'I just felt that I should convey something . . . And I left it to John to use his experience to know how to handle that.' Gibbons' reaction was swift. Whatever was wrong, it was now clearly apparent that that the debate could not go ahead without First Minister Donald Dewar being told. So that afternoon, Dewar was secretly smuggled down to Holyrood for a meeting. 'I told him I didn't know whether it was malignant,' Stewart explained. 'I didn't know what the real prognosis was. I knew he was going to have an operation, and we were obviously hopeful that this would be OK.' All news that was known was passed on to Presiding Officer David Steel. The surgery was known to be risky, extremely difficult, and there was a danger of side-effects. The critical thing for the long-term prognosis was how Miralles had come through the operation – and he had come through it alive.

Within days of his operation, Miralles sent his colleagues another fax. It was brief, but showed a near-miraculous improvement. His handwriting was entirely back to normal. Although Edinburgh had not involved him in the debate – 'it was too difficult for Enric to have such an emotional shock,' explained Tagliabue, over the coming days he would keep in touch regularly, almost euphoric about Holyrood and raring to get back to work. He spoke to John Gibbons frequently on the phone from Houston, and his voice, his manner and the length of the conversations all suggested that he was improving day by day. However, one subject was never broached frankly. 'We never talked directly about the illness,' said John Gibbons, 'he didn't want to, and we never did.' As always with Miralles, the facts lay some way beneath the surface, and required some effort to extract. But what was becoming clear from his conversations was that his treatment was beginning to catch up with him. Two courses of intensive therapy were having the usual side-effects, and the long-term seriousness of his condition remained uncertain. But despite the fact that not all the tumour had been removed, he was clearly lucid, and humorous. 'That's why we shouldn't jump to conclusions,' Brian Stewart explained to the documentary team at the post-debate party. 'We simply don't know what the state of his health is . . . nobody should jump to conclusions. But I just know that he is urging us to keep going, and I don't support the view that the project should stop.'

As Miralles' condition rapidly improved, he began to work again. 'He couldn't disconnect and sometimes he was angry with himself because he couldn't disconnect from what he was used to do[ing],' a smiling Tagliabue confided. 'He wanted in a way to change a little, no? He thought maybe something in his way of life had caused this illness to come – but it's not true.' The daily routine was structured. Miralles would work for half a day, then spend the rest of the day having treatment, or recovering from it. Despite the success of his operation, there were physical problems. But he was writing again, and he was steadily recovering. And what was more, he was on his way back to Barcelona, to recuperate in the hills. Arrangements were made in Edinburgh for a working visit to see him. But before the team could leave, Mick Duncan – alone in his RMJM office – received a terrible call from Miralles' studio. Suddenly, and completely without warning, Enric Miralles had suffered a brain haemorrhage. He was dead at 45.

Within hours of the dreadful news breaking, a hasty statement was released to the Scottish press. 'Enric's legacy to the Parliament and Scotland is a fantastic design which was recently approved by the Parliament,' declared Sir David Steel. 'As is clear from the on-site construction, and despite this terrible shock to all concerned, there is no doubt that this project can and will be completed.'[3] It was a sentiment echoed by new

Progress Group convenor Lewis Macdonald, who added that he was 'absolutely confident that this project will be completed on time and within its budget'.[4] Given the suspicion with which Holyrood briefings were now received, it was hard to imagine a worse approach. Scotland's press and the project's opponents were entitled to suspect that they were being given neither the full nor the final story. And what Holyrood really didn't need at a moment of such crisis was politicians reciting more official line. The shock announcement was to have profoundly upsetting repercussions. Almost immediately, events in Barcelona would unleash a storm of claim, counter-claim and allegation. And it would be both distasteful and violent – even by Holyrood's brutal standards.

Within hours, the Miralles backlash had begun. While some commentators – in Scotland, the south and internationally – lamented the loss of a talented architect, for others Miralles' death opened up a whole new set of questions. These were, declared a sickened John Gibbons, both 'distasteful and demoralising', and formed a mainly Edinburgh-based story 'muckraking over what plots might have been hatched about [Enric's] death'. At the front of the charge strode blonde standard bearer Margo MacDonald, who greeted the tragic news with regret, and a very serious charge of deception. Arguing that work at Holyrood should be put on hold as a mark of deference until after the funeral, she declared that many outstanding questions still required answers, and suggested that the parliament had been either misled or lied to about the seriousness of Miralles' condition.[5] 'There was no statement at the start of proceedings,' she declared to the documentary team, 'there was no prior notice given to Donald Gorrie and myself – who were moving what amounted to a moratorium . . . for the new parliament building – we were not told that Enric Miralles was ill. We most certainly weren't told how ill he was, and during the course of the debate it came about inadvertently that the Presiding Officer had to say that Enric Miralles was quite unwell.'

Margo's clear belief was that David Steel's statement had

been prompted less by Miralles' illness, than by a story run in the *Evening News* – and picked up by politicians – on the morning of the debate.[6] Within the parliament, however, her statement provoked a curt and dismissive response. The SPCB noted 'with regret the inappropriate and tasteless comments from one MSP', and refused to respond any further.[7] Yet Margo was not to be cowed. Branding her reprimand 'unseemly',[8] she penned an article for the *Evening News* that would sensationally whip any moral high ground from beneath her own feet. The parliament building, she argued, was now no longer Miralles' concept, and was a compromise of his initial dream. Raking over the history of the project so far – and calling Miralles' approach into question as she did so – she stated her intention to ask parliament again to cancel the building she so vehemently opposed. But it was her closing statement that scraped a new low for the Holyrood saga. 'Whatever the building at the foot of Holyrood Road might be,' she argued, 'it's not Enric Miralles'. It's a cut-price compromise that should be allowed to die with him.'[9]

As the row over Miralles' death unfolded, the questions and allegations grew. Claims were soon being made that the architect had known he was going to die as long ago as February,[10] and the news that he had attacked the behaviour of Scotland's 'lying' politicians was run – by one paper – as 'an amazing death bed rant'.[11] 'Now all of the myths about February,' explained an emotional Brian Stewart to the film team, 'and claims that people knew. [Enric's first fax] is clear. This is a tragic situation which was just unfolding on an hour by hour basis at the end of March beginning of April. No one knowing precisely what the real situation was, not even Enric.' Questions were now being raised about both the percentage of fee Miralles had been paid before his death, and the degree to which the design could now be called a Miralles project, given that Scotland was paying for the work of a famous architect who was no longer involved.[12] Bovis' Alan Mack was incredulous, 'Nobody knew he was ill: we didn't know he was ill,' he stated in disbelief. 'And all this nonsense about "when was it first known that . . . he was sick?" and "how much has he been paid?" and "has he been paid too much?" It's awful, absolutely awful and people like that you ignore! You don't expect to have people like that in public office.'

On 8 July 2000, five days after Miralles' death, and with speculation growing about the future, Brian Stewart and Mick Duncan issued a press statement. Responding to the 'understandable concern[s]' being raised in the public arena, Miralles' partners confirmed that their friend's death had been totally unexpected, and that the remaining partners intended to go on.[13] 'Enric was working with us on the project right up to the end of last week,' the statement declared, 'and there is ample testimony to his close involvement with the Stage D scheme design which was recently agreed by the Scottish Parliamentary Corporate Body.' If the statement was intended to reassure the public, however, in the hostile environment surrounding Holyrood, it would achieve just the opposite.

Within a day, Margo MacDonald went public again with more Holyrood questions – this time about the extent of Miralles' input into the building's most recent designs. 'As an elected representative,' she argued, 'I have the responsibility of calling to account the people who have issued this latest statement. I would suggest that they can allay suspicion as to the precise quantity and nature of the input from Enric Miralles in the last two or three months of his life by publishing his last drawings and plans. They must publish the notes by the people who claim to have discussed details of the project with [Miralles] within the last fortnight.'[14] To the documentary team, however, Margo's reaction would be far more explicit. 'I can't tell you how disgusted I am by the claims that Enric Miralles was able – between the time of the first diagnosis of his illness . . . and the completion of . . . the scheme design . . . – I can't tell you how disgusted I am at the claim that it was Enric Miralles who did that,' she argued with obvious passion. 'For goodness sake, the man was so ill he couldn't have been possibly expected to do it. I wouldn't have expected him to do it, and anyone in their right mind knows that he was unable to do so. And I think it's a downright lie to claim that he did.'

To Miralles' widow Benedetta Tagliabue, none of this public storm made sense. Her husband's death remained, she told the film team, 'a story that I always have in my mind, because I still really don't understand . . . We knew that everything was difficult but we didn't expect such an abruptly [sic] end. And even the doctor didn't expect that.' As for suggestions that his illness must have prevented the architect from working, they were untrue. 'You want to find hints that what was happening to him . . . and he didn't show any hint,' she confided. 'He displayed an enormous amount of energy . . . he didn't leave any instruction but he left everything totally ordered . . . a lot of notebooks perfectly done and perfectly ordered and all the projects with the ideas well explained . . . So really he produced more in this last year than . . . in the previous one . . . I don't know, it's surprising.' Even at Holyrood, serious discussions had been had with the architect about the building's detail in the last days of his illness. Miralles, it appeared, had made one last gargantuan effort. 'It's very strange, it's very strange,' his widow mused. 'Maybe because he knew . . . I believe that your body – if it knows that it's in life danger – must transmit in some part of your personality, this danger of life. And maybe he was reacting in the way that he knew. It was with a lot of energy with giving the best of himself. Really the best.'

While Tagliabue struggled in Barcelona with personal and professional tragedy, for the team back in Edinburgh, the impact of Miralles' death was immense. EMBT/RMJM had passed through some serious periods of difficulty, but despite its differences, the working consortium had grown strong. 'I don't think . . . there was ever anything said on either side that went deep,' explained Brian Stewart, struggling to articulate the team's evolving relationship, 'so, you know, we sort of always cleared the air and started to understand one another better and then built on that . . . I think they . . . maybe were productive actually in some senses.' For him, the problems the architects had faced in the political and public arenas had only served to make them stronger. 'I think the nature of the project and the pressures of the project . . . meant that you almost had to sort of frequently join hands and sort of deal with the outside world,' he confided in the film team, 'so that was a sort of bond.'

For a tearful John Gibbons though, whatever the problems of the past had been, Miralles' relationship with his design partners was now absolutely clear. 'Well, Brian thinks they've had their ups and downs,' he confided, smiling sadly. 'I think to Enric it's a form of friendship. If you can get fairly wild, aggressive, shout and rant and rave, you know, you only do that to your mates . . . They've certainly . . . had their ups and downs, but by and large there's been a clear friendship developed. They are very similar people in many ways.' Brian Stewart's feelings about his colleague's sudden death were certainly beyond doubt. As he attempted to read for the film team from the faxes sent at the height of Miralles' illness, a struggling Stewart flicked through the papers before breaking down completely. Putting the papers aside, his voice broke, and his eyes filled with tears. 'I can't do it,' he wept.

Yet perhaps most tragically of all in this dreadful situation, the behaviour of some of Scotland's press had made Enric Miralles' last days intolerable. Before his illness, the architect had been increasingly upset and angered by the coverage of his building in some of Scotland's newspapers, and at his last meeting with the documentary team he had returned to the topic of the papers again and again and again. 'Enric thought he could control the press', explained Tagliabue. 'Here in Spain . . . the press really listens to you. [And] he was absolutely annoyed by spending a lot of time trying to explain to someone . . . and see[ing] that everything was manipulated and what . . . was written was not what he was saying.' In the last days of his life, the architect had been unable to bring himself to look at Scotland's newspapers at all. 'He couldn't think about the press,' confided Tagliabue. 'This may hurt him very much . . . he couldn't look at it.'

For those inside the project in Edinburgh, distaste at the Scottish media – and at some of Scotland's politicians – had now spilled over into outright disgust. 'Over the year I've become more and more cynical,' declared Alan Mack, stand-ing in Holyrood's 'non-existent' car park, 'and it's just like water off a duck's back now. I mean, probably Elvis will be seen in Holyrood next, Elvis will be in the car park . . . [It's] scurri-lous diatribe . . . that's exactly what it is. It's garbage, shite, keich.' But whatever problems the project was facing in the outside world, what Holyrood was about to encounter would be the most profound upset it had suffered since the project began. With terrible irony, Miralles had died just as the client had resolved what it wanted, a new client body for the build-ing had been put in place, and the Stage D report for the project had been approved.[15] But the pressures Holyrood was about to come under would not originate outside the project. This time, they would be at the very heart of EMBT/RMJM.

Notes

1. Interview, 1 August 2000.
2. Enric Miralles to RMJM, Fax, 28 March 2000.
3. *Parliamentary News Release* no. 036/2000, 'Sir David pays tribute to Enric Miralles', 3 July 2000, http://www.scottish.parliament.uk
4. Quoted in Robbie Dinwoodie. 'Parliament a memorial to architect; Miralles dies before his vision is fulfilled', *Herald*, 4 July 2000.
5. Margo argued that the alternative to this was that ministers and the SPCB had been badly served by civil servants duty-bound to investi-gate and report both on the state of Miralles' health and on his capa-bility of completing the building. In an interview with the film team, she gave what she believed were the reasons for the information being withheld: 'one was the perfectly understandable and perfectly human reason of the Miralles family . . . not wanting . . . to have this discussed openly, and not wanting people to be speculating about whether or not he would live or die, because that was the seriousness obviously of the operation. So I can perfectly understand that . . . I think we were not told because there were a number of vested interests in the project. There were obviously the vested interests of the people who had con-

cluded contracts, who had already done work on it, who had committed a lot of their company's time and energy to it, I understand that well. There were also the vested interests of the people who had advised the First Minister, Donald Dewar, on first of all the site, secondly the choice of architect, and thirdly on the type of contract that would be used, this management construction contract, and so therefore there were people who had made decisions, and had given advice who frankly had to cover their backs. That's what I think. Those were the two groups of reasons why we were not told the truth about Enric Miralles' illness.' Interview, Margo MacDonald, 26 October 2000.

6. Karen Rice and Ian Swanson, 'Hurt Enric steps back', *Edinburgh Evening News*, 5 April 2000; Interview, Margo MacDonald, 26 October 2000.

7. *Parliamentary News Release* no. 037/2000, 'Corporate Body expresses sympathy to Miralles family', 4 July 2000, http://www.scottish.parliament.uk

8. David Scott, 'Miralles's death "not a surprise"', *The Scotsman*, 5 July 2000.

9. Margo MacDonald, 'Holyrood folly is no tribute to architect', *Edinburgh Evening News*, 5 July 2000.

10. Karen Rice, 'The lies and dirty tricks', *Edinburgh Evening News*, 4 July 2000; 'Secrecy must end', *Edinburgh Evening News*, 4 July 2000.

11. 'Death bed outburst of Holyrood architect', *Daily Record*, 5 July 2000.

12. Hamish MacDonnell, 'Blow to Holyrood plan as its mastermind dies: a man of sensitive imagination', *Scottish Daily Mail*, 4 July 2000; Ian Swanson, 'Now is the time for Holyrood answers', *Edinburgh Evening News*, 10 July 2000.

13. *Parliamentary News Release* no. 040/2000, 'Parliament welcomes statement of commitment to building project', 8 July 2000, http://www.scottish.parliament.uk

14. Quoted in Joanne Robertson, 'Miralles team deny cover-up over his health', *Sunday Times*, 9 July 2000. Margo also tabled a parliamentary question asking whether the SPCB would publish 'authenticated drawings, design sketches, diagrams and any other documentation on the Holyrood project produced by Enric Miralles between February and July 2000' (S1W-9259). David Steel replied that the approved Stage D drawings were available for inspection, and the SPCB had 'no reason to seek any ancillary material from the architect in support of that submission', http://www.scottish.parliament.uk

15. *Extract from Note of the Scottish Parliamentary Corporate Body Meeting*, 'Scottish Parliament Building; Stage D (Scheme Design)', 20 June 2000, http://www.holyroodinquiry.org. The film team, however, would be told that Stage D at the point of Miralles' death was only 75 per cent complete. The Fraser Inquiry would hear, 'The situation on site as at the end of July 2000 was that although the Architect had presented a

Stage D: Scheme Design which had been approved, it was not a co-ordinated Stage D: Scheme Design. It was an architectural Stage D only with the design information provided by the Structural Engineer and the Mechanical & Electrical Engineer not equivalent to Stage D.' Alan Mack and Brian McQuade, 'Precognition', para. 7.1, 2004, http://www.holyroodinquiry.org

11

Spiralling Out of Control

'I will be the public face now, we were two partners, it's me now and I'm very committed.'
Benedetta Tagliabue[1]

IN A SMALL bar round the corner from EMBT's Barcelona studio, John Gibbons, Brian Stewart and Mick Duncan stood in tense and worried discussion nursing untouched beers. It was 1 August 2000, and all three had flown to Barcelona to meet Miralles' widow and try to find a way forward in the aftershock of his sudden death. The reception they received was something none of them had expected.

Within three weeks of Miralles' passing, Benedetta Tagliabue had flown to Edinburgh for meetings at Holyrood. She looked shattered, and had given no thought to the project – or work on site – at all. It had been her first visit to the building site since construction had begun, and the day had been spent showing her round, and explaining what work she would need to look at. For those inside Holyrood, Tagliabue's view of the future was unclear. She had two small children, a business to run and many projects besides the parliament to consider. And given the way her husband had suffered at the hands of Scotland's politicians and press, there was great concern that her decision could go one of two ways. 'She will either say "to hell with the project,"' worried Bovis' Alan Mack. 'I mean, I suppose she could take a view that "it killed my husband" . . . and I'll take my children and go and do something with my life that is meaningful, and leave these miserable buggers in Scotland to their own devices. Or she will get passionately

involved to make sure it gets completed. I hope it's the latter –
and I'm sure it will be.'

By the end of Tagliabue's visit, two things were certain.
Miralles' widow was utterly determined that her husband's
vision must be realised. But what was equally clear was that she
had very little knowledge of how the project had developed
since EMBT/RMJM's competition win. 'I think I do understand the project,' she explained sincerely to the film team,
'and I was always with Enric here in the atelier, deciding things,
deciding [changes] . . . and living together with a team . . . We
were really acting as "compensation" in a way . . . I was using
my creativity in a way to be next to him and to comment [on]
things with him . . . and of course I was also assuming a lot of
roles that he didn't have the time to assume, or maybe he was
not very good at.' Tagliabue's role at Holyrood, it now seemed,
had not been as Miralles' equal partner. But with the parliament's signature architect dead and the political focus sharp-
ening up, one question increasingly called for an urgent
answer. If Enric Miralles was no longer leading the Holyrood
project, who was now in charge?

Inside Holyrood, the answer to this question seemed obvious.
EMBT/RMJM had three surviving directors within the partnership, all of whom were totally committed to delivering the
project. But Miralles had also had a closely trusted right-hand
man in Barcelona, Joán Callis, who had worked on the parliament complex from the beginning and designed almost
instinctively in the master's style. The quietly spoken Callis
had stated his total commitment to completing Holyrood, and
it seemed that the perfect 'replacement' for Miralles as director was simply waiting patiently in the wings. Dealing with the
personal impact of her husband's death, however, Tagliabue
had not been fully involved in discussions about the
company's future, and when she had re-emerged at her office,
her reaction to Callis' potential elevation had been an
unequivocal no. The alternative options soon laid out on the
table were worrying. Either her father – a successful wine pro-

ducer in Italy – should replace her husband, another eminent Spanish architect should take the role, or – perhaps – it should be a lawyer. Each of these solutions would prove unacceptable, so in order to equalise the balance within EMBT/RMJM, it had been suggested that the Edinburgh end should drop one of their two partners. Utterly aghast, Brian Stewart and Mick Duncan refused.

With Tagliabue now back in Barcelona, a lengthy standoff over the leadership of the architects was already beginning to unfold. While Miralles and his Scottish colleagues had – at times – had a difficult relationship, a strong professional respect and friendship had gradually emerged. But it seemed that Tagliabue had never viewed RMJM as equals, and on at least one occasion apparently indicated that the only important constant on the project was EMBT itself. With her involvement at Holyrood minimal, it had been an uncomfortable situation but one that could be skilfully managed. However, Miralles' death had had a profound effect on the company's internal dynamics. 'It totally changes things,' Mick Duncan would later explain to the film crew. 'The whole difference between the past and the future was that single event of [Enric's] death, because that affects the whole nature of his office, and it affects the relationship therefore between us and them.' Miralles' death, an immediate tragedy, would have unexpected long-term consequences. And although nobody yet knew it, it would set off a chain of events that would affect the partners for years to come.

For Holyrood lynchpin John Gibbons, the situation he now faced was unenviable. Repeated attempts to contact Tagliabue personally had proved impossible for well over a week, and with progress at a standstill and a resolution increasingly essential, an EMBT/RMJM board meeting had been proposed in Barcelona. Gibbons – yet again – would play a crucial mediating role. 'We're here because we were finding great difficulty in somehow conveying to Benedetta the urgency of this,' he confided, depressed and worried as he drove through the streets of the city. 'Obviously it has to be done very sensitively in the circumstances, but . . . we did need to move forward.' The next forty-eight hours would demonstrate just how impossible the situation within Holyrood had now become.

Before arriving for the crisis meeting, John Gibbons had faxed Tagliabue twice to say that he, Stewart and Duncan would be arriving at EMBT's offices at half past one. But as they dropped their bags in the elegantly cluttered hallway, the visitors learnt that she wasn't present – would they like to wait for her in a back room? It was the worst possible start. With bad blood between the two sides beginning to simmer and the Edinburgh team taking off two days that they could ill afford, all were concerned that what they now faced was a mixture of delaying tactics and the dismissive attitude to RMJM that Tagliabue was said to have displayed all along. However, things were about to get much worse. When the team emerged from their waiting room unexpectedly, a very embarrassed Tagliabue was caught slipping out of EMBT's front door. Flustered and cornered, she asked to rearrange the crucial meeting for four o'clock. Gibbons, Stewart and Duncan retreated to a bar round the corner – and there they waited, frustrated, angry and deeply upset. In a volatile political situation, the signs for a swift and amicable resolution were now looking very far from positive. 'Well, it has to be the last crisis,' Mick Duncan laughed wryly. 'It's either the last one or it's the first of a lot many more. Which do you prefer? . . . One really desperate crisis or another?' Unfortunately, the answer to his question would not be what anybody hoped.

EMBT/RMJM's crisis meeting – when it eventually transpired – was awful. Despite the public affirmations of commitment following Miralles' death, the architectural partnership was now under intolerable strain, and with Tagliabue feeling vulnerable and outnumbered, a bad-tempered meeting had seen strong words – and even some accusations – being thrown. After years of dedication and pressure, the situation Stewart and Duncan now faced presented an enormous dilemma. 'There are split loyalties,' Mick Duncan confided, 'split loyalties . . . of the past, the present, the future and . . .

how do you deal with the future. What's the right way, what's the appropriate form for that to take?' One fundamental question facing the Edinburgh architects now dominated, as a worried Duncan explained. 'Well, can you continue under the new circumstances?' he pondered. 'Is this the correct way to deal with the problem? Can you actually deliver a building in the spirit [in] which it was originally set out . . . Is it possible, is it right, is it necessary?' For the Edinburgh architects, the emerging situation had placed huge strain on a resolve that had already been sorely and continually tested. But for Tagliabue and EMBT, the situation Holyrood now faced was entirely different. And it was also painfully personal.

As Holyrood had developed into an intensely scrutinised, politically pressured and media-driven project, the pressures on Enric Miralles – it seemed – had had a galvanising effect. Following the competition win, every morning he would enter his company's offices and state, '"We're going to win the competition," because . . . every day was . . . something different and we had to fight and survive.'[2] The result had been a promise made during his illness that his EMBT team would continue with Holyrood until he came back. With Miralles the target of fierce criticism in Scotland, what very few Scots had realised was the extraordinary loyalty and love that Miralles inspired in those who knew him well. And with the architect suddenly dead, these feelings had crystallised into an unshakeable resolve. 'We go on,' explained one EMBT architect, '[it] is the only thing that we can do, because for us he's still alive . . . Everybody is saying he is dead. He is not dead. He left a lot, and for me he's still alive, because I keep it in my heart. And he will never die.'

This attitude was one that persisted with heartbreaking consistency throughout EMBT's workforce. And for Benedetta Tagliabue herself, it seemed that keeping going with the company's projects was a source of crucial energy and strength. 'Maybe it's a kind of survival tool,' she argued privately, in an interview that deeply upset the documentary team, 'but it's important for everybody here in the office to work as if he's still there. And he actually is – he is still there. We remember what he wants, we have a lot of sketches . . . so in a way the project is very, very detailed, is very much [advanced].' It was a topic she returned to frequently, and with disturbing frankness. 'We are acting with him at the side, and so in a certain sense not very much has happened,' she insisted, 'just that he will not be present physically . . . [It] is the easiest thing I can do, because to me it's really a way to be always in the same situation – to be near to Enric and to go on . . .' Bereaved for less than four weeks, Tagliabue seemed to see in Holyrood a way of carrying forward her late husband's last wishes. But whatever the tragedy facing her in private and pro-fessionally, the loss of Enric Miralles – and Tagliabue's reaction to it – was about to result in a critical problem. And it would be the first major issue that the newly formed Progress Group would have to confront.

As an exhausted Gibbons, Stewart and Duncan left Barcelona for the airport, Benedetta Tagliabue pressed a letter into their hands. It regarded the partnership, and in it all the work, dis-cussion and negotiation of the last forty-eight hours were blown apart.[3] 'It seems to set out a legal position which to me should have been the starting point for the two-day period,' explained Gibbons, utterly deflated. 'We could have debated what her legal advice was. And we now find ourselves going back to Edinburgh to look at what her formal position is, when we've had the opportunity [in Barcelona] to discuss it and to try to see what issues we can accept, and what issues we can't accept.'

What Tagliabue now appeared to be proposing for Holyrood had taken the Edinburgh end completely aback. With Miralles gone, it seemed that she – the least experienced of the remaining directors – now wanted to take over as key consultant. It was a totally unacceptable proposal. Following the wrangles of 1999, responsibilities within EMBT/RMJM had been restructured, with Miralles and Tagliabue retaining design responsibility for the project, and management and implementation left with Brian Stewart.[4] With EMBT's input largely complete, responsibility now mainly lay with the Scottish end – a situation that Tagliabue didn't seem to recognise. 'We've been presented at the end with a fait accompli – or almost a fairly heavy threat – that this is how she will take the project forward . . .' Gibbons continued. 'She proposes now to become very involved; but she's starting almost from a zero base of knowledge and . . . we are in a somewhat volatile, critical environment, very tight budget, very tight programme. This calls for the greatest expertise we can focus on the project everywhere. Everywhere. So there's no opportunity for anybody to cut their teeth or to try to take this in a different direction. The risks are too great.'

Tagliabue's proposal now presented enormous practical difficulties. With Miralles' widow in charge, it could be almost impossible for EMBT/RMJM to deliver in terms of insurance, and an additional fear was that Stewart and Duncan – both embattled and exhausted – might simply decide to resign. Stewart himself, it was said, had made a commitment that the building could be delivered to budget by the 2002 deadline, but with the changes now being proposed by the Spanish end, both money and timescale were looking under threat. The Scottish team, hurt and offended, had now taken legal advice themselves, and their response to Tagliabue had provoked shock, surprise, and a claim that her innocent letter had been misinterpreted. Again, John Gibbons' task was to build bridges, and get the Holyrood show back on the road. The two sides were now being helped to communicate through his delicate mediation, and it was essential to get the problem resolved before the story – inevitably – hit the press. 'There's the whole presentational thing,' argued Progress Group mandarin Robert Gordon, 'you know, who's in charge?' And I mean, throughout we have said that Benedetta was an architect. And . . . if she chooses to go public with some of this . . . you can imagine the fun the *Evening News* would have.'[5]

On 17 August 2000, only eight days after Gordon had sounded his warning, an exclusive interview with Benedetta

Tagliabue appeared in the *Edinburgh Evening News*. In it, Miralles' widow stated her intention to continue as the project's 'public face', and reaffirmed what she believed was now her Holyrood role. '[Enric and I] didn't have to tell each other that I would take over,' she stated. 'It was not as explicit as that. We knew we could rely on each other, that was our deal.'[6] The only mention of RMJM in the article was a statement that they had been kept informed of Enric Miralles' condition. Within Holyrood, the impact of the story was immediate, and in the light of what had unfolded since the visit, her interview could hardly have been more damaging.

On 9 August 2000, shortly after the team's return from Barcelona, the new Progress Group had gathered for its routine meeting. But instead of being presented with moves towards resolution, it was told that the situation between the architects had barely progressed at all. A decision had been made to send all three partners a letter setting out the 'timetable and . . . terms on which the Client would expect to see the commission moving forward',[7] and by 14 August, progress was being made, and the project team had given themselves until the end of the week to find an understanding. By the 18th, however, Tagliabue's news article had had a dramatic effect. Brian Stewart was depressed, Mick Duncan had had enough, and John Gibbons had been talked out of walking off the project twice in a single week. Yet just three days later, a solution looked to be just around the corner. On the 22nd, Tagliabue dined with her partners and with John Gibbons, and all indications suggested that the Progress Group meeting the following day should pass without incident. Given the history of Holyrood so far, all should have anticipated that it was not to be.

On 23 August, the Progress Group met again. There was, convenor Lewis Macdonald declared to the film team, 'no sense of crisis', and it appeared that a resolution remained very much on course. Half an hour before the meeting, however, all that changed. A fax had arrived from Tagliabue, and in it – arguing under Spanish law – she restated her position of total control.[8] The move was an almost direct repeat of how events had unfolded in Barcelona, and with the architects now locked in negotiations at RMJM's offices, it seemed that the situation was back at square one. 'The positions are entrenched – totally entrenched,' explained John Gibbons, just off the phone with the designers, 'what Benedetta is quite clearly arguing for is total control of the project, otherwise . . . she will withdraw.'[9] Brian Stewart had hoped to bring the problem to the Progress Group, but had been told that it didn't want to see the architects until an agreement had been reached. 'We'll never reach an agreement,' Stewart had confided to John Gibbons. 'Well, you need to communicate that in writing to us,' Gibbons had replied, 'and then . . . we'll consider termination of contract.' 'And that's,' he reported to Lewis Macdonald, 'clearly rattled him.'[10]

The situation between the directors was now critical. Tagliabue was prepared to sign a letter drafted by Brian Stewart, but only on the condition that she could add a clause rejecting its two key issues. There were concerns about her references to the design being incomplete, and Brian Stewart, worried, was arguing for more time to find a solution. As the Progress Group took a short break for lunch, a firm decision was taken. The architects must come back that afternoon with a proposal – or an acceptable timetable for getting one – or the termination of their contract would be considered. With the Progress Group tucking into sandwiches, the film team rushed its camera to RMJM's offices to see how discussions were progressing. The pressure applied, it seemed, had had the desired effect. After five hours of deliberations, an agreement had been reached, and although it was certainly not ideal there now looked to be a basis from which to move forward. It was not to last.

By the end of the day, the stalemate within EMBT/RMJM had once more revived. A late night meeting between the architects and John Gibbons had seen Tagliabue making progress, then repeatedly return to restate her original position. And within twenty-four hours, the situation was yet again at crisis point. After talks that had gone on until 3 a.m. in Stirling, genuine progress seemed to have been made. But as Tagliabue left to go to the airport, she hugged John Gibbons – and gave him another letter. It was written on behalf of EMBT/RMJM, but neither Stewart nor Duncan had any knowledge of its contents.[11]

With the situation unravelling, the Holyrood film team – longtime impartial observers of the process – were now being pulled into the fray. When they raced to meet Tagliabue at the airport, she greeted them, then handed them a copy of the Companies Act, which she had been given to help break the deadlock. It was too heavy to carry, she told them, and anyway, she wouldn't read it. 'I just would like to be sure that my participation . . . is as it has always been together with Enric,' she argued firmly, '. . . someone who has the power to decide things, because this is the only way I can assure [that] I can do my best. I wouldn't like to be put in the contract just as a decoration, let's say. And this is the greatest danger I really will not accept.' With Tagliabue on the way back to Barcelona, another round of non-communication was set to start. The desperate circumstances would culminate in a telling exchange with the film crew. With Benedetta Tagliabue uncontactable, one of the project's leading figures – only half joking – would ask for a favour. Could the film team give them a phone call if it managed to speak to Tagliabue first?

For the Progress Group, the options now left to it were both stark and unpleasant. The situation between the architects was increasingly frustrating, and with the deadline slipping from week to week, the need for a resolution was becoming desperate. On 30 August, the Progress Group met again. No single response from EMBT/RMJM had been received with three signatures on it. What had been obtained, however, was Tagliabue's handwritten letter given to John Gibbons, and a typed-up version of the same letter signed by Brian Stewart and Mick Duncan.[12] Stewart and Duncan had asked Tagliabue to sign it before the meeting, but Tagliabue had not. Instead, a copy of an earlier letter had been received by the Progress

Group that morning, in which she again restated her position and went back on what had been said in her most recent communication. Enclosed with it was an explanation for her non-attendance – and a request to reconvene on another date.[13]

Within the Progress Group, the prospect of taking legal advice was now up for serious discussion. If the architects could not agree on a way forward, it was stated, a solution may then have to be imposed upon them. Whatever happened, the situation now had to be brought to a conclusion, and the time had come for the Progress Group to talk tough.[14] John Gibbons had offered to meet Tagliabue anywhere in the world to try and reach a resolution, but the situation seemed to keep changing from day to day. In the event, however, and despite a terrible week, a final resolution came with surprising swiftness. In mid-September, after weeks of torturous discussion, a letter was received signed by all three partners, which agreed to joint responsibility, with no replacement for Enric Miralles being put forward. It took everybody watching the process by surprise.[15]

'I think a bit of it is a mystery and will always remain a mystery,' confided Progress Group secretary Sarah Davidson, 'and I think it may be . . . an illustration of the fact that there were larger misunderstandings than we thought there were. Genuine misunderstandings, not different positions. And that when everything came together, in fact what everybody was looking for was not as far apart as they had thought it might be.' For John Gibbons though, the resolution had been both a surprise and a relief. 'I was expecting that . . . there would be another period of negotiation, that the final agreement would be conditional,' he remembered. 'I mean, that . . . final letter . . . had in fact been available in that form, and been discussed by everybody, over a period of two and a half weeks, so it wasn't a new document . . . I mean, the position changed over a fifteen-minute period . . . We set up a meeting [where] we were expecting to have to give some very harsh long lectures, and in fact we were just simply told that the position [they'd] reached was acceptable – and so peace broke out.'

Finally – and unexpectedly – it looked like the Holyrood

project was back on track, and a public announcement on the future could be ventured. However, in reality, the problems between the EMBT/RMJM directors would continue, and problems would resurface between the Barcelona and Edinburgh partners in the years to come. But if Enric Miralles' death had been a tragedy for Holyrood, fate had one final and cruel blow that would be dealt within just weeks of the hard-won resolution.

After heart surgery, and a fall on the steps of his official residence, Donald Dewar, Scotland's First Minister, and the architect of the entire devolution process, was dead. 'I couldn't assume to have a close relationship with Donald Dewar,' Brian Stewart would remember, 'and I . . . couldn't assume that what we were doing really mattered to him . . . My experience of communicating with him, and working with him was all of the . . . good things that are said about him are true. I think that he always felt we were really under the microscope. We were suffering daily the scrutiny of the project, and we were bearing that and trying to deal with it and cope with it . . . He was always interested, and he was clearly . . . really sure that what he was doing was right.' Holyrood had lost its architect, and now it had lost its champion. Only one, small, ray of hope remained on the horizon. Perhaps the appointment of Alan Ezzi, Holyrood's third Project Director, would see things turn the corner. Or then again, perhaps it wouldn't.

Notes

1. Quoted in Karen Rice, 'Enric died as he lay beside me', *Edinburgh Evening News*, 17 August 2000.
2. Interview, EMBT architect, 1 August 2000.
3. Benedetta Tagliabue to Brian Stewart and Mick Duncan, Letter, 1 August 2000, http://www.holyroodinquiry.org
4. Enric Miralles and Brian Stewart to David Steel, Letter and structure chart, 4 October 1999, ibid.
5. Gordon's related concern was at what stage the directors' problems might impact on project progress. At the meeting of 9 August, John Gibbons would confirm that the relationship at a working level between Edinburgh and Barcelona continued to be very good.

6. Quoted in Karen Rice, 'Enric died as he lay beside me', *Edinburgh Evening News*, 17 August 2000.
7. *Minutes: Holyrood Progress Group Meeting, 4th Meeting, HPG/oo/4/M*, para. 2, 9 August 2000, http://www.holyroodinquiry.org
8. Benedetta Tagliabue to RMJM, Fax, 23 August 2000, ibid.
9. John Gibbons described this as 'a somewhat loose interpretation' of Tagliabue's position that the project would stop due to her rights of control.
10. The threat of termination appears to have been a strategy to reach a successful conclusion.
11. Benedetta Tagliabue to the Progress Group, Letter, 24 August 2000, http://www.holyroodinquiry.org
12. Brian Stewart to Benedetta Tagliabue, Fax, 29 August 2000, ibid.
13. Benedetta Tagliabue to John Gibbons, Letter, 29 August 2000, ibid.
14. Lewis Macdonald to EMBT/RMJM directors, Letter, 31 August 2000, ibid.
15. Benedetta Tagliabue, Brian Stewart, Mick Duncan, 'EMBT/RMJM Limited signed agreement', 13 September 2000, ibid.

12

Who's in Charge?

'An author of soap operas might, for a plot, be tempted to draw on the saga of the Scottish Parliament enterprise. The only problem is that the public would never believe it.'
Donald Gorrie, MSP[1]

ON 7 NOVEMBER 2000, the Holyrood film team travelled to meet new Project Director Alan Ezzi as he prepared to take up his post. Ezzi was a small man with an immensely strong presence, and a manner that could turn from charm to steel in a matter of seconds. He had been – in consultation with Progress Group convenor Lewis Macdonald – a personal appointment by Parliament Chief Executive Paul Grice, whose main concern now was to bring Holyrood in by its December 2002 end date and within the £195 million cap. By the end of the film team's visit, two things about Ezzi were certain. If anyone could bring Holyrood in on time and on budget, it was him. But he had absolutely no experience of operating in a political environment.

As Ezzi sat in his office nine weeks later, the distinction between him and his civil service predecessors was plain. In some ways, Ezzi's lack of government experience was beneficial. His future employment prospects were not at risk by the way he dealt with people, and he certainly had the determination to push his remit through. 'There are the "small p" political considerations that [civil servants] would have to take into account which I don't have to take into account . . .' he explained to the documentary team. 'I mean, there are nuances of the way that one deals with people that float around this place that just go over my head completely. And I don't have to worry about that because I'm an ignoramus when it comes to that kind of thing.' With budget and timescale paramount, and the political focus as sharp as ever, Alan Ezzi's parameters were simple: Holyrood must be on time, and it must be on cost. Although he didn't yet know it, he had been handed a virtually impossible task.

With Alan Ezzi now engaged at Holyrood, a new question dominated. The job he had been appointed for had caused enormous complications for even the shrewdest political operators. Was there any way it could be achieved by an 'outsider'? His early impressions of the task in hand were clear. Holyrood as it was currently designed was unlikely to be completed within £195 million. And if his remit was to be achieved within a 'horrendously tight' budget and timescale, some hard – and potentially unpopular – decisions would have to be taken. Essentially, Ezzi believed, the cost cap had been imposed at a point when no one could be certain that £195 million was a realistic total. And with the constraints of cost and deadline being mutually exclusive, the room to manoeuvre was extremely small. 'I would *love* to see this building complete[d] exactly as it is on paper at this point in time,' he declared enthusiastically. But there was a significant caveat. 'We can build "a building", we can build it in that time frame,' he confided, 'but I suspect it won't be as is shown on the drawings at this point in time.'

What Alan Ezzi didn't realise, however, was that the terms on which he had been engaged at Holyrood would turn the entire approach to the parliament building on its head. From the earliest stages right up until the architect's death, the integrity of Miralles' concept had been absolutely paramount. But when asked what effect his employment parameters would have on the parliament's design, Ezzi's response had been this. 'I really don't know . . .' he pondered, 'either the Scottish Parliament will have to find more money, if they particularly want the details as we know them . . . or they will have to accept that there's going to be a change in these details.' For Ezzi, this didn't mean a 'dumbing down' exercise, nor did it mean a reduction in quality. Holyrood had some very expensive details, and if the money wasn't there to pay for them, the design would have to be revised. Miralles' death would not be the issue with the greatest impact on Holyrood's eventual design, the new Project Director argued. Practical, external factors would have far more influence. And this was a situation not unique to the parliament project; it was simply a matter of fact.

To John Gibbons, however, back in his office, the employment of Alan Ezzi would soon raise some very serious concerns. 'I think the reasoning was that his appointment very much was a demonstration that action was being taken . . .' he confided, '[and] I think Enric . . . would have recognised in Alan a reincarnated Bill Armstrong – a project manager with very clear, firm ideas of cost control, with not a lot of appreciation or regard for design.' Holyrood, essentially, was a complicated designer project operating in a political environment with which it was completely incompatible. And with the process now started, for the building to be delivered at all – let alone with any resemblance to Miralles' initial concept – was a masterpiece of manipulation, strategy and spin.

In a new and 'open' democracy, it was an unpalatable, if necessary, evil. But with Alan Ezzi an outsider in this world of political manoeuvring, his determination to fulfil his obligations was already under threat. 'As far as the design team is concerned there is one client in this project, and that will be me . . .' he stated firmly. 'If the design team choose to take instructions from someone else other than through me, then they won't get paid for it. And I'm the one that signs their cheques.' It was a determined strategy, aimed to reduce the miscommunication caused by too many people at the Holyrood helm. But in the environment in which the building was being delivered, it had two, potentially fatal, loopholes. Ezzi's approach would effectively reduce the input of the Progress Group – and it had much more influence than he imagined. But even more crucially, the emerging project team

structure would remove John Gibbons from the heart of decision-making. And John Gibbons was the man who had kept
the entire show on the road from day one.

Yet whatever the problems lying in store for Alan Ezzi in future,
what would become starkly apparent as he arrived to observe
his second Progress Group meeting was that Holyrood still
faced far greater problems than anybody knew. When the new
project director's appointment had been announced, the
Progress Group had taken the chance to confirm the resolved
arrangement between Brian Stewart, Mick Duncan and
Benedetta Tagliabue. 'It is abundantly clear that the vision of
the Parliament was deeply held and understood by all the
members of the partnership,' Lewis Macdonald had
announced. 'I am confident that they will continue to work
together – as they have done in the past – to deliver an outstanding Parliament building.'[2] As the architects appeared
together before the Progress Group just weeks after signing
their agreement, it swiftly became clear that this was not
entirely the case.

As Brian Stewart began the presentation approved by the
project team twenty-four hours earlier, something extraordinary suddenly happened. Tagliabue interrupted, and began to
project her own – unauthorised – slide show over the top of it.
The tension and embarrassment in the meeting room was
agonising, and as Lewis Macdonald struggled for a diplomatic
way to get the meeting back on track, Tagliabue charmingly –
but firmly – argued her case. In one brief and illuminating
moment, the problems between the architects were crystallised. Tagliabue appeared not to accept, or understand, the
protocol of the rest of the project. And as far as she was concerned, she was still in charge.

As the ruined presentation staggered to a close, the
Holyrood film crew followed a furious and frustrated Brian
Stewart back to his riverside office. Arguments with Miralles
had – ultimately – always been productive. 'His involvement is
clearly missed,' he argued, 'and what it needs now . . . it needs

confidence . . . and that's the practical thing that's missing . . . We would always find the right solution . . . The logic and the reason from both sides would be there, and then we would reach a conclusion.' With Miralles gone though, the relationship between the partners was now fundamentally different. And although Tagliabue and RMJM were ultimately fighting for the same aim – an Enric Miralles building – the difficulties in communication apparent in Barcelona had essentially continued as before.

'We'll sometimes wonder . . . does anybody really know how Enric would do this project?' Brian Stewart agonised to the film team. 'I wouldn't assume. I don't think anybody else should assume either. No one should assume that they would understand how one person would have completed this project. We can be sensitive, and we can look at everything very hard and form a judgement. But we form our own judgement . . . we're not forming Enric's judgement . . . and I think that's the right way to proceed, and I think that's how he would expect the thing to proceed.' For Tagliabue, however, recently interviewed in the *Herald*, the situation seemed to remain largely as expressed before. '[I]f I don't struggle now it's saying goodbye to everything,' she had confided, 'so I'm obliged to do this. I really will try to maintain Enric's idea, and have the authority to say how it should be done. I was always with him when there were problems, so it's not new to me, but to be honest now is not an easy moment.'[3] To John Gibbons, able to observe the architects' problems with more detachment and objectivity, the situation seemed to have another, altogether more worrying, side. 'Benedetta's point of view is that the intellectual rights to the design were Enric's, and that as the heir to Enric's estate she's automatically assuming his role,' he had explained to the Progress Group at the height of the partnership problems in August, 'and the two other directors can't accept that or understand that.' The architectural partners, it seemed apparent, remained far from having their internal problems resolved.

By early November 2000, Tagliabue's ongoing role within

EMBT/RMJM was still uncertain. 'Well, it's not good,' Stewart confided, when asked about the current state of the working relationship with their Spanish partner. 'I mean, that's just a fact . . . The current relationship is not good. I'm trying very hard to ensure that it doesn't actually impede the project in any way. We're trying really very hard to keep mobilising and keep going. And I think we're alright . . . we are managing to do that to a degree . . . I really have tried very hard to understand where the deep-seated problems are . . . and I think the client has tried very hard to do that and be very sympathetic to it. But I think it's like everything, you know: there is only so much patience there.'

However diplomatically Brian Stewart tried to couch his opinion, four months after Miralles' death, Benedetta Tagliabue's role at Holyrood remained indefinite. 'We are doing our utmost to carry on,' Stewart explained haltingly. 'I think that – practically – it's not getting in the way, not too much. But precisely how Benedetta fits, what role she plays, and how it impacts on the project is not really very clear yet . . . I think I know what I'm doing. I think I know what Mick's doing. I think I know what thirty-five people downstairs are doing. I'm not absolutely quite sure I know what she's doing yet: maybe she doesn't know.' If any illustration was needed of just how disengaged Tagliabue remained with events in Edinburgh, an interview with *Newsnight Scotland* would offer valuable proof. Describing the deaths of both her husband and Donald Dewar as a 'real disaster', she claimed the legacy of the building would reflect the desires of both men, and Scotland could be 'proud of spending a lot of money for something that you will then love and will be proud about'.[4] To a country already blaming Dewar and Miralles for the entire Holyrood fiasco, and increasingly angry about the building's spiralling costs, it was hardly welcome news.

Yet while relations between the directors continued to be uncertain, what was now becoming apparent was that a set of new problems was already beginning to brew. This time, they were right at the heart of the project team. With Alan Ezzi settling in as Project Director, the new change of management was causing unprecedented upset. And while Alan Mack at Bovis believed that Ezzi was probably a good choice for the position, others were already less than sure. 'I think he's a very honest individual,' Mack concluded, standing in the rain on the hills overlooking the site, 'so he will be quite direct, and . . . I believe that they've employed him to be so . . . because we don't have time left, you know, if we're going to hold on to this programme . . . There are issues that have been not handled or addressed directly, which have caused us some problems. Issues about budget and all this good stuff . . . and [they] are gonna have to be addressed in the immediate future. And he's running with those now; and some of them are gonna be thorny.'

While Ezzi was certainly not in awe of the political context that surrounded Holyrood, the sensitive realities of the situation were already beginning to have an effect. Holyrood – whatever the terms of his appointment – was not all about pragmatism and cost control, and the 'nuances' and sensitivities of which Ezzi had already professed ignorance were absolutely essential to surviving in the job. Before Barbara Doig had left, she had warned the documentary team of what she believed her successor would be in for. 'Well, I don't think they can be under any illusions as to what they're coming to,' she had claimed, laughing, 'it does rather conjure up a kind of picture of the kind of person . . . who might be prepared to take this on . . . I think there must be terrific temptation to appoint somebody who will come in macho-style: "Just leave it to me . . . a bit of good control is needed." But I don't think that's had a track record of success . . . a more flexible approach is probably better.'

With Paul Grice's appointment of Alan Ezzi, Holyrood now had exactly the kind of project director against which Barbara Doig had warned. '[When Alan] first arrived, I think [he'd already taken] the view that to achieve the savings that he'd been asked to achieve, he had to take a very firm grip on the design team . . .' John Gibbons explained to the film crew, 'and in practice I think felt that he would stop them attending Progress Group meetings, and that he would represent the views of the design team to the client.' Stories abounded round site that Ezzi had threatened to 'kick the shit' out of the design team, and already others had been angered at what they regarded as a direct questioning of their professional role. 'In the case of the engineers,' Gibbons remembered, 'Alan was told in no uncertain terms that . . . if he was challenging their professional ability as designers of structures, then he'd better be prepared to take the consequences when they fall down. And [they were] really very, very concerned that he was suggesting to them economies that he thought they hadn't looked for – and so they got rather upset.'

Within the project team itself, Ezzi's restructuring programme had left a closely bonded team totally and massively demoralised, and several were now either leaving, or reconsidering their futures on the job. Undoubtedly, Ezzi was capable of delivering what he'd been asked for. The question was, was what he'd been asked for in any way compatible with the Holyrood post? 'I think he's in a very difficult position,' Alan Mack would confide to the film team in mid-January 2001, 'because . . . from what I see of him . . . he's not a political animal. And I think he's gonna find it difficult possibly to work within the politics that exist . . . I mean, for two years now I kept saying, "I'm not going to get involved." But you do – you get sucked in . . . I'm not sure that he's gonna be able to be so kinda clear cut and direct as he would like to be . . .'

For John Gibbons too, the problems that Ezzi would now face had been entirely predictable. 'Well, it is a very difficult job, and I think the first few weeks of really getting to get to grips with all the complexities of it have made him sit and think,' he pondered. 'I think to come in from the outside really in Alan's situation is very, very difficult . . . I think he's got the basic skills, but whether he can apply those quickly enough and catch up with everything else . . . I think it's very difficult

... if you want to bring about a culture change if you haven't yet understood the culture of the organisation.'

With Holyrood again dogged by internal problems, and pressures on to agree a cost plan by the end of August, the project – as ever – was headed for difficult times.[5] And as if matters weren't complicated enough, the latter part of 2000 saw the publication of three new reports on the building project. In September, the Auditor General for Scotland's report became public, in October it was the report by the Finance Committee, and in December Margo MacDonald released her own findings, based on the report from the Auditor General, John Spencely's review and the answers received to multiple parliamentary questions and letters. Of the three, it would be the Auditor General's report that would have the greatest impact.

As the Auditor General had himself suggested, conducting an audit examination in the middle of an ongoing project was unusual.[6] For some on the inside track at Holyrood, the need to retrace old ground and then appear before the parliament's Audit Committee was disastrous. Resources had had to be diverted from pushing the project forwards to providing retrospective information, priority issues had had to be re-aligned, and the impact on morale had been enormous. Interim conclusions reached – although they related to past issues – raised the danger of impacting on the project's operation in the future. And the risk of this disruption was especially acute if there were implied criticisms of the experience and competence of the team. 'These are still the same people who are working here,' John Gibbons confided to the film crew, 'and they don't then address the current problems with quite the same vigour that they would ... if we had been ... trying to motivate them in the conventional way.'

For Brian Stewart, however, the impact of the audit and its aftermath had been altogether different. With various key figures called to give evidence to the parliament's Audit Committee, it looked like the project's waters were only becoming more muddied. 'It's forced people to post-rationalise things and take positions which are not really absolutely accurate,' he pondered. 'I'm not saying that they're wrong, but it's an interpretation of grey areas. And I think there's a fantastic amount of post-rationalising going on.' For one member of the film team, it was a moment of sudden and terrifying revelation. Having been inside the Holyrood project almost from the beginning, it was now clear that whatever reports and investigations were now conducted into the parliament building, there were only two people who could try to tell the project's true story. And she was one of them.

Yet as always within Holyrood, whatever the current problems and pressures, there were always more lining up around the corner. Just before Christmas, John Gibbons returned from teaching in Boston. He bumped into Alan Mack in the car park, and as they chatted, Mack revealed that some changes had been made. 'I was told third-hand that the Project Director wished me to move from the building,' explained John Gibbons to the film team, 'and amongst a package of wishes that he had was that he wanted to reduce my influence on the project.' It was the first that Gibbons had heard of his removal under Alan Ezzi's tenure, and he was bitter, angry, and very, very upset. Miralles was dead, Donald Dewar was dead, and now – suddenly and without warning – John Gibbons, architect of the entire Holyrood process, was out in the cold.

Notes

1. *Scottish Parliament Official Report*, col. 1886, 21 June 2001, http://www.scottish.parliament.uk
2. *Parliamentary News Release* no. 044/2000, 'Holyrood Progress Group welcomes new leadership of Holyrood project', 13 September 2000, ibid.
3. Quoted in Michael Tierney, 'Building on Enric's dream: Benedetta Tagliabue, widow of renowned Catalan architect Enric Miralles, faces a daunting challenge – to ensure that the plans for the Scottish Parliament building are realised', *Herald*, 7 October 2000.
4. Quoted in 'Miralles widow defends Holyrood cash', *Herald*, 1 November 2000.
5. Cost consultant Hugh Fisher told the Fraser Inquiry, 'The objective was

achieved in that [the] team bought into the provision of a figure [of] £108m in line with the Client's instruction. The exercise was not successful insofar as the design associated with that exercise was not actually delivered. In other words, the risks that were removed from the estimate to get to £108m never went away. That was why . . . the overall figure shot back up almost immediately after the date that the £195m was produced.' Hugh Fisher, evidence session, para. 253, 18 February 2004, http://www.holyroodinquiry.org. Colleague Ian McAndie had earlier told the film team, 'If [the design] wasn't reined back, the costs wouldn't come back to the 195 [million pounds] . . . It was obviously going to be broken without changing the design, and nobody directed the design to be changed.' Interview, 30 April 2002.

6. *Scottish Parliament Audit Committee Official Report*, col. 299, 19 September 2000, http://www.scottish.parliament.uk; Auditor General for Scotland, *The New Scottish Parliament Building: An Examination of the Management of the Holyrood Project*, p.1. September 2000, ibid., http://www.holyroodinquiry.org

13

A Penny Saved is a Penny Gained

'I think they all think that I'm blinkered and that all I've got are dollar signs in front of my eyes – which is true to a large extent. I mean, that's my job . . . I was brought in here because the job had a dire history of overruns on costs . . . where does it stop?'
Alan Ezzi[1]

WITH JOHN GIBBONS 'removed' from control at Holyrood, the internal dynamics that powered the project were, by January 2001, becoming increasingly and damagingly exposed. It had always been clear that the atmosphere surrounding the parliament building was as much political – with a small 'p' – as it was party political. But with Gibbons at the helm, everything had been expertly juggled and presented to ensure that the project could get where it needed to go in the face of extraordinary external machinations. To the outside world, Holyrood remained an embarrassing catastrophe which continued to spiral wildly out of control. But within the project, the view was entirely different. Holyrood may have been a cock-up, but there was no doubt it would have been far worse had John Gibbons not been at the helm.

As with all Holyrood dramas, however, the story behind the events was as surprising and compelling as the events themselves. That Gibbons remained deeply hurt and angered by his removal was not in doubt: he absolutely, categorically refused to set foot in the site offices. But the procedure by which he had been sidelined was clearly not as straightforward as it had first appeared. It seemed that Parliament Chief Executive Paul Grice had personally assured John Gibbons that he wanted him to stay on at Holyrood, and on this basis Gibbons had turned down a teaching job in America. However, Alan Ezzi – it appeared – had been told an entirely different story; he believed that Gibbons' future role was up to him. When asked by the Holyrood film crew who his key team members now were, Alan Ezzi reeled off a list of names. John Gibbons featured nowhere on it. And when Gibbons contacted Grice to see where their prior agreement now stood, Grice's reaction had been, 'a little bit on the fence. It was that the Project Director was a new appointment [and] he couldn't be seen not to be supporting his Project Director on the one hand, but on the other hand he was quite clear that he wished me to continue, and that we could all sit round a table and talk it through, and that would be the grown up way of doing it.' To describe the situation as confusing was an understatement, to say the least.

With all this bubbling away, Alan Ezzi had begun to re-organise the project team's office accommodation. Instead of John Gibbons' current work space, Gibbons observed wryly, it now seemed that he would be put 'in a cleaning cupboard, I think, down at the other end of the site'. His humour masked a deep resentment. Ezzi clearly felt that Gibbons should remain involved in *some* capacity at Holyrood, although that involvement would be massively curtailed and its nature was still uncertain. Yet John Gibbons saw his continuing role entirely differently. 'To continue here . . . I had to have certain assurances about accommodation and about the need for [my] role,' he confided. 'I certainly didn't want to work somewhere where I was not wanted.' Whatever the tensions between the two men, however, they were beginning to be overshadowed by other – equally serious – problems. The coming months were going to see some tough and unpopular decision-making if £195 million and December 2002 were going to be achieved, and how this would impact in terms of the Progress Group's involvement remained uncertain. '[Their remit is] not precise; it's quite vague,' Alan Ezzi argued to the film team, 'and therefore they think that they are entitled to comment and make decisions on a lot more issues than I think they're entitled to do.'

Ezzi believed that a time was coming when some issues wouldn't be referred to the Progress Group at all; they were matters that should be dealt with swiftly and directly by him. For John Gibbons, this approach – combined with his own removal – rang a series of loud alarm bells. '[He had] really – to me – quite serious misunderstandings of how we could ever make progress . . .' Gibbons worried. 'This smacks of the worst days of the criticism from the Corporate Body; of the old days of not getting information . . . There is absolutely is no way – quite rightly – of preventing the client hav[ing] a very loud voice at discussions about finishes and issues that will affect their working lives.' For Ezzi, however, the job he had been employed to do needed to be done. And the fact that he had become the latest in a growing line of Holyrood project directors offered him a measure of increased security in his pressured and complex role. 'I think that if somebody decided to get rid of me in the course of the next two years then as many questions would be asked of the people employing me as . . . would be of my professional capabilities,' he stated. Ezzi was absolutely right. And although Paul Grice had assured him at his interview for the Holyrood job that 'if you think that we're some kind of hire and fire outfit, I can assure you that that's not the case,' the seeds were already sown for Alan Ezzi's tenure at Holyrood to be both short and stormy. After just seven months of his employment, Holyrood's new Project Director – a deliberate appointment to demonstrate that 'something was being done' – would be gone.

On 17 January 2001, with Alan Ezzi still at the Holyrood helm, the Progress Group gathered for its regular fortnightly meeting. The past few weeks had been tense, and John Gibbons was still blowing hot and cold about the project, despite the fact that he had now worked out a position that both he – and most others – seemed to be happy with. Ezzi, it had been noted, was beginning to realise the huge pitfalls of the job he had taken on, and with a new Progress Group member – the Liberal Democrats' Jamie Stone replacing recently promoted Tavish Scott – the

Holyrood project was undergoing change at many levels. Gibbons, the film team observed, now seemed to take a lower-key role within Progress Group meetings, sitting further down the table during discussions, and separated from the meetings' key players, convenor Lewis Macdonald and secretary Sarah Davidson. To all appearances, John Gibbons was being side-lined. But although Alan Ezzi may not have known it, his predecessor as Project Director remained a powerful and influential figure in the wings.

From Gibbons' 'bird's eye' perspective, morale within the project was now far from buoyant. Both the Progress Group and the architects were unhappy with the direction in which the project seemed to be heading, and the honeymoon period between these two teams would itself soon dramatically be over. The new year would see the architects complaining of unclear instructions and lack of consistency in what they were being asked to do, while there was a view that the Progress Group would be suspicious not only that its designers were guilty of wilful misunderstanding, but also that they were being less than swift in coming up with savings suggestions. Whatever the situation, it was not the only upheaval going on at the heart of the project. In his first major suggestion for cost cuts, Alan Ezzi had recommended that Portuguese granite be used for the building instead of the Scottish Kemnay stone the Progress Group preferred. The saving incurred would have run into hundreds of thousands of pounds, but it would have meant the loss of a Scottish material for a foreign one – something that was already raising press and professional concern. The new Project Director had reputedly declared that the Portuguese material fulfilled all the criteria the project required, and that Kemnay granite would only be used on the building 'over my dead body'. In the event, nothing so terminal would be required. When Alan Ezzi left for a holiday, the contract for Kemnay granite was issued behind his back in what looked like a gesture of defiance. It was a move broadly interpreted by those in Holyrood's inner circle as a firm two-fingered gesture to the project's new leadership.

However, the meeting on 17 January would mark a new low in internal relationships, even by Holyrood's increasingly fraught standards. The day had apparently begun behind closed doors with the 'mother of all battles' between Brian Stewart and Benedetta Tagliabue, although the two maintained an impermeable public bond of professional unity. With the pair still discussing their internal arrangements, a settlement appeared to have been reached just before Christmas. But, as John Gibbons explained, shortly before the meeting 'Benedetta saw Brian and expressed concern about some of the arrangements that she had agreed to . . . on the basis that she didn't fully understand the implications of them . . . I understand some were fee related, but others were control related, and particularly control in terms of veto over design changes.' If the day had started badly, however, it was about to get far worse.

In late November, an instruction had been given to analyse potential savings – some more drastic than others – on the MSP office building, which would help reduce costs as part of an ongoing site-wide savings exercise.[2] The meeting, it was suggested, could give the designers a steer regarding which of the more radical cost cuts the Progress Group considered acceptable. With planning implications, impact on environmental standards and the potential knock-on costs or delay of making changes all possible, it was a delicate and difficult balancing act for those on all sides. But while the architects' presentation was about to cause angry eruptions, the really bad news was still to come. With the cost plan only recently agreed,[3] the tenders for the structural frame of the east end of the site – including the complex debating chamber – had come in worryingly over tender, despite significant, prolonged and partially successful attempts to bring the costs back down. With no substantial change in design in this area over the last nine months, it seemed that a dramatic increase in the price of materials, Holyrood's reputation, the need for additional steelwork, and delays and pressures caused by the buildings' complexity could all have been part of the problem. But whatever the reasons, the project now faced a major predicament. There was no way – at this stage – that this area could be brought in under budget. And with Holyrood operating to an incredibly tight timescale, the package would have to be let as it stood to beat programme commitments and avoid a significant rise in cost. It would mean an unpalatable and worrying decision. Some of the contingency money set aside for emergencies was going to have to be spent.

To the Progress Group, it was the worst possible news. Nobody could quantify how much of the contingency would be needed until a value engineering exercise had been carried out to rein the costs back. But with the structural design of the area so complex, there was no way that this could be set in motion until a steelwork contractor had been brought on board. The Progress Group was locked in an intractable situation. And what infuriated them most was that if the tight time restrictions were to be adhered to, the package had to be let by the following Monday. By the time the Progress Group heard the news, it was already ten o'clock on Wednesday morning. While the group protested angrily that a gun was being held to their heads and Alan Ezzi explained the mechanics of why the bombshell had been so sudden, it was left to Alan Mack to take a typically pragmatic view in private. 'I could've . . . responded and jumped up and down and [said] . . . the project team actually knew the level of problem from November last year when we got tenders opened and we were working with them and . . . the cost consultant actually wrote to the project team in early December and said in his opinion the cost was going to be £22.5 million . . . But there was nowhere to go with that, and there was no point in having a pissing contest across the table.'[4]

However, if the news of the cost increase had been a shock, the meeting itself would see a quite spectacular fallout between the Progress Group and their architects. The cost savings the design team had been asked to present covered a broad range of options, from those that would have no real impact on planning permission, quality or the project's brief to those that could cause significant change. As Brian Stewart himself conceded, 'you may say well this is . . . a bit bloody-minded because we're attacking [the] brief, and we're attacking every-thing else . . . These are the only areas that are left [to make savings] because of the stage of the whole construction process . . . We can't say that we support every one of these because we do think they impact on the function, and the quality to some extent, in a *disproportionate* way to the saving . . . [but] we're trying to get a balance.' Even Alan Ezzi, fiercely committed to his remit of 'on time, on cost', had warned the Progress Group that it was not going to like everything that was put before it. But nobody could have predicted what was about to happen.

As Brian Stewart introduced the savings he'd been asked to deliver, it was clear that the mood of the Progress Group had become significantly colder. But when the issue of swapping granite on the MSP block with a cheaper substitute was raised, the meeting unexpectedly erupted. 'I'll be very, very honest: I think some of this discussion is just ridiculous,' stated SNP member Linda Fabiani crossly, 'because there is absolutely no way that anybody here is going to agree that we should get rid of granite on the whole MSP block . . . So for a potential saving to come up to us . . . I feel, Brian, it's absolutely ridiculous. We placed the order for the MSP granite . . . I mean, I now have to say that I have no faith in any of this. If that's the level it's been come at, I don't feel I can seriously consider this paper. And I think we're wasting our time sitting here if that's the kind of thing that's being put in front of us.'

It was Ezzi who leapt swiftly to the architects' defence. 'I don't think it's a waste of time at all,' he argued firmly, 'because the design team – remember – are in a situation where they have met the brief, they have brought this MSP wing within budget . . . It is we as a client who are instructing them to come up [with] blue sky visioning, looking at where we can save any money that we can potentially save.' But Linda Fabiani remained trenchant. 'I can see why you've done it, Brian, 'cause you're under a lot of pressure,' she stated, 'and I would say to you, Alan, that for me . . . coming in here and getting faced with this, I find really out of order. Whether it be that this should have been discussed with other members of the project team before it came to the Progress Group; perhaps that should have been done. But I really feel to be sitting here faced with this, and just handed to us today is ridiculous to expect us to be giving you any steer at all.'

With a prior engagement at the parliament's chamber, Fabiani had to abruptly leave the meeting. And with Brian Stewart left shaking his head with resigned disbelief in the corner, it would be up to John Gibbons to clarify exactly what the fallout had been about. 'The reason for the particular outburst . . . by Linda,' he would later confide, 'was that she didn't attend the briefing meeting where the background to the saving paper was explained in great detail. And I think had she attended she would have seen that a lot of the issues that she was addressing in her outburst had already been discussed with the design team, and there had been no attempt . . . by [them] to be just obstructive, or devious or rude, but they were simply saying to us, "Hey, you've just made a decision to spend three-quarters of a million pounds when you didn't need to, you know. How often are you gonna do that, Mr Client?"'[5]

As the meeting drew to a close, Brian Stewart – usually deeply troubled by client conflict – emerged into the site car park chuckling quietly. 'How do we describe it? They want their cake and eat it, and diet at the same time,' he told the film crew, 'and it's just . . . it's daft!' Did he think he was getting any consistency in his instructions? 'They're all over the place,' he laughed. 'They're not engaged; they're really all over the place.' As the film team dug deeper into the situation however, the confusion underlying the savings meeting only seemed to become worse. 'I think there's another issue about the granite, which . . . was really the design team challenging a decision which had only been made within the last week by the Progress Group about the material to be used in the exterior of the Parliament,' John Gibbons explained. 'The decision to use Scottish granite was essentially made on aesthetic grounds. And to challenge that so quickly after the decision had been made to use Scottish granite was a somewhat courageous proposition by the design team . . . [and] they might have expected the people who made the decision to come back at them fairly hard.'

With the Portuguese/Kemnay granite battles to all appearances over, it now seemed that Alan Ezzi had instructed the architects to raise the issue again. So had he? 'The design team will argue – have argued – that they were actually asked to do that,' Gibbons confided, 'were told to do that . . . by Alan Ezzi, which I understand was true. It's hearsay as far as I'm concerned.' To Alan Mack at Bovis, however, it was clear where the problems now lay. 'Well, the design team are obviously working very hard to hang on to the concept, hang on to some of the feature details that were one of the reasons why Enric's design was chosen . . .' he argued. 'Obviously [with] the pressures of the budget you can see that the MSPs themselves are starting to feel very uncomfortable about money being spent on a working building if the whole thing is in jeopardy budget wise and, you know . . . over the months you're almost getting the view that they want almost like a hole to crawl into. It's becoming almost sackcloth and ashes: "Just give us a couple of plasterboard walls, guys, and we'll be happy."'

With the architects having bitten the bullet, confused messages were now coming in from the client. And for both Mack and the designers, it was having an unexpected effect. 'I mean we're getting a bit frustrated,' Mack confided, 'but that's good, because we're starting to get a bit ballsy now – a bit more attitude. You know, like, "Well, we're gonna build this thing . . . even if you fucking don't want it!" . . . In many respects that's kind of brought the design team and ourselves a bit closer together, so now we're kind of . . . swivelling round on a common enemy, you know? We're gonna get the thing built.' With the design team and Progress Group at loggerheads, however, within weeks, the common enemy was set to change. And the man who would soon be in the firing line would be Holyrood's new Project Director, Alan Ezzi.

As the fallout from the Progress Group meeting continued, tempers within Holyrood flared. John Gibbons and Brian

Stewart had a one and a half hour row after Gibbons backed the Progress Group's view that some of the savings the designers had pursued had been ruled out on two previous occasions. The Progress Group was angered that the cost information it was getting from the design team and construction manager seemed to be inconsistent, with different figures being quoted for the overbudget east-end frame.[6] A letter issued by the Progress Group to Alan Ezzi – stating their dissatisfaction at the design team's performance – had still to be translated formally to the architects a week after the meeting, although Brian Stewart had been told of its contents by John Gibbons in order that the team could keep moving. And Brian Stewart himself remained adamant that the instructions the architects were being given were inadequate, and that savings options that did not damage the building had been 'rigorously' addressed. Did John Gibbons foresee more project casualties? 'Er – depends what you mean by casualties!' he laughed thoughtfully. 'We've had a lot of casualties on the project . . . I suppose the answer must be there must be more casualties . . . but we are getting so close to finishing.' With the pressure on to make savings throughout the site and ensure that £195 million could now be met, a radical series of cost-cuts was now utterly paramount. It would unite the Progress Group and the architects in a way that in January 2001 had seemed almost impossible.

In the first week of March, the Progress Group met to discuss the Project Director's latest report. The preceding months had seen a sporadic flurry of newspaper criticism of the Holyrood building, culminating in a damaging article which had appeared in the *Edinburgh Evening News*. In it, Martin Hulse of Edinburgh's heritage group the Cockburn Association had described the canopy over the building's public entrance as looking 'like a bus shelter, but not a very good one', while Tory MSP Brian Monteith sniped, 'I'm worried there will be people queuing up on a Saturday morning waiting for it to open and looking for their trolleys.'[7] In *Scotland on Sunday*, Margo MacDonald claimed the protruding 'think bubble' windows in the MSP offices were simply 'blisters . . . there to fool us into thinking that this very over-priced but ordinary building will be special and worth the price'.[8] But the more serious and growing criticism centred on just who was responsible for the parliament building's design. It was Peter Wilson, architect and one of the Holyrood building's increasingly vocal critics, who had offered the most damning conclusion. Responding to the building's recently unveiled plans, he argued this: 'It's another example of changes made to give the appearance of Miralles' geometrics and shapes,' he was quoted as saying, 'but in reality [it] is expedient and reactive design development.'[9]

In fact, the architects and Progress Group were now locked in an anxious battle to hang on to Miralles' concept in the face of overwhelming cost pressures. The site-wide savings exercise, it had been hoped, might claw back some of the contingency set against the over-budget east frame package. But as Ezzi delivered his savings options to the Progress Group, it was clear that he had worrying – and very bad – news. 'Even if we can accept every one of the proposed savings that I've put in that paper,' he explained, 'it shows that we will have used up almost all of our contingency, and we're left with something in the order of £500,000 out of a £10.8 million [sum].' For all concerned on the project, it raised an impossible dilemma. Clearly, all the options must be considered to minimise another budget overshoot. But with some MSPs now stating privately that quality mustn't be compromised, and with Miralles' design now far advanced, the Progress Group's concern was that radical change now could have significant and damaging impact.

For the architects at EMBT/RMJM, Ezzi's most radical suggestions were nothing short of horrifying. The dramatic suspended cantilever opposite historic Holyrood Palace now faced being returned to an earlier design where it had rested on the Canongate's pavement. Or another option proffered could place columns underneath it to help reduce the cost. The cantilever had been one of Miralles' last touches before he died, and, for Brian Stewart, a revisit now just meant more costly going around in circles. Just as worrying, concrete vaulting in the building's public entrance – a feature integral to Miralles' overall concept – now might be swopped for cheaper render on a preformed metal mesh. 'I mean, as an architect the idea of some form of mock vaulting there in such an important part of the building really is appalling,' John Gibbons confided. 'I think . . . the design team around Enric all shared the philosophy that he brought to this, which was an honesty of structure: that the building was what it was . . . The building that was designed had an honest expression of what made it stand up basically. And, as I said . . . the column and the barrel vault was very much an integral part of that.'[10]

What was now emerging at Holyrood was the clash of ideologies that had been obvious since Alan Ezzi's arrival. On one side stood John Gibbons and the architects, passionate about Miralles' concept and equally convinced that it was too late for major savings to be made. And on the other stood Project Director Alan Ezzi, attempting to fulfil the terms on which his contract had been based. 'Now I'm uncomfortable with what happened today,' he told the documentary crew after the meeting, 'because I don't believe that we've got the same aims. I can understand [the Progress Group's concerns] perfectly . . . they're MSPs, and they believe that we should be getting the right building for the Scottish Parliament. And I absolutely agree with that, we should be getting the right building. But if that building is gonna cost more than £195 million, it's outwith my capability to give them that.'

As ever it was John Gibbons – always frank about the problems Holyrood was facing – who provided an insightful perspective into where the situation now lay. As long ago as January, he had predicted with startling accuracy how Alan Ezzi's tenure would unfold. 'I don't think it will take very long before . . . [Alan's] able to assess . . . that it perhaps isn't possible to go back to 195 [million pounds],' he had told the film team, 'you know, that in fact his terms of reference are virtually impossible to deliver . . . I think . . . from [Alan's] point of view . . . he has to examine what he's being asked to do, and whether it's do-able, whether it ever was do-able . . . And, well, certainly if I were in his shoes that is what I would be doing, would be addressing whether it could be done – ever.' With the Progress Group looking increasingly likely to go for concept over cheapness, and the pressures on the budget now intolerable, going back to parliament for more funding was all a matter of timing. But although no one in Holyrood could have guessed it, they were about to get a helping hand from a very unexpected source.

Notes

1. Interview, 7 March 2001.
2. 'The Project Director has been instructed to review the total cost of the MSP block with the cost consultant and, having done so, he will no doubt wish to discuss a range of options with the Design Team.' John Gibbons (for Alan Ezzi) to Brian Stewart, Letter, 29 November 2000, http://www.holyroodinquiry.org. '[W]e are not at all happy with the initiative to establish a range of cost options resting solely with the Project Director and the Cost Consultant. DL[&]E concur with this view.' Mick Duncan to John Gibbons, Letter, 4 December 2000, ibid.
3. Lord Fraser's report would conclude, in line with the Auditor General's report, that there was 'at best only "qualified agreement"' achieved. *Holyrood Inquiry*, ch. 11, para. 11.14, September 2004, ibid.
4. A paper from the project team would explain their end of the story in March 2001: Martin Mustard, *Paper – Procurement of East Frame (Trade Package TP 2605)*, 20 March 2001, ibid.
5. Fabiani's explanation of her outburst was quite different. 'Well, quite often I feel that we suffer as elected members from being given information that perhaps the civil service, perhaps the project team, design team feel that we ought to have,' she argued. 'And sometimes I think there's a lot there that we should be getting told, and that we, you know, just aren't being told . . . I want to know it all, and then I can make a proper decision . . . [But] it was more than that last week . . . We had asked for a schedule of potential savings that we could look at, and make decisions on, and I realised halfway through the report that some of the savings that we were being presented with were not potential at all. They were absolutely impossible. And I felt we were getting treated with a wee bit [of] contempt.' Interview, 24 January 2001.
6. 'My understanding before the meeting was that we were looking at the end of the day at £2–3 million, but as much as £5 million was mentioned at the Progress Group meeting and I think that really was what caused a lot of the difficulty for the Progress Group. I think they were

expecting a more fixed, fine-tuned estimate of where we were ... I don't think there was any mystery or deviousness in [the different figures]. I think there were just different views on the state they're at. I mean to manage down the package like that, the various players are very, very actively doing things, and I think they all perhaps are separately arriving at different conclusions. But there was a good deal of frustration at that meeting that this had arrived without notice, as it were.' Interview, John Gibbons, 24 January 2001.

7. Quoted in Karen Rice, 'Is it a parliament . . . or a supermarket?', *Edinburgh Evening News*, 10 February 2001.

8. Quoted in Murdo Macleod, 'Holyrood think bubbles at £17,000 each', *Scotland on Sunday*, 17 December 2000. In fact, the MSP window was an original Miralles idea, as project architect John Kinsley explained: 'Mick and myself were in Barcelona on a visit, probably in early '99 and we were talking to Enric and suggesting to him it would be nice to have a bay window in the MSP room and to have a space in there that offered the potential for reflection and so on ... And Enric very, very quickly said, "Fantastic idea – we'll have a curve here to rest your back against, a seat to sit on, a well for your feet and some steps here to put your feet up on or to store personal objects and books, a window to look out of and we'll finish it with a roof like that" and he just drew this bay window in about twenty seconds flat and it was just this utterly, utterly unique shape and form and ... I mean Mick and myself, the jaws just dropped. You know, you're aware that you're in the presence of somebody fairly special when they can do that kind of thing.' Interview, 21 August 2003.

9. Quoted in Karen Rice, 'Is it a parliament . . . or a supermarket?', *Edinburgh Evening News*, 10 February 2001.

10. Progress Group meeting, March 2001; interview, March 2001. Brian Stewart, Mick Duncan and Benedetta Tagliabue stood absolutely united on this issue: Mick Duncan to Lewis Macdonald, Letter, 'Scottish Parliament Building, Holyrood: cost saving exercise', 27 February 2001, http://www.holyroodinquiry.org; Benedetta Tagliabue to Lewis Macdonald, Letter, 5 March 2001, ibid.

14

With a Little Help from our Friends

*'The Holyrood project has been used as a political football from the start
and it is about time that that stopped. We all have responsibility for the
outcome. It is nonsense to think that we will not all be judged on the final
outcome.'*
Pauline McNeill MSP[1]

ON 10 MAY 2001, the Scottish Parliament gathered for
debate number three on the Holyrood project. The previous months had seen yet more worrying upheaval. With
Progress Group member Tavish Scott having already left the
committee due to promotion, in March it was the turn of convenor Lewis Macdonald to depart in the ministerial Mondeo.
'It was a considerable blow,' explained Progress Group secretary Sarah Davidson, 'partly because we were at quite a difficult time in the project and – whenever isn't it a difficult time?
– but I just remember . . . [I] felt particularly insecure at the
thought of losing him. He was a consummate chairman. He
handled things very well and very carefully and . . . I think I was
genuinely rather scared . . . and daunted at the prospect of
having to start from scratch with someone all over again . . .'

The handover – to Labour MSP John Home Robertson –
had actually turned out to be relatively seamless. But as always
with the building project, any news was fodder for opponents
to attack. The motion to approve Macdonald's ministerial
appointment had led to more political pot-shots, with Tory
leader David McLetchie sniping that the appointment gave 'a
real lesson to ambitious members of the Labour and Liberal
Democrat back benches . . . that the fast track to promotion

in the parliament is to become a member of the Holyrood Progress Group.' For new First Minister Henry McLeish, the statement left a wide-open goal. '[T]here is no prospect at all for any Tory advancement,' he retorted, 'because the Tories still will not sit on the Holyrood Progress Group and consider the parliamentary issues involved.'[2] In the public domain too, the pattern of attack remained familiar. 'Confusion as head of parliament group quits' the *Evening News* trumpeted boldly. It continued: 'The group meant to keep a grip on the new Scottish Parliament building has been plunged into confusion after the MSP in charge was made a minister.'[3] If the tactics were predictable, however, the new convenor's enthusiasm certainly did not help. 'I have spoken in the past of my hope that future generations of Scots will come to identify with the Holyrood building,' Home Robertson had declared loyally, 'and that we will have the confidence as a nation to take a pride in it as well. It's a healthy project, I've no reason to believe it isn't . . .' For arch-critic Margo MacDonald, the opportunity he offered was far too good to pass by. If Home Robertson believed he was inheriting a healthy project, she argued with some justification, it was apparent he had come late to the scheme.[4]

For those inside Holyrood, however, the weeks since the March Progress Group meetings had been ones of worried and intense analysis. With Ezzi's major savings options rejected, it was now clear that the £195 million cap was going to be breached. But how the cost situation had arrived at this point remained confusing, and – as ever – depended on who you listened to. For Alan Ezzi, the answer had been straightforward. '[It's] too simplistic [to say that DL&E[5] got the cost plan wrong]', he had told the Progress Group on 7 March, 'That's not the case. We know that at the time everyone signed up to this deal, the development was on the table at £130 million. DL&E said this; all the designers knew that. Yet they still signed up to producing a design which would effectively be at £108 million.'[6] For Ezzi, this had seemed a clear example of failure by the architects to do what they were being paid for. And with the savings exercise coming in with a fee tag for redesign work, his proposal had been that this money – and the costs of engineering changes that also might be needed – should be coming out of EMBT/RMJM's fee. To John Gibbons though, the allegations against the company had proved deeply disturbing. 'Well, I think these are very serious accusations against the architect of incompetence . . .' he had argued gravely. 'I mean, these are very serious termination of commission allegations . . . Have these been put to the architect yet?' The answer – alarmingly – had been no.

With Alan Ezzi blaming the architects, John Gibbons suggesting that DL&E's advice may be changing, and the Progress Group indicating concern about comments recorded on the record by the time it met again a fortnight later, the situation was now as confusing for the film team as it had ever been to date. What *had* become clear, however, was that the £195 million figure agreed by parliament in 2000 now appeared not to have included inflation. The decision taken at the time had been that attempts would be made to manage inflation out of the equation, with savings being found to compensate for this sum. But news of the cost situation – when explained in a letter from Paul Grice – had caused consternation at a Finance Committee meeting in February.[7] Six weeks later, when the *Evening News* ran a story headlined '£195m will give "lower quality" of parliament', the political reaction to the news was predictably incensed. 'I hope that the Scottish Parliament will put short shrift to this third requirement for yet more taxpayers' money to lavish on the Scottish Parliament building,' declared Tory leader David McLetchie. 'It is absurd to suggest that a suitable building cannot be produced with a cap of £195 million.'[8] For the Tories, the opportunity to state their case formally was about to come round in May. And it would have an outcome that no one outside Holyrood could possibly have expected.

Within the Scottish Parliament's structure, opposition parties have set times when they can choose topics for debate. And in May 2001, the Scottish Tories selected Holyrood. For those inside the project, the motivations behind their selection seemed clear. 'I think the Conservative Party in the UK have launched their election manifesto today,' John Gibbons confided wryly on the morning the debate was scheduled, 'and it's been clear for some time that Holyrood was going to figure in their strategy to . . . [illustrate] the management capabilities of the current government. I mean, that's speculation, but it's hard to think that it's an accident, that the debate is taking place coincidentally with the launch of the UK national Conservative policy.' Progress Group member Jamie Stone was less diplomatic. 'It's a stunt', he stated plainly. 'There's a general election coming around and I think that's why the Conservatives tabled it . . . Personally I think they've misjudged it, because people are saying to us, "Get on with [the building]; finish it" and so on . . . But that's what it's about, [isn't] it?' Yet again, Holyrood was ammunition in a peripheral political conflict. But with the Tories completely misreading the signals, Holyrood debate number three would have an entirely unexpected outcome. And for once, the Holyrood project was going to benefit.

The launch of the Scottish Tories' election campaign had itself got off to a spectacularly embarrassing start twenty-four hours earlier, when their campaign poster had been unveiled to reveal not the intended attack on Labour, but an advert for a twenty-four hour Tesco store in Stevenage. It was a gaffe that had garnered the Tories acres of unexpected news coverage, and provoked one of the most animated performances of First Minister's Question Time so far. Still more humiliating, however, had been the revelation made forty-eight hours before the debate was due to take place. The Tories' own David Davidson had been appointed Finance Committee reporter on the Holyrood building, and his report delivered on 8 May had drawn the following conclusion. Spencely's price range expectation had been made at a point when design difficulties still remained outstanding. And as a result, 'the motion put to and passed by the Scottish Parliament . . . for a fixed cash sum . . . of £195m, was somewhat optimistic and, in light of the complexity of the tender and control process inherited from the [Scottish Office], naïve for such a complicated and . . . unique design'.[9]

Given that Davidson's own party was about to spend an entire debate insisting that not a penny more should be spent on the building, the timing of his findings could hardly have been more embarrassing. And for those inside the project, the current situation seemed to generate an unusual measure of calm. 'Well, I think you've gotta step back and say, you know, this is part of a political process,' John Gibbons rationalised quietly. 'We're providing a building in a political context, so healthy democratic debate is fine . . . In terms of progressing the project, we could do without it. But in terms of a point along the way it could turn out to be very helpful.' With a separate exercise already underway for the parliament to be told of the current financial position with Holyrood, a heavy defeat of the Conservative motion would mean only one thing. Instead of ensuring that the cost cap of £195 million would be reinforced firmly, the Scottish Tories could actually achieve the reverse. Uniting all parties against them, the new building's £195 million cost cap – far from becoming final – would have the ground prepared for its lifting within a matter of weeks.

As the chamber in the temporary parliament filled with murmuring politicians, in a quiet office at Parliament Headquarters Mick Duncan and Benedetta Tagliabue sat watching the unfolding debate on TV. It was the first time Tagliabue had seen the political battleground into which her husband's building was emerging, and, as the session continued, it would provoke her laughter, applause and dismay. 'It's a parliament, and they have a system which works . . . with oppositions and games of power,' she explained to the Holyrood film team, 'and of course they use this as a game of power . . . Yes I'm shocked, but I also can try to look at [it] from far away.'

Yet while some of Tagliabue's reactions would confirm her semi-detachment from the process, there was one contribution that would clearly rock the architect on her heels. Its source would be Holyrood nemesis Margo MacDonald. 'We are never, ever going to hear the admission we should hear that misleading information was given . . . about the exact state of Enric Miralles' health,' the building's opponent declared firmly. 'I do not expect ever to have an apology from where I ought to have one, to say that I was right in saying that the poor man would be unable to see his concept fulfilled and that anything following that would be a hotch-potch job.'[10] For Margo, the situation remained that if the signature architect was not there to see the project through, his vision 'should perhaps be reassessed in the light of reality'.[11] But for Tagliabue, who always maintained an impermeably composed public demeanour, the comments provoked a sudden flash of disgust and pain. 'Well, I'm absolutely shocked,' she stated, disbelieving. 'I think [there is] no reason at all to say these things . . . I couldn't think that someone could think *that*! . . . The project is there, and it's Enric's project . . . But when I hear things which are absolutely not true, of course it's difficult [not to get] touched by that. I try not.' On the journey to the airport later, her assessment of MacDonald's comments would be blunter. 'Today was the first day I heard Margo MacDonald,' she would confide in the film crew plainly, 'and I really thought that, today, she didn't really have anything to say.'

If Margo's comments had provoked disgust within Holyrood, however, what would really set this debate apart from its predecessors was the role to be played by a newly published, and highly critical, book. Launched on the day of the debate, its author was David Black, key critic of the Holyrood process, and the organiser of the public 'information' session which had preceded the debate post-Spencely a year before. In the months since Miralles' illness, Black had become an increasingly visible presence. In April 2000, he had appeared in the *Evening News*, declaring that it 'would make sense' for Benedetta Tagliabue to take the lead in Miralles' absence; RMJM, he argued, were 'completely the wrong people to deliver a parliament'.[12] In May, he was in the *Evening News* again, suggesting that a newly won contract by Miralles meant that his Holyrood contract should be re-examined.[13] By August, having called for a public inquiry, he was expounding his theories about the project in the *Herald*.[14] And by early spring a year later, one of Black's numerous criticisms was beginning to come to the fore. Holyrood, he declared, could top £300 million, bringing it in an eye-watering 3,000 per cent over budget.[15] It was a prediction that would be seized upon by opponent after opponent in the Holyrood debate. But what – exactly – did Black's £300 million consist of?

The answer to this question was simple: quite a lot that made it incomparable to any other sum. 'A quick computation on the back of an envelope,' Black's book had declared, 'indicated that if one included all the costs of avoiding Calton Hill, such as the reports by Spencely and the Auditor General . . . the cost of parliamentary time spent on the issue, the cost of researching and answering almost 150 written questions . . . between June 1999 and October 2000, the £7.7m spent on refurbishing the Mound, the cost of hiring special advisors from outside the civil service at up to £750 per day each, the cost of all the knock-on effects of increased traffic circulation in the Old Town, and probably the £1m which Edinburgh ratepayers had had to hand over to Harvey Nichols after EDI's initial Calton Hill scheme had been binned, then there was no realistic chance of seeing a penny change out of £300m.'[16] It was a method of calculation that could have arrived at almost any total; indeed, it seemed remarkable that the cost of bus tickets hadn't been factored into the sum. Yet despite this, opponent after opponent employed Black's figures as ammunition. 'It's like the Bible!' Tagliabue laughed as the SNP's Mike Russell waved the volume in the air. Mick Duncan, however, was more frustrated. 'Well, they're doing the same thing,' he explained, unhappy, 'they're playing with figures; they're influenced by this man Black. Why's all of a sudden he become a god, that they [are] waving the book and *quoting* one man's view of life? I find that very upsetting.'

With the debate on Holyrood drawing to a close, and MSPs spilling into the famous black and white corridor, the Progress

Group's Linda Fabiani and Jamie Stone were clearly relieved. 'I can see why they brought it up, and it's perfectly valid – it's a general election,' Linda Fabiani confided, standing in the afternoon sunshine. 'But I don't think [the Tories] prepared very well for it; they went off on the wrong tack. And I think they've just ended up looking a bit silly.' With the Tories almost certainly facing defeat, Holyrood, for once, was savouring victory. And with the £195million cap set to be lifted, the originally envisaged quality for the building was back within reach. 'The motivation of absolutely everybody in the group, not just politicians but also including the independent members that are there . . . and I would go as far to say the entire design team and all the civil servants that are involved,' explained Fabiani, 'we're really at a one in getting a quality product at the end of this. That is absolutely crucial . . . [But t]he kind of procurement we're using, the way the construction industry works. Until we sign the final contract . . . [n]obody actually knows what this is gonna be costing. All we can do is do our best to contain it as much as possible.' With this now clearly apparent, it raised one fundamental issue. If the client wanted quality, quality was going to cost more money. And if more money was going to be called for, it would have far-reaching effects. With Alan Ezzi employed to deliver Holyrood on time and on budget, one question now predominated. If all were now choosing concept over cost issues, where did this leave his job?

Notes

1. *Scottish Parliament Official Report*, Session 1 (2001) vol. 12, col. 592, 10 May 2001, http://www.scottish.parliament.uk
2. *Scottish Parliament Official Report*, vol.11, no. 8, cols 886, 889, 22 March, 2001, ibid.
3. 'Confusion as head of parliament group quits', *Edinburgh Evening News*, 23 March 2001.
4. 'Outlook is healthy at Holyrood says chief', *Edinburgh Evening News*, 28 March 2001.
5. DL&E, Davis Langon and Everest, were the parliament building's cost consultants.
6. Cost consultant Hugh Fisher would explain to the Fraser Inquiry: 'The

£195m was a politically required figure . . . The project proceeded and, as cost consultants, it was incumbent on us to say to the Client, "That is all very well, but there are significant risks and things to which this project is exposed that have not yet been managed out . . . therefore, as they have not been managed out, we are going to put them back into our reports until somebody does manage them out, because they remain threats to the project".' Hugh Fisher evidence session, para. 257, 18 February 2004, http://www.holyroodinquiry.org

7. Paul Grice to Nick Johnston, Letter, 6 February 2001, http://www.scottish.parliament.uk; *Scottish Parliament Finance Committee Official Report*, Meeting no. 5, 2001, cols 1126–30, 27 February 2001, ibid. Despite the reactions of the Finance Committee, the SPCB's response to John Spencely's report had advised the exclusion of inflation, although their statement that the design could be delivered for a total budget of $195m may have led to confusion. *SPCB Paper 99*, paras 20, 3, ibid., http://www.holyroodinquiry.org

8. Karen Rice, '£195m will give "lower quality" of parliament', *Edinburgh Evening News*, 11 April 2001. Margo MacDonald raised the issue of the £195 million cap being broken at a question and answer session with the Progress Group on 7 February. As the project progressed, Margo's increasing frustration at not receiving adequate answers through official channels would be apparent. 'I've got to verify things,' she told the film team, 'and most of the time, if I couldn't verify it and I thought it sounded reasonable, it checked off something else, then I asked a question. But the whole idea of asking questions and then getting rubbish replies, that was disrespectful of me . . . as an MSP – or of any MSP who would have asked questions.' Interview, 2003.

9. *Paper F1/01/11/5*, 'Interim Report on the Holyrood Project'. Finance Committee, 8 May 2001, http://www.scottish.parliament.uk

10. *Scottish Parliament Official Report*, col. 588, 10 May 2001, ibid.

11. Ibid, col. 589.

12. Quoted in Karen Rice, 'Wife with designs on Enric's job', *Edinburgh Evening News*, 28 April 2000.

13. 'Parliament architect in fee cut call', *Edinburgh Evening News*, 27 May 2000.

14. David Black, 'The final grim twist was the tragic death of the Parliament's architect', *Herald*, 12 August 2000.

15. David Black, Letter to the *Herald*, 6 March 2001.

16. David Black, *All the First Minister's Men: The Truth behind Holyrood*, Edinburgh: Birlinn, 2001, p. 217.

15

Did he Jump or Was he Pushed?

'I suppose theoretically it could get to the stage where if every one of my recommendations were rejected by the Corporate Body then they might ask questions and I might ask questions myself about my role here. But I don't think that will happen.'

Alan Ezzi[1]

O N 19 JUNE 2001, the Scottish Parliament issued an unexpected press release. 'Mutual expectations have not been fully realised,' it stated, 'and, having reflected on the current position and looking ahead to project completion, the Scottish Parliamentary Corporate Body has accepted Mr Ezzi's resignation on agreed terms.' Sarah Davidson, it concluded, 'closely involved in the project at a senior level for more than a year', had already been appointed as his replacement.[2] For a project that had provoked outrage and controversy from its very earliest days, the reaction to this news could not have been described as unprecedented. 'There may well be professionals in the building industry looking at this,' arch-critic Margo MacDonald declared firmly, 'and wondering whether their grandmother could get a job on the final design to pass away the hours.'[3]

Alan Ezzi's demise – despite the problems of the preceding months – had been as secret as it had been sudden. That there was an emerging schism within the project was beyond doubt, but with the announcement of Ezzi's departure made just two days before the crucial debate on Holyrood, the timing could hardly have been worse. So why had things come to such an abrupt conclusion? The answer, it soon became clear, would take some finding. No one, it seemed, was to be told the details of Ezzi's departure; and that included the documentary team, who had charted the process for years. Producer Stuart Greig had met one of the Progress Group politicians the night before the announcement. All, he had been assured, had been well. With interviews to establish the facts proving largely fruitless, the team realised that establishing the truth would be an even greater battle than usual. The question was, where should they start?

On 20 June 2001, the film team travelled to meet John Spencely, who was taking a rare day off on his yacht. The preceding weeks had seemed the catalyst for Alan Ezzi leaving, and Parliament Chief Executive Paul Grice had responded by asking Spencely for lunch. 'And so we had lunch . . .' recalled Spencely, 'and he said, "Of course, I'm not really looking for free consultancy advice *but* would you go and have a wee chat with Alan?", because he clearly could see there was a problem there, that Alan wasn't being diplomatically well skilled.'

Spencely had arranged to meet Alan Ezzi a week before the surprise announcement, and it had been clear that the Project Director was not a happy man. 'I mean, this was last week,' Spencely remembered, '[and it] was perfectly clear to me that he wasn't gonna stay the course, but I didn't realise it was gonna be next week. I mean, he gave me to understand it would be a year . . . or whatever before he pushed off.' Ezzi's central problem, as had been clear since he began at Holyrood, was with the Progress Group. '[To say that it] saw him as an . . . enemy is putting it too strong,' Spencely confided, 'but he was quite clearly seen on the other side of some dividing line. He wasn't seen as "one of us", and that – I think – was Barbara's problem as well, and maybe John Gibbons' . . . That somehow nobody on the client's side has ever been able to see these people as anything other than "one of them", who are trying to put one across on us. And that of course is disastrous, and that's utterly unusual.'

For new Project Director Sarah Davidson, settling into her office on site, the story was much the same. 'We observed over

time this increasing separation between what project management appeared to be believing was the direction which we
should be going, and the politicians believed was the direction
they should be going,' she explained to the film crew discreetly,
'and the politicians had some concerns . . . that what they
wanted was not necessarily central to what was happening, but
also that – and I don't know whether this was fair or not – but
they began to believe that there was a move to set them up as
the people who were to blame if the project didn't meet its
targets on cost and budget, and so on. And there were a
number of people who they felt were running away from any
blame, and the Project Director was one of them.'

With the relationship disintegrating, the problems of Ezzi's
appointment were becoming clearer. As early as January 2001,
concern had been raised that the new Project Director's role
had created a no-win situation. If he succeeded in cutting
costs, there were fears that the building might end up the 'el
cheapo hotel' derided by political opponents. And if he didn't,
what would be the impact if he left the project, and then went
public with claims that his proposals had been ignored? As if
this was not enough, the relationship between Ezzi and Brian
Stewart was itself under increasing and worrying pressure, and
a decision that members of the design team would continue to
report directly to the Progress Group – contradicting Alan
Ezzi's wishes – had created additional strain. By February,
Ezzi's relationship with the design team was no better, and the
Progress Group was now concerned about the way he was
relating to it too. But the build-up to the Project Director's
sudden departure had really begun in April.

On 25 April, with Alan Ezzi absent and colleague Martin
Mustard deputising, the Progress Group met as usual.
Concerns were raised that the strong line Ezzi was taking on
fees may not, in fact, be deliverable, and it was suggested that
the Project Director was failing in his role to pull the members
of the team together. With some of the Progress Group concerned that it was being 'set up' as those responsible for exceed-
ing the project's budget, the rot had clearly set deep into the

relationship. Ezzi, it was argued, did not appreciate the political sensitivities of the building, and he failed to 'give due weight' to the Progress Group's central role. Worse still, it emerged that the developing design for the building's foyer roof was over £3,000 per square metre – not the £500 allowed for in the cost plan.[4] A week later, the Progress Group met again, and by now the situation had worsened. In an attempt to achieve savings, the Group believed, Ezzi had actually divided the design team 'to a degree which was now having a serious impact on the project'.[5] And by June, the situation would be worse still.

On 6 June, the Progress Group met once more. Over the previous three weeks, two special emergency meetings had been held, as well as several others during the evenings. Holyrood was in serious difficulties, and for the Progress Group, Alan Ezzi was partly to blame. Both John Gibbons and Sarah Davidson had been on the verge of quitting the project, and Paul Grice, now re-clasping Gibbons to his bosom, had been called in and questioned on whether Ezzi's role had been made clear. The meeting on the 6th was a disaster. Ezzi was unable to give reassurance on the foyer roof, arguing that he had not been fully aware of the group's depth of feeling. And worse still, he reported that Brian Stewart had not returned his calls for over a fortnight.[6] For the Progress Group, enough was finally enough. The issue now was whether Ezzi should leave, a meeting was called with Paul Grice, and a letter was presented detailing the group's acute and growing concerns.[7] On the 19th, the press release detailing his departure was made public. Project Director number three had left the job.

Unsurprisingly, Alan Ezzi's version of events was rather different. Following his appointment to the Holyrood project, Grice had sent him a letter detailing the Project Director's complex role. Ezzi must liaise with and be guided by the Progress Group, but he had also been named as the single focal point for day-to-day management.[8] To the film crew, the two roles had seemed destined to collide, a fact Ezzi himself would quickly realise. 'I had believed . . . when I started in the project,' he told them, sitting in his Edinburgh living room, 'that the Progress Group . . . were going to act as a strategic project board taking the strategic overview. In fact, it turned out that they wanted to be much more operationally involved, and . . . as far as I'm concerned, project management by committee doesn't work.' With two members of the group replaced during Ezzi's short tenure, lack of consistency was problematic. And with the deeply trusted John Gibbons readily available, Ezzi believed his own authority with the architects was being constantly undermined, a fact only made worse when the Progress Group rejected his savings. And as if all this was not enough, these problems – it seemed – were not the only hurdles.

For Ezzi, what had proved deeply frustrating had been the newly re-structured Progress Group meetings, which had excluded him completely from decision-making. 'The Progress Group sat down once a fortnight,' he remembered, 'they had their meetings, I was given an agenda on the things that I was to present to, I went in there and presented for twenty minutes and then at the end of the day they went into a huddle and a puff of white smoke appeared, and I would get this list of things that I had to do.' For someone expecting to act as Project Director, it was an infuriating method of management. But what had made him particularly uncomfortable had been the conflicting nature of some of the instructions that emerged. 'On the one hand, I was being . . . instructed by the Holyrood Progress Group to mend relationships within the design team,' he would later remember, 'and yet, on the other hand, I was being asked to attribute responsibility for cost overruns and delays between those individual design team members. I clearly could not do both.'[9]

To the film team, the rift between Progress Group and Project Director merely highlighted what had been obvious to them for months. 'I don't think those two ever understood each other, really,' Sarah Davidson pondered in confirmation. 'I think they professed to understand each other, but they didn't really. And I think also the Progress Group were naturally always suspicious from the very beginning of somebody who was going to come in and drive forward the project from a project management point of view. And that wasn't necessarily fair, but I think their view was: "He will always try to persuade us of something that's not so beautiful, that's not so artistic." And . . . once they had that view they were unlikely to really accept his recommendations.' For Ezzi, however, it seemed that the chapter of his departure was still not finally closed. Who did the project need to lead it, asked the film team's Susan Bain, as neither a civil servant nor a building professional had lasted the distance? 'Oh, you're looking at him,' Ezzi replied firmly. 'There's absolutely no doubt about it; and I hold myself ready and willing there. [If] the phone call comes tomorrow and says . . . "We think that we need you after all," I'll go back there and I'll do it. Because I think that absolutely and definitely what it needs is a building professional; that the inter-relationships of the design team and the contractor, and the client are such that it needs somebody with my skills to make it happen.'

For Sarah Davidson, now thrust into the spotlight as Project Director number four, the task that lay in front of her was daunting. Twenty-nine years old, Oxford taught and strikingly attractive, she was certainly *not* a building professional but yet another career civil servant. It was a distinction not lost on the project's greatest opponent. '[I]f it required a year ago someone of Alan Ezzi's professional qualifications – which the advertisement for his job made very clear were absolutely essential . . .' Margo MacDonald argued, 'and a proven track record was equally essential, then why, at a crucial time of the development, have you chosen to go down market, and go for a superb administrator rather than someone qualified in construction? . . . We've appointed someone with no track record in construction, and we have not interviewed anyone else for this job, even though it's the most prestigious construction job in Scotland.'[10]

Margo's point was a fair one, and certainly more sensible

than some of the comments emerging elsewhere. 'I wouldn't trust this woman to cut my finger nails, far less build a project like this,' the *Scottish Sun* quoted Donald Gorrie as sniping – a soundbite he would publicly disown,[11] while an unnamed 'construction industry expert' stated, 'If I wanted information on Caravaggio, I'd go to Sarah Davidson, but not if I wanted a parliament building . . . I'd give her six months.'[12] Susan Dalgety at the *Evening News* offered a more flippant analysis. '[T]he job of building Scotland's parliament,' she wrote, 'has been given to a young woman whose main qualification for the job seems to be that she once played the oboe.'[13] These criticisms – as they had with Miralles – raised suspicions of a far less pleasant agenda. 'In any other project, had a bright, able, young Scottish lady advanced in this manner, we would have said "Amen" and "Hallelujah to that,"' Progress Group member Jamie Stone would argue in the chamber, 'but because it is the Holyrood Project, she has been shot at . . . Because Sarah Davidson happens to be female and young, it is suggested that she is incompetent. That is disgraceful.'[14]

So how did Sarah Davidson end up in the Project Director's post? And was she really qualified to do such a complex job? The roots of the new appointment stretched right back to the days of Barbara Doig. As part of management restructuring post-Spencely, the SPCB had split Doig's huge job into parts. The Project Sponsor role was shared between a Project Director and Financial Controller, and the function of project completion was delegated to Paul Grice. But there had also been another change, as Davidson explained. 'About this time last year,' she told the film team, 'what we wanted to do was to have a slightly different way of running the project, and we recognised that one person just couldn't do it all in the way it was at that time.' The solution had been to have someone employed to look after the technical side, and another to look after the politicians. With Alan Ezzi's appointment, it had been hoped that he and Davidson could work side by side, to create a better whole. But in practice, this had never happened, and the two halves of the project had begun to drift apart.

'The kind of restructuring we've done is to try and move the client back into the centre again . . .' Davidson explained, '[because] if [the job] doesn't take into account every single step of the way what the client wants, what the politicians want, and what the users of the building want, then it's just not going to be what we would call fit for purpose . . . And as I've been the person who's always dealt with trying to interpret what the client wants, they've put my role much more at the centre.' Once again, it was being acknowledged that the job was highly political, a fact that had become all too apparent to those inside the project over the years. With Davidson's acute political radar, technical back-up from the project team and interpersonal skills that were the polar opposite of Ezzi's, it was an arrangement that certainly looked like it could function. Yet for architect John Spencely, the future was not assured. '[Alan] tells me that they want, now . . . to provide more space for people,' he worried, 'and that's an undisciplined client body . . . The fact that they've lost confidence in him is a two way process . . . They appointed him knowing full well – because I told them – what their problems are, [the Auditor General's] told them what's the problems, and they know fine themselves what the problems are . . . The building is being built; it's being well built, and it'll be finished. But it'll be finished late.'

On 21 June 2001, the Scottish Parliament gathered again. A week earlier, the SPCB had published its sixth progress report on the Holyrood project, and in it the projected outturn cost – barring outstanding inflation and risk related costs – had been £198 million.[15] With construction industry inflation predicted to add at least £10.4 million to future packages, design risk assessed at £14.2 million, and £12.1 million for construction risk, the potential grand total for the Holyrood building now stood at £234.7 million. The £195 million cap had been well and truly breached.

Despite this bad news, however, debate number four would mark something of a sea-change. Clearly, there was still anger about the decisions of the past. But there now seemed to be an acceptance – albeit grudging – that the project was going ahead. The real question henceforth seemed to be how best to manage it. 'I mean, to some extent nobody knows how to finish this,' the SNP's Mike Russell told the film crew as he arrived at the parliament's chamber. 'This is like a huge morass. And what I'm trying to do . . . [is] say "Let's have some honesty about it."' With the SPCB proposing that the project should be completed without compromising quality, the SNP's amendment calling for a new financial plan, and the Tories again calling for the £195 million cap to be enforced, Holyrood was now certain to go forward – in some form.[16] And given the result of debate number three, it was unlikely to be the route favoured by the Tories. 'You couldn't have capped it at £195 million last year,' Mike Russell explained dryly. 'This year what are you gonna do? Leave the roof off, you know? . . . Forget to build a wall? . . . That's just nonsense, it can't be done . . . I wish it could be done, it can't be done. So the Tory amendment is – frankly – mince.'

For some insiders, though, standing outside the chamber with Brian Stewart, the way ahead could not have felt less triumphant. The SPCB would – ultimately – claim victory, but Stewart seemed only exhausted, deflated, and sad. 'I'm not sure it makes, really, an enormous amount of difference,' he confided quietly. 'We're doing our best on the project, we always have done and we always will do . . . I mean, obviously, the motion on how to manage the finance is an important issue, so I mean, that has to be raised. But you don't get that issue without all of the other baggage that goes along with that . . . You know, crawling over the history's really not very, very helpful.'

Hours later, over coffee, the extent of Stewart's disillusion became clear. '[You and I have] spent hours and hours discussing this project,' he confided frankly, 'and I think you just reach the point where it's exhaustion. You know, you reach exhaustion . . . where you have issues which are not . . . specific[ally] project-related, that are constantly influencing and affecting what we're doing . . . You get exhausted with that. And it's not to say that the project isn't special. Of course it is; it's a special project. But you just get exhausted with all the periphery, and you need a rest.' From the client end, the Progress Group had been told that Stewart would be 'dipping out of the process',[17] and there had been mutterings that he was now irrational, stressed and had developed a 'huge' persecution complex. Yet for Stewart himself, the situation was quite plain. 'I think some of the events sometimes just are a bit sickening,' he admitted, 'and you just – phew – you know, you just say, "Oh, I've had enough of this . . . Is my involvement in this making it easier or better to get this done?" And I reached that point.'

With Holyrood given the green light, the £195 million cap lifted, and the Finance Committee due for quarterly reports on the project's costs, it looked like the worst was finally over. The relationship with the Progress Group was working, Sarah Davidson – backed by John Gibbons – was at the helm, and relationships within the team were relatively stable. 'In many ways a lot of the issues that have been prominent in the whole process have evaporated,' Brian Stewart pondered, 'the major political thrust has now gone, hasn't it? . . . The sort of struggle to undermine the project, or defend and support the project is over . . . That struggle's done . . . There may be some different struggles ahead, but I think that one's done. And that obviously was a key issue which stimulated interest from the press and the media in general.' He smiled at the film crew impishly, 'So I think it's dull and boring now . . . I think that's the way it is, you know. Do you want to come and see some reinforced concrete?'

What Stewart could never predict, however, was that trouble was about to re-emerge from quite a different quarter. For the first time in years, things at Holyrood were looking hopeful, and if the project's history was anything to go by, that could only mean bad news. In this case, the coming developments could hardly have been more destructive. Enter the SPCB.

Notes

1. Interview, 18 January 2001.
2. *Parliamentary News Release* no. 0042/2001, 'Parliament Project Director resigns', 19 June 2001, http://www.scottish.parliament.uk
3. Quoted in Michelle Nichols and David Scott, 'New storm as Holyrood chief quits', *The Scotsman*, 20 June 2001; Andrew Nicoll, 'Holyrood boss quits', *Scottish Sun*, 20 June 2001.
4. *Holyrood Progress Group, 7th meeting, 2001*, HPG/01/7/M, paras 3, 4, 9, 15, 25 April 2001, http://www.holyroodinquiry.org
5. *Holyrood Progress Group, 8th meeting, 2001*, HPG/01/8/M, para. 3, 2 May 2001, ibid.
6. *Holyrood Progress Group, 12th meeting, 2001*, HPG/01/12/M, paras 17, 6, 6 June 2001, ibid.
7. John Home Robertson to Paul Grice, Letter, 13 June 2001, ibid.
8. Letter of Appointment, 17 January 2001; Ibid, Annex A, ibid.
9. Alan Ezzi evidence session, col. 450, 10 March 2004, ibid.
10. Transcript, Progress Group question and answer session, 20 June 2001.
11. Quoted in Andrew Nicoll, 'I wouldn't trust new parly boss to cut my nails', *Scottish Sun*, 21 June 2001; *Scottish Parliament Official Report*, col. 1886, 21 June 2001, http://www.scottish.parliament.uk
12. Quoted in Karen Rice, 'From girl next door to construction chief in two years . . . can it work?' *Edinburgh Evening News*, 22 June 2001.
13. Susan Dalgety, 'Thank God it's Saturday: for those about to rock . . . the boat', *Edinburgh Evening News*, 23 June 2001.
14. *Scottish Parliament Official Report*, col. 1880, 21 June 2001, http://www.scottish.parliament.uk
15. Scottish Parliament Corporate Body, *Holyrood Project – June 2001, Sixth Progress Report to Parliament*, 13 June 2001, ibid.
16. Motion S1M-2012, amendment S1M-2012.3, amendment S1M-2012.1, ibid.
17. *Holyrood Progress Group: 12th Meeting 2001*, HPG/01/12/M, para. 6, 6 June 2001, http://www.holyroodinquiry.org

16

Who Rules the Roost?

'Those who are greedy of praise prove that they are poor in merit.'
Plutarch

O N 1 JULY 2001, the Scottish Parliament reached its second anniversary. Birthday one had been marred by the death of Enric Miralles, and the year that followed had seen protracted difficulties between his widow and the co-directors in Edinburgh. Birthday two, by comparison, was relatively quiet. In Wales, however, a recognisable drama was unfolding. The Richard Rogers Partnership, architects of the Welsh Assembly building, had left the project amid rows of spiralling costs, with Assembly members voting that they had lost confidence in the company. For some observers, it all seemed horribly familiar. And within weeks, another worrying pattern was about to re-emerge. Holyrood was set for yet another fallout. And this time, it would not be the architects at the centre, but the SPCB and Progress Group – Holyrood's political clients.

On 29 August 2001, a delegation from the Progress Group flew to Barcelona. The meeting had been planned for at least a fortnight, and was the first time that the body had visited EMBT. 'Coming to Barcelona's always been a bit of a difficult issue,' explained Project Director Sarah Davidson, 'and we've had a fair number of arguments – some more public than others – about whether or not it's the right thing to do . . . I think it was very, very important that they came, and John Home Robertson as convenor . . . believes passionately that he's got a duty to come and see what's happening here.' For Progress Group member Jamie Stone, the visit was equally essential. 'I mean, did you ever hear of a project – you know, 200 plus million – where you can't go and actually talk to the people who are designing it? I mean, that's ludicrous!' he argued. Unfortunately – for all concerned – the SPCB had far from shared this view.

Twenty-four hours before the Progress Group's departure, Home Robertson had given his regular report to the SPCB. 'Well, my telephone went absolutely ballistic yesterday,' Stone explained to the film team. 'I received a text message from Sarah and telephone calls to say there could be a problem.' The Progress Group was in the happy position of not having to clear its travel with the SPCB, a fact the SPCB – it seemed – had failed to realise. And on breaking the news of the visit, Home Robertson had unleashed a very nasty response. 'When I took on this job of responsibility for progressing the construction of our parliament building I knew that it was going to be difficult,' he confided firmly, 'I knew that there was a lot of flak flying around, and I was expecting some aggravation from the press and from some other people. I was *not* expecting aggravation from the Scottish Parliament Corporate Body.'

With the visit already unanimously decided by the Progress Group, the SPCB had subjected Home Robertson to an uncomfortable cross-examination in front of his officials. 'I think it's a bit like Christopher Robin; you can't go to Buckingham Palace without first consulting me, that sort of type of attitude,' explained a clearly exasperated Jamie Stone, 'but, I mean, in actual fact – technically speaking – it wasn't the Corporate Body's decision. It's actually up to Paul Grice.' For Home Robertson, the whole experience had left him infuriated. 'I was bloody angry,' he told the film team. 'I went there for the . . . regular routine report . . . about progress at Holyrood, and there was stuff about millions of pounds worth of tenders being signed off and the rest of it. And to my astonishment a number of members of the [SPCB] started niggling and nitpicking about the cost of £1,000 for sending some members of the Progress Group out here to meet Benedetta on the spot, and to see what the team are doing in their office.'

The roots of the row, it appeared, were buried in two quite separate issues. 'Inevitably with the media attention there is around these things, there were some people who felt very strongly that it was just asking for trouble to get on a plane and go to Barcelona,' Sarah Davidson explained, 'and risk accusations of junketing and sitting in the sun rather than actually getting any work done . . . [But] so far so good: we're here and as far as I know there's only a small story on page fifteen of the *Evening News.*' The other reason, however, would prove to be far more serious. The relationship between the two client bodies had left the SPCB holding legal control of the project. But on a day-to-day basis, it was the Progress Group who actually did all the work. 'I think there's 150 different ways of interpreting the term "day-to-day responsibility",' Davidson would ponder, 'and when it comes to really key areas like the debating chamber and the committee rooms, I think everybody wants to get their hands on it, particularly when things are going a little bit better . . . And I think [there'll] be some difficult issues over the next few months about who actually takes the lead in pushing some of these issues forward. And it's very difficult to work out who's taking the final decisions.'

The row over the Barcelona trip, it now seemed, had turned into a struggle over who was holding the tiller. 'There developed this debate about who was actually in charge of the project, and who was making the decisions,' John Gibbons confided, 'and members of the [SPCB] made it very plain that they considered that . . . major decision making was something that they should be involved in.' On a fast-track, high-profile project already suffering from political meddling, the dangers of this stance were simply immense. 'If we stop to seek authority every two weeks,' he continued, 'there are some dangers that there'll be programme slippage again, and programme slippage means budgetary increases, and one can quickly slip back into a less controlled position'. For Home Robertson, however, the problem could be summed up with far more candour. 'We take day-to-day responsibility,' he stated, 'as you know we spend hours and days going through details, and plans, and talking to people . . . de facto we're in charge. I'm not sure that all members of the Corporate Body fully understand that point . . . It needn't cause aggravation if there was mutual understanding and mutual trust. But there's some people playing silly buggers, there's some people playing politics. And it is disappointing that the Corporate Body, which is meant to be representing the whole of the Scottish Parliament on a very big historic issue, should descend into such silly niggling.'

What the Barcelona visit had exposed was yet another fracture at the heart of Holyrood. And for some key observers, the SPCB's reaction had provoked a wry response. Introducing the group's annual report in late spring, chairman David Steel had written, 'As one of the Parliament's key principles is openness we recently agreed that our minutes should be published on the Parliament's website . . .'[1] What the minutes of *this* meeting would state, and what appeared to have actually happened, would prove an illuminating example of just how 'open' the SPCB had now become.

According to Jamie Stone, Home Robertson had left the meeting with the Corporate Body apoplectic. 'I think [the SPCB] took the line that, you know, "We make the decisions and we haven't given you permission to do that." To which John – I think quite correctly – said, "Well, hang on a minute. You have delegated to the Holyrood Progress Group to do this," and he drew himself up to his full height and said, "Look, I am the chairman; we actually . . . cop responsibility for this, we have to take the flak in the chamber" . . . so it was sort of eyeball to eyeball. And John was incandescent.' 'Certainly I found it a very uncomfortable meeting,' John Gibbons confirmed frankly. 'Not a meeting that as an official I enjoy, where, you know, you have . . . the convenor in this case almost being lectured to by some of his colleagues . . . And I think undeserved really. I think what was said was more said for effect than there was any real need to say it. I know the political members of the Progress Group fully understand the relationship they have with the [SPCB] . . . No one is challenging the authority of the Corporate Body.'

What appeared to be prompting the stand-off was the project's current position. With the £195 million cap lifted, things had been progressing better. And the SPCB, it now seemed, was wanting to take all the praise. 'It's fine and dandy to say, "Oh, things are a bit rough – step back," which they did ... last year,' said Jamie Stone bluntly. '"We'll let these other blokes take [it all]" ... We've just heard that the chamber's going to come in within budget, and then [they] start to interfere. Well, wait a minute – you can't have it both ways.' Home Robertson, it appeared, had threatened his own resignation – a move he denied tactfully, but which was confirmed by virtually everyone else present at the time. And for him, it seemed, the importance of the visit far outweighed the short-term 'niggles' it raised. 'I said I was bloody angry,' he told the documentary team, 'and I said that if that was what the Corporate Body felt then I would just come out here at my own expense – by bus if necessary – because I think ... it would have been an abdication of responsibility not to come here and see what's happening.'

With Home Robertson furious, Jamie Stone exasperated and the SPCB's re-emergence threatening serious problems, the relationship between the two client bodies was now at an all-time low. 'It is disappointing, the sort of discussions that occurred on Tuesday,' John Gibbons would worry privately, '... the fact that there's not that clarity [of role] is not helpful to the project at all. Issues of like who's going to approve the design of the debating chamber ... [it's] somewhat late in the day to start to be arguing over relative responsibilities.' For Home Robertson, however, the situation had provoked a wry smile. 'I don't really care [if they want to elbow us aside],' he told the film team, shrugging, 'I didn't come into this job for personal glory . . . Some people might think that they're out of the stormy waters and it's going to be plain sailing, and people can bask in reflected glory – in which case those of us who've been doing ... the donkey work might be shoved aside. I don't particularly care about that ... The important thing is to finish the job and do it well.' To Jamie Stone, perhaps some schoolboy tactics were now in order. 'I can tell you, I think that John and

I and all of us have some issues to address with the Presiding Officer,' he asserted gravely. 'And David Steel was very good about this; he did his level best. But I think – you know – we need to just have a wee wordy with these people: take them round the back and say, 'Well, what's your game, you know? Is this how you're gonna run it – meddle in every dash thing?'

So how *had* the SPCB 'openly' recorded the biggest client crisis since the Progress Group's creation? The answer, despite all the rhetoric, was perhaps more illuminating than it might think. Point seven of an eight-point summation recorded the astonishing encounter thus: 'Some members of the Progress Group would visit Barcelona on Wednesday 29 August to meet the team and to view the large landscape and working models of the chamber and committee rooms. It was agreed that any future travel should be agreed in advance by the SPCB.'[2]

With the row over leadership still simmering, however, it seemed that external political problems were already beginning to emerge elsewhere. Linda Fabiani, the SNP member of the Progress Group, had not made the trip to Barcelona, the official line being that she hadn't seen the need to go. 'Well, I didn't think it was necessary, it was that simple,' she would tell the film team later. 'I felt that there was nothing I could learn in Barcelona that I couldn't learn here, and I also felt that it was a bit silly . . . for everybody to run off to Barcelona just at the end of the summer recess and it could engender bad publicity, which was in some way justified. So I . . . chose not to go.' According to other sources within Holyrood, the reality was somewhat different. During the run-up to the June 2001 debate, it had become clear that Fabiani was having problems within her own party. 'There are times . . . when I sit on the Progress Group . . .' she had told the documentary team, '[and] I do sit and think, "Why am I bothering?" because I feel sometimes very much that I don't get the support of [the SNP].' With her party's position – and that of its more vocal members – generally opposed to Miralles' building, Fabiani's role on the Progress Group was considerably harder than most. 'There's times I feel like walking away from it,' she had stated sincerely, 'because I think with some of the publicity that comes out, my own personal credibility is sometimes at stake because people – I hope unwittingly – sort of besmirch my reputation . . . and there are those of course who would do this purely for self-promotion and really don't think about how it affects their colleagues.'

As the trip to Barcelona had drawn closer, it had begun to look like Fabiani's role was on the line. One source had already made it clear that Linda did not have her own party's backing, and it looked like her place on the Progress Group may well end up going to someone else. With the group's only opposition member in an uncomfortable and precarious position, it seemed the diplomatic solution had been to find a date that made it hard for her to attend. 'She had to make a political judgement,' Jamie Stone conceded under questioning, 'and I respect her for that. Myself and John Home [sic] also, you know, we said, "No, we understand exactly where you're coming from, and that's no problem at all" . . . It's never easy trying to work three political parties. But we do it . . . it's partly 'cause we're pals; we get on well. So there you go.'

With the Progress Group's visit coming to an end, Fabiani staying in position, and a tricky political face-off narrowly avoided, the worst of the current crisis seemed to pass without disaster. As always though, there was trouble waiting in the wings. It had been agreed with the SPCB that the Barcelona trip would be treated positively, with no nasty leaks appearing in the papers. But within days of the Progress Group's return, it seemed a leak was exactly what occurred. '[They've got] power without responsibility,' John Home Robertson would worry in the back of an Edinburgh taxi. 'Individual members [of the SPCB] appear to feel free to say what they like about [Holyrood], when in fact we're trying to do a job of work for them . . .' He felt it was galling, when doing a difficult, time-consuming, demanding job for the Corporate Body, to read nasty stories in the press alleging that that outing to Barcelona for twenty-four hours was some kind of a junket. The fallout

of late summer might be over, but the clash between the clients
had only just begun.

Notes

1. Introduction, *Annual Report of the Scottish Parliamentary Corporate
   Body, 2001*, http://www.scottish.parliament.uk
2. *Minute of Scottish Parliamentary Corporate Body Meeting*, pt 9, 28
   August 2001, ibid. Documents provided to the Fraser Inquiry would
   confirm that the SPCB kept two sets of minutes. The issue is covered in
   Lord Fraser's Inquiry Report, *Holyrood Inquiry (SP Paper No. 205)*, ch.
   9, para. 9.26, September 2004, http://www.holyroodinquiry.org

17

Blame the Builders

'If it's a success, it will be the client's great clairvoyant, clear thinking at the time, and "Weren't we clever to do it?". If it's a failure, well, it's always the builder. Brian will say it's the architect, but it's always the builder.'
Alan Mack[1]

O N 26 SEPTEMBER 2001, the Progress Group met for its fortnightly Holyrood session. The current occupation date that all were working to was May 2003, an enormously symbolic deadline which would allow the Scottish Parliament to start its second term not in rented accommodation, but in its brand-new, purpose-built home. It would be a new start, a bold statement that the parliament was moving forwards, putting all the hiccups, tragedies and embarrassments of the first term behind them. But as the Progress Group meeting unfolded, one thing became absolutely certain. If nothing was done to get back on schedule, virtually the entire east end of the site was already running up against the end date. And the press tower – along with Miralles' spectacular debating chamber – was itself lagging four to five months behind that. With Alan Mack insisting that there was no slack in the programme and an end to change was now essential, one thing was undeniable. If the next few months panned out according to Holyrood's past history, there was no way the May 2003 deadline was going to be achieved.

Within a week, and with programme problems now topping the agenda, the Progress Group met to consider its options. 'What I found intolerable at that last meeting,' bristled John Home Robertson, 'is that . . . for months now . . . we've been getting these programme reports saying that, "Oh, we're . . . within a few weeks of where we want to be," and not flagging up any problems at all. But all of a sudden out of the blue last week we're told that we're months adrift . . . and people [are] running for cover . . . blaming each other, and blaming the engineer, or blaming somebody else.' For Linda Fabiani, there was another – equally serious – issue. 'What I found disturbing' she stated with quiet indignation, '[was] suddenly dropping something in as if it has always been the reality, and everyone's known, when in actual fact it wasn't . . . All of a sudden there seems to be three elements of completion. We have construction completion, we have fit-out and commissioning completion, and then we have a completion that allows the buildings to be habitable . . . I would like very firm terminology used about what is actually meant by completion . . . and not this constant moving of the goal posts . . .' To Alan Mack, however, the situation was entirely under control. 'This is what pisses me off so much,' he told the film team, frustrated. 'This is not a car that's out of control, this is us in a car driving along the road saying, "Guys, the brakes aren't working; we need to fix the brakes at the next possible stage," or "The exhaust is a bit iffy – we need to fix it." We know all the stuff that needs fixing, and we are addressing it. It's the speed of response of everyone around . . . and the speed of response of the client . . . [They] can't start fannying about saying, "Well, yeah, you know, that's a lovely office, but we'd like to convert it into a wine store."'

The roots of the Progress Group's concerns, it soon became clear, were buried in the form of its reporting. The information they got fortnightly from Alan Mack was largely made against progress on site. But to the project team, headed by Sarah Davidson, it had been clear there were problems building up behind the scenes. 'The engineers have had to start designing some parts of the building before the architects had fully resolved their designs,' she confided to the film crew, 'and in an ideal world you wouldn't hand over an architectural drawing to a structural engineer until it was absolutely fixed and frozen. A combination of the speed that we've been trying to go at, and the fact that there's an awful lot of pressure from time to time for changes . . . from the client . . . mean that . . . the engineers are constantly having to revisit their drawings. That inevitably causes delay, and it ties up staff both in the engineers' and the architects' office on revisiting drawings when they should be moving on to the next part.'

For Brian Stewart, standing in the site car park, there were other factors also impacting on time. 'Structural engineering'll say, "It's much more complicated than I envisaged . . ."' he pondered slowly, 'so design development between the team then becomes protracted . . . [And] you remember the inordinate amount of time that was spent looking at site-wide cost savings . . . that were never adopted . . . It's a deflection of resource into these sort of areas . . . I think it's a series of factors that have impacted on the flow of information, particularly on that package. And that package now appears to be the critical [one].'

Whatever the myriad reasons, delay was having domino effects. And with information coming in behind schedule, Alan Mack's team was now under serious pressure. We have a problem: we can't construct it – so now I've got to find some way of constructing it, cladding it . . . and finishing it faster . . .' Mack explained. 'So we're in a situation now [where] we're trying to condense a lot of activities . . . We're trying to change the sequence of events; maybe do some things in parallel that we would prefer to do perhaps singly . . . The problem when you do all of that is if you make a mistake during that period, the repercussions of that mistake are obviously more extensive than if you've got time to go back and rework it . . . so you're being very focused on trying to make sure that the information that we get now when we get it is suitable for construction straight away.'

As if all this wasn't enough to contend with, Holyrood was also in the midst of its biggest contractual hit to date. Flour City,[2] winners of a major contract on the west end of the site, had been served with notice of termination – and the SNP's

Fergus Ewing would soon be pursuing the case. If Margo MacDonald had proved tenacious, Ewing's questioning over the years to come would provide some serious competition. 'The [SPCB] has noted that [your] 36 questions are in addition to the 113 [you have] already asked about the Holyrood Project,' David Steel would reply to him in February 2003. 'Accordingly, I shall write at length to [you] in due course, placing a copy in [the Parliament's Information Centre].'[3]

With the May 2003 date under severe pressure – even before difficulties with the preferred glazing contractor were taken into consideration – one issue was now focusing everyone's minds. Should the east end of the project be accelerated to hit its political deadline, or should the end-date be extended to let the building finish at its own pace? Neither option offered a palatable answer. Accelerating the building – especially over a long period – was both risky and uneconomic: a broad-brush assessment put the cost at £15–20 million. But not accelerating was itself likely to cost another £10–15 million, with contractors entitled to recover costs for work that had overrun. It was a scenario with which all were now acquainted: damned if you do, and damned if you don't. And as John Home Robertson confided, the implications of either decision would have long-term repercussions. 'Well, it's a balancing act,' he told the film team sincerely, 'I don't want to sacrifice quality, you know. This building has got to stand for a hundred years or more . . . We don't want rough edges and shoddy finishes, it's gotta be done right. But you know, that shouldn't be beyond the wit of man. We've got good contractors, we've got good architects. If we can get them to stop blaming each other and to start working with each other, we should be able to achieve it.'

Back on the Holyrood frontline, where those under fire were all toiling, the pressure – as always – was on. With the client clearly exercised about the end-date, strenuous efforts were being made to deliver. But with the east end of the site problematic, there was no way the answers could be rushed. 'I think we all left the . . . meeting last Wednesday . . . with a fairly clear expectation . . . that Alan Mack was going to give all the members of the design team the programme which he . . . put on the table . . .' Sarah Davidson explained to the Progress Group on 3 October, 'and that they would all be spending the time between last Wednesday and now looking very closely at the dates to ascertain whether or not they could sign up to them . . . I think to be charitable one could say that Alan Mack was being hopelessly optimistic . . . because it's quite clear from the discussions we've had about what's involved in programming this, there was no way they could have had it in the hands of the design team in time for them to have input today.'

With everything hanging on the east-end frame package, scrutiny from architects and structural engineering was essential to see that the dates could be delivered. And at Bovis, Mack was unequivocal about what now had to be achieved. 'Is anything realistic?' he asked the film team, frustrated. 'I mean, it's what has to be done . . . Whether it can be done or not is another matter . . . We're staffing up . . . [but] the question's been said to me several times [that] we're not driving people hard enough. I'm not sure quite what they mean by that because the only thing left that I can do right now . . . is to draw the fucking thing myself . . . We can manage everything else, and we're telling everyone else what we believe is necessary. But I can't bloody design it; that's not my role.' Despite Alan Mack's best efforts, however, serious questions were now being raised about his company's performance. 'I mean, I'm a bit fed up – or getting a bit fed up – with Bovis,' Jamie Stone had stated at the meeting on 3 October. 'I've put my trust in what Alan Mack's been saying . . . "Oh, we're only a week here, two weeks there" – whatever. And Bovis must have known, mustn't they, more about this? I don't know, I've just got a question in my mind.'[4] For Mack though, the situation could be summed up with characteristic colour. 'I don't think any of the people that we work with . . . wake up in the morning, and say . . . "How're we gonna frustrate the process today?"' he told the film crew with a wry flicker. 'We all turn up because we say, "Look, we're gonna make this happen" . . . and we're stupid enough to say,

"Yeah, it's just like migraine, you keep banging your head against the wall, eventually the pain goes away and it's finished." And we'll get there. The incentive is to get rid of the pain as quickly as possible . . . We'll get a result 'cause that's what we're here for. We will get a result.'

On 10 October 2001, with the end-date still topping the agenda, the Progress Group gathered again. The project team had been reviewing proposed revisions to the programme, and with some major risks still outstanding it was clear the east end could not be accelerated until more certainty had been achieved. With 'speeding up' not proposed until the later stages of the project, an eye would have to be kept on whether compression of the timescale remained productive. And with the cumulative effects of delay immensely damaging, it was becoming crucial that monitoring was put in place to pin down exactly what happened when information was altered or delayed. 'Can I ask just how suicidal you were when you were doing all this?' the Progress Group's Linda Fabiani joked to Project Manager Martin Mustard. Mustard rubbed his hair bashfully. 'I nearly threw myself out of a window,' he smiled.

What should now have been clear to everyone, however, was that whatever the client aspired to, the revised programme could only be met if crucial issues fell into place as they were required. 'It's based on the fact that we're gonna get – obviously – all the information when we need it,' explained Alan Mack. 'It's based upon the fact that . . . we're going to get road closure on 17 October, that we are able to bring the design to a freeze point, and agree that there are no further changes.'[5] When did the design freeze have to start? Fabiani asked carefully. 'I – er – I don't mean to be flippant,' came the deadpan reply, 'but I would probably say about a year ago.'

With the proposed revisions now on the table, the question remained – could the design team buy into them? The answer, it seemed, was achievement was going to be tough. 'The reaction that we've got immediately,' John Gibbons had told the film team, 'is that they are – well, they're not unrealistic [targets]. They're pretty tough dates in certain places, and the consultants need to look to see whether they've got the resources to deliver, or indeed whether they can get additional resources and how they can manage [them] to deliver on some of these dates.' So what was the result? At the architects', Brian Stewart was cautious, but optimistic. 'The completion of the . . . [debating] chamber structure [is] a tall order,' he told the Progress Group haltingly, 'but [we] collectively feel that we're getting to a point where we can satisfy this programme . . . I suppose in some way we've got to say "We'll deal with this." Obviously there are a number of issues and there are potential impediments which might get in our way.'

So could this at last be a final, achievable programme? For those asking, the answer they got from John Gibbons was extremely frank. 'No,' he stated bluntly, 'I don't think one can really ever say that 'cause you never know what's just around the corner . . . So I mean it would be wonderful to think that nothing else happened . . . and we were able to just calmly sail through till the end of the project, but somehow I think there will be other things that we shall have to deal with.' Brian Stewart, certainly, was concerned at what he was being asked to agree. 'Well, we can't not sign up to it,' he shrugged, resigned and unsmiling at the meeting, 'it's just a fact of life.' While the architects believed more information about the east end was needed if they were to redeploy their troops effectively, for Bovis, it appeared, the amount of information that remained to be put forward would not dramatically alter anyone's view. 'It's becoming really quite difficult to manage this whole thing,' Stewart worried, unhappy. 'But, I mean if we've got to accept something in the abstract . . . then we'll have to accept it, and just duck and dive and resource in any way we can.'

As October 2001 drew to a close, with frustrations apparent on all sides and the programme still causing concern, Holyrood did not look like a project that would meet its political target. A meeting with the SPCB had endorsed the deadline, and with the Progress Group told to provide them in a month with a costed acceleration programme, the pressure – for everyone – remained high. 'The word "exasperation" is exactly right,' David Steel would tell the film team, 'we are exasperated . . . and of course we don't yet know the reasons why there is this slippage, we don't have the costings of what it will do to correct the slippage. We're hoping to get that in detail in a month's time.' For some at the heart of Holyrood, his words were an extraordinary insight into the SPCB's management. And despite the client's own lack of grip on the story, it seemed that Bovis too was not yet off the hook. Concerns were now being raised that the client was getting cornered in 'procurement cul-de-sacs', and that the project team would have to inveigle itself more into the process earlier to manage the problems out. 'I mean, it seems a bit weird to me that Bovis [has] come to us with programmes that the design team seem to be a bit unaware of,' John Gibbons worried to the Progress Group in late October, 'whereas I would have thought . . . speaking to the design team before you put a programme together was quite important.'

To the film team though, who had watched the whole crisis unfolding, the most revealing insight was going to come late in the day. On 24 October, a subdued Alan Mack updated the Progress Group, and one subtle exchange would say more than discussions all month. 'You'll not be surprised to hear that we had an interesting session with the [SPCB] yesterday,' John Home Robertson told him, 'and they are taking exactly the same line as all the members of this group . . . that it's absolutely imperative that this job is completed in time for the opening of the next parliament . . . We are – disappointed is the wrong term to use – we're bloody furious about the fact that . . . it's suddenly emerged that we're this far adrift.' Alan Mack's face was a picture. If it had 'suddenly emerged' to the Progress Group that the programme had had serious problems, and if Mack's expression was anything to go by, it certainly hadn't been for want of him flagging it up elsewhere.

Notes

1. Interview, 2 December 1999.
2. Flour City Architectural Metals (UK) Ltd.
3. David Steel, *Written Answers*, 12 February, 2003, http://www.scottish.parliament.uk
4. This response was qualified by some of the Progress Group's other members.
5. See also, Alan Mack to Sarah Davidson, *'Target Strategic Programme – September 2001 Review – Rev 5A Draft'*, 18 October 2001, http://www.holyroodinquiry.org

18

Sacking Barcelona?

Stuart Greig: *'How do you manage a problem like [this], when you've got a design team that's effectively split?'*
John Home Robertson: *'I have some limited diplomatic skills, but I'm not a psychiatrist.'[1]*

ON A BRIGHT autumn morning in 2001, the documentary team joined John Gibbons in his Holyrood site office. The last few weeks had been extremely stressful, and with programme problems now dominating, Gibbons' role was proving even more draining than usual. For at least one project insider, it was time that John gave himself a break; he was exhausted, overworked and suffering from being the focal point of information and support for all sides. It was said that Gibbons was on the point of quitting Holyrood, and finding it hard to think of a reason to go on. If this was true, it meant four years of near-constant trauma had finally caught up with the man who'd held Holyrood together. But as October slowly unfolded, it became clear that however exhausted Gibbons had now become, there were issues within Holyrood that still required the touch of his expert input.

On 26 September 2001, the Progress Group met at Holyrood. With the project's end-date in jeopardy, a serious obstacle to the programme seemed to have emerged. 'I mean, completion is still the prime sort of objective if you like,' John Gibbons would tell the film crew. 'We're going to have to do whatever is necessary to achieve that. What we heard . . . at the Progress Group meeting . . . I think really from every member of the construction team . . . was criticism of EMBT, and in some way saying that if they had to point to a single issue or problem that was not helping the situation, it was the EMBT involvement – for a variety of different reasons.' Suggestions had been made that Barcelona was revisiting costed and agreed designs – thereby causing delay – and the two halves of the partnership were said to be 'at war' over the appointment of a signage consultant. Bovis was in the throes of preparing a 'very strenuous complaint' about late design interference by one of EMBT's architects, which was risking delay and increase in cost, and sending 'completely the wrong messages to the package contractor that he was going to be messed about forever'.[2] As the Progress Group meeting continued, a startling choice would emerge. It was thought the programme couldn't be achieved if EMBT remained part of the architects, and a change would have to be negotiated. The question was, what?

Within days of the worrying meeting, the documentary team was back at site again. After more than three years of intensive research and filming, it was hard to believe that removing Barcelona was really a feasible option. But it now seemed the possibility was being considered more seriously than before. 'Well, I mean we have to be sort of brutally confrontational in the sense that if this can't be resolved then I think one has to look for a more fundamental way of moving forward,' John Gibbons explained frankly, 'because what we're facing is the need to move forward in the most efficient way possible . . . At the end of the day I don't think any of the individual players in this are as important as what we're trying to achieve in completing the building. So if there have to be sacrifices anywhere . . . [and] we have to adjust how we're gonna get there . . . one would rule nothing out of the situation, no.'

While it was still hoped that things could be managed without resorting to such drastic measures, for Project Director Sarah Davidson, the choice was exactly the same. 'The most important thing now is that we deliver it, and deliver it as well, as cost effectively, and as timeously as possible,' she confided. 'My own personal feeling is that if faced with a choice between that or the negative, probably fairly short-term negative consequences of splitting up the partnership, the client would be inclined to go for the split. But I think that's a decision they'll have to take.' So did Progress Group convenor John Home Robertson believe now was the time to say 'enough'? 'Oh Lord, I wouldn't go that far,' he told the film team bluntly. 'This whole concept started with Enric Miralles . . . It's unthinkable that EMBT should not be involved in the completion . . . No, we need to keep them working with us, but that's the key point; they've got to be working with us, and working with the rest of the team. So if there's a problem, it's got to be addressed. And . . . if we can achieve that in the next few days and weeks, so much the better. If not, we've got a problem.'

By 24 October, however, a problem was exactly what would emerge. The preceding weeks had seen discussion about a possible change from construction management to a form of contract that could – at a cost – see a guaranteed completion date and maximum price for the building. The likely penalty for such a transfer? 'I think we can be certain,' Sarah Davidson had told the Progress Group, 'that if we moved to a management contract Bovis would not accept . . . Barcelona; they would insist that we sacked EMBT/RMJM.' With discussion then ensuing that sacking the architects was not, in fact, what was intended, the group's Linda Fabiani had again been of the opinion that the Progress Group was being manipulated. 'If we're going to sack them, sack them,' she had stormed, indignant. 'If we're at the point of saying, "They're not delivering, they can't do it";[3] sort it. Don't then look for other ways of doing it.' To the film team, she would be equally as candid. 'I'm very annoyed,' she confided after the meeting. 'I feel I've been here before, which is that feeling of a politician being asked to be in control of something, being asked to be aware of all the facts and suddenly realising that I'm being given the information that they think I should have rather than the full picture from which I can make decisions. It seems that every so often I have to have a wee tantrum just to make sure I get the right information – and I suspect I had another one today.'

If early October had provoked a Fabiani tantrum, events by the end of the month would be cause for stronger reactions still. On 10 October, Benedetta Tagliabue had attended a Progress Group meeting, and – in her only contributions during the entire session – had assured those present that she was in total agreement with Brian Stewart, and that the architectural company was working well.[4] For the Progress Group, it was an entirely unexpected declaration of unity. 'I think I would go for the cock-up rather than conspiracy theory on this one,' explained Fabiani when pressed on the issue. 'We had a new secretary doing [the] minutes, and she sent out copies . . . to everyone who had . . . attended the meeting rather than just to members of the Progress Group . . . And we had . . . discussed concern about the relationship between Benedetta and Brian Stewart . . . and indeed ourselves, and we expressed it in quite strong terms. And I think when Benedetta read that she probably got a shock.'

When the film team had raised Tagliabue's comments with Brian Stewart after the meeting, their question had provoked an amused smile. 'Yeah, one word from me and she does what she likes,' he joked. 'It's important to us that we complete the project as a joint venture,' he continued sincerely. 'I mean, that's really vital. How we best get through . . . this next critical phase is a matter that I've discussed with her. And we just need to try and make sure that . . . we as a team don't create any impediments and don't create any frustration in the client. Clearly the programming issue is . . . important for us, for our credibility . . . This joint venture . . . is complicated and needs a lot of very sensitive management. But I don't want us to fail, collectively, frankly. I don't think it would be right, and I don't want to.'[5]

Within a fortnight though, it seemed clear the situation had moved on. At a meeting to discuss the way forward, Tagliabue and Stewart had appeared to be in harmony. But when Sarah Davidson had written to confirm the agreement, a letter had come from Barcelona rejecting almost everything it was thought had been agreed. Worse still, it looked like Tagliabue was now involving her lawyers.[6] Brian Stewart – furious and concerned that he could now not give assurances about hitting the end-date – had threatened resignation. But worse was still to come. When John Gibbons had spoken to Tagliabue about the situation, her reaction had been entirely unexpected. 'I phoned Benedetta to discuss it further and say, "What's going on?"' he told the Progress Group on 24 October. 'I also phoned to tell her that I'd just had Brian on the phone telling me that there was no way forward; this was the end as far as he was concerned, and as far as RMJM were concerned. And she expressed surprise about the meeting. "What meeting?" were her words . . . and I said, "Well, the meeting that we agreed all of this." And she said, "I never agreed anything!" I said, "We all agreed it, we all sat round the table." And she said, "You're a liar."'

With the situation apparently in crisis, the Progress Group's job now was to find the best way forward. 'I mean in practical terms what has happened is I've wasted five days, Brian Stewart's wasted five days, and Sarah the same,' John Gibbons explained to the film team. 'And tomorrow [the Progress Group is] meeting not to . . . discuss the results of five days of concentrated design effort to get us back on to programme, but five days we've wasted dealing with correspondence about an issue which . . . should not be central to the plot here. You know, we should all be about recovering the programme slippage.'[7]

For the group, the issue now raised a daunting problem. Davidson had asked all principals to note perceived impediments to achieving the current end-date. By the morning of the 24th a reply had arrived from Barcelona, and appended to it was an out-of-date programme for the project.[8] 'I think what concerns us in this letter that arrived this morning', Sarah

Davidson worried, '. . . is [Benedetta's] understanding of the EMBT role as being one of reviewing. And it's clear that . . . whatever [RMJM] are in the lead in doing at the moment, she sees the job of her people to come in and review it and see whether or not it really is what they want.' With the situation thought to be threatening delay – and hence cost – things could not be allowed to continue unchecked. A letter would be sent setting out the basis on which the client wanted to continue with the joint partnership, and a meeting arranged in which the details would be discussed.[9] With talk of termination again in the air, the situation was once more critical. 'It's fair to assume that Benedetta's not gonna be happy about this,' John Home Robertson pondered. 'Yes,' replied Sarah Davidson bluntly. 'Eminently fair.'

As the letter to the architects left Holyrood, the situation seemed only to be getting worse. Word from inside the project suggested that more disturbing correspondence was still incoming, and with relations between the directors deteriorating, fears were that termination might be triggered by mistake. Worryingly, no one seemed quite sure what Tagliabue was doing, and when this did become clear, it was apparent that she would not be available for a meeting until 14 November. On 31 October, word came in that she had been in Scotland since the beginning of the week. And with lawyers now talking to lawyers, the situation was certainly not on the mend. Brian Stewart now seemed more serious than ever about going, and there was real concern that any meeting might result in him simply walking out. With people now queuing up to 'accidentally fire' Tagliabue, it was just as well the outside world had its attention focused elsewhere. With First Minister Henry McLeish's 'Officegate' story dominating the headlines, for one project source the political scandal engulfing the Executive had at least one silver lining. It was 'very decent', they joked, of Henry McLeish to cause a diversion.[10]

*

On 13 November 2001, Benedetta Tagliabue arrived for a meeting on Holyrood's future. And as the crisis session unfolded, the documentary crew was left in the corridor pondering events. From the Progress Group's perspective the situation had seemed simple. But as always with the Holyrood building, interpretation of the story depended very much on where you stood at the time. Stewart and Tagliabue were undoubtedly personally hostile – yet despite the pair's differences, the film team's interviews had displayed a considerable amount of professional common ground. And on the issue of the EMBT end causing problems, the two directors had been largely united. Was it fair to claim that Barcelona was slowing things down?, the film team had asked Brian Stewart. 'Not really, no,' had been his reply. For Tagliabue, the Progress Group minutes that she had been sent by accident could only have 'rel[ied] upon a lot of ignorance' to make the suggestions they did. So what would be the impact of a meeting to iron out the partnership?

For Brian Stewart, the worry was an escalation in tensions. 'Well, I think it's like anything of this . . . nature,' he explained, thoughtful. 'They're probably just looking for clarification of leadership . . . and I don't think that's unusual to seek that . . . [But] I think what invariably happens when a client has set down how they would like to see things work that . . . creates – potentially – difficulties between us as joint venture partners . . . And that's unfortunate because then that does tend to drive difficulties between us. I'd be lying to say it's smooth and . . . everything works perfectly. It doesn't. But it works.' Tagliabue's view, days later, would be very similar. 'At the beginning [there were problems],' she confided, 'because we were very naive. We were not able to make . . . on a piece of paper, "We will do this, you will do that." . . . But then we did it, together with Enric. Then when Enric died, this happened again . . . And we were able . . . in the joint venture to go further in the writing of the documents so that it's even more detailed . . . And I think this was able to maintain the relationship correct[ly]. But of course as in every relationship, [it's] a question of power. And in every kind of relationship . . . you have to kind of control it, no? To give roles to everybody in a way that everybody can maintain the equilibrium. Breaking the equilibrium to me, it's the worst thing that can happen.'

With the Progress Group preparing to impose its own 'equilibrium' on the project, however, Brian Stewart instinctively feared that the client reaction was out of proportion. 'I'm just going [to the meeting] to listen,' he told the film team, frustrated. 'I didn't create this, I don't want it . . . It's just a complete distraction. It's a complete waste of time. There are too many other things to do. And that's got to be the most important thing, is to get it done and then reflect on all of this.' For Tagliabue too, it seemed that post-meeting nothing had actually changed. 'To me this was just a phrase which will signify in the future that something has been done,' she explained intently. 'Actually the situation is absolutely the same as before . . . And anyway, I don't know what can be changed to make the situation faster . . . The only solution I see is to put more people [on the project] . . . More people working and more effort. That's it.'

To the Progress Group, however, it was clear that an important project problem had been tackled. 'I think we've reached an agreement,' revealed a relieved John Home Robertson, 'but I'm a wee bit nervous because . . . I've spoken to Lewis Macdonald and others who've been involved in this project for longer than I have, and I gather we've been here before; that there's been a row, it's come to a head, there's been a meeting, everybody's smiled and plugged each other on the back, and said, "OK, we're going to work together in the future." There was a bit of that today, but what we've got is a clear, specific, firm agreement to come up with a written-down management structure which will designate Brian as the anchor-man for the remainder of this construction project . . . and provided we get that, and provided everyone acts on that, I think we're out of the woods.'

Linda Fabiani, a veteran of Holyrood's past, was less hopeful. 'We actually insisted today that fine words were great but we need it in writing,' she explained. 'We need it in black and white and we need to know how they're gonna monitor it to make sure that it's translated into action. So they've got four days to come up with this plan about how we're all gonnae achieve this completion date. Monday night we shall see if this plan arrives . . . I suspect there'll be a phone call on Monday saying that they need another day or another couple of days. I certainly wouldn't be happy with that because it's not that difficult. If they're already doing it like they state, where is the difficulty?'

The answer – at least in part – was that the difficulty remained with a worried Tagliabue in Barcelona. In talks with the Holyrood film team, Miralles' widow was now clearly seriously concerned about the way her company was being treated. She worried that suggestions in Sarah Davidson's letter were not legal, and was obviously still upset about the comments in the minutes she'd received. 'Really I would like someone else to explain to me,' she confided, animated, 'because I really don't understand what is happening. I really do not understand. As I don't understand how this minute could have been written . . . I think there was no problem that . . . could be attributed to our way of working . . . So it's strange to change the internal agreement of this company – because of what? . . . And if they want to give more power, or having Brian as the key person . . . this was already happening.'

More worrying, however, was the lack of trust Tagliabue now had for the building's client. In a hostile public environment, she understood that information given must be diluted. Yet she was now concerned that information given bore very little relation to what she had agreed. 'If they want to . . . give my head to say, "Ah, this is the cause of everything," I don't like that,' she told the film team, 'I don't like that at all. First of all it's not true. I know it's very useful and very easy because it's a head coming from abroad – so it's even easier . . . I know that most of the time . . . this is secret, the other thing is secret, the thing gets reported in this way, the thing gets manipulated in the other; you cannot go and talk directly with this, you cannot talk with the newspapers. I understand that this must be important to maintain the well-being of the client. And I accept it. I absolutely accept it until this darkness is . . . used against me . . . I mean, nobody can understand anything in this job because it's so woooah! The information is so diluted and manipulated. But then [it] is not nice to use this darkness to go against someone.'

Within hours of the critical meeting, it seemed all was not working out as had been hoped. One report claimed that EMBT/RMJM's directors had returned to separate rooms at RMJM's offices, where Brian Stewart had begun drafting the arrangement agreed at the meeting, and Tagliabue had started writing another letter. Two days later, Tagliabue was on the plane back to Barcelona, and Stewart was producing the structure chart on his own. With the client threatening to invoke the 'deadlock' procedure on its architects, it seemed that there was nowhere for Tagliabue to manoeuvre. Yet as ever within Holyrood, solutions were less certain than they seemed. By Monday evening's deadline, two structure charts had been delivered to the client – one from each half of the partnership – and a combative letter had been sent from Barcelona to Brian Stewart.[11] With fears growing that Tagliabue was using the media to fight her corner, it seemed essential that the issue was resolved. Yet another meeting would now be called, for 26 November. The question was, would the Progress Group achieve what it required?

On 26 November 2001, EMBT/RMJM's directors met with a reduced Progress Group. The passing days had seen settlement grow more distant, and there were now concerns that Tagliabue's fears were causing attempts for more control. It was, confided one insider, the project's worst-ever scenario. If the architects said they couldn't agree, the only solution was legal action – and that meant they'd need another architect. In the event, however, such a radical restructure would prove unnecessary. Stewart, Tagliabue and Duncan turned up with a single management chart, and Tagliabue confessed that she hadn't understood. After weeks of angst and manouevering, it was all over in the space of forty minutes.

'If it was continuing like this,' Brian Stewart had confided weeks earlier, 'then it would jeopardise everything . . . these things have to be put to the side. They can't be allowed to interfere with the work. They just can't be allowed to interfere.' With the architects again having reached the required solution, it seemed Holyrood – again – was back on track. But this hard-won calm would prove both brief and quite deceptive. Because yet another row at Holyrood was about to erupt. And this time, it was between the Progress Group and the SPCB.

Notes

1. Interview, 23 October 2001.
2. John Gibbons, Progress Group meeting, 10 October 2001.
3. It should be stressed that this was only one perspective on proceedings.
4. While Tagliabue and Stewart had their problems, at lower levels of the consortium the working relationship was good – particularly with Enric Miralles' right-hand man, Joán Callis.
5. Tagliabue's explanation of the allegation of EMBT changing things would be this: 'I really don't see the fact that EMBT has been changing. You know, the process is a difficult process. The process of arriving to a coherence, when we have so many people acting is very difficult. Especially with a structural engineer, sometimes you can laugh, no? You give them a phase and they arrive to something which is irrecognisable: "But I gave you [these] drawings – what did you give me?" . . . Then you go back to them, and you say, "Please try to make it more similar to what I gave it to you." So this is, consider the amount of change of what we have been doing. And, I think EMBT is really now going in the direction of not making any changing since a long time ago.' Interview, 10 October 2001.
6. Sarah Davidson to Benedetta Tagliabue, Letter, 17 October 2001, http://www.holyroodinquiry.org; Benedetta Tagliabue to Sarah Davidson, Letter, 18 October 2001, ibid.
7. Brian Stewart would be adamant that the problems at director level did not percolate downwards, and a letter from Benedetta Tagliabue of 23 October seems to agree that this was the case. Benedetta Tagliabue to Brian Stewart, Letter, 23 October 2001, ibid.
8. Benedetta Tagliabue to Sarah Davidson, Letter, 23 October 2001, ibid.
9. Sarah Davidson to Brian Stewart and Benedetta Tagliabue, Letter, 26 October 2001, ibid.
10. The 'Officegate' affair erupted when it emerged that Henry McLeish, when a Westminster MP, had sub-let part of his constituency office in Glenrothes, and had not declared the income from the sub-lets when he claimed his office expenses.

11. Benedetta Tagliabue to John Home Robertson, Letter and structure chart, 19 November 2001, http://www.holyroodinquiry.org; Brian Stewart to John Home Robertson, Letter and structure chart, 16 November 2001, ibid; Cristina Busch to Brian Stewart, Letter, 19 November 2001, ibid.

19

Access all Areas

*'Why pick on disabled people? I think it's an odd thing
to have done but that's for them to explain.'*
John Home Robertson, Convenor, Holyrood Progress Group[1]

ON 23 OCTOBER 2001, the film team's Stuart Greig and Susan Bain were in the mood for celebration. After almost two and a half years of exclusion, the SPCB had at last granted access to a meeting. Cameras were allowed, biscuits were provided, and the pair would finally get to see the client group in action. What the film crew could not have anticipated, however, was how the SPCB would interpret 'access'. As the Progress Group filed in part-way through proceedings, the 'open parliament' was about to shut its doors. 'Can I ask if you ladies and gentlemen have got enough now, could you kindly leave us?' David Steel stated smiling. 'Or just watch the others coming in? You've got more than you bargained for really.' But the request had been to film the client bodies together. 'Well, two minutes only, then you really must go,' he declared firmly, 'because it's slowing us down.'

With just minutes left to record, what the film team would see of the meeting would prove more telling than they had anticipated. 'Would it be fair to say that the [SPCB] give off the appearance of not really being fully informed, or not being on top of the job?' Stuart Greig would ask the Progress Group's Linda Fabiani. Fabiani sighed. 'Well, I think they do give that impression,' she replied, thoughtful, 'it's whether or not they deliberately give that impression as a way of alleviating responsibility, or whether it is actually the case.' And did they have confidence in the Progress Group, Greig continued, worried. Fabiani pondered. 'I don't think they have confidence in anybody,' she replied. 'I think they start from the premise that they can't be seen to be blamed; therefore their first thought is, "Whose fault is this?" . . . I'm maybe being bad towards them by saying that, but I quite often feel that that's the case.' Certainly, indications within the meeting did not look hopeful. When John Home Robertson complained about press leaks following the Barcelona trip, an indignant response from Andrew Welsh suggested tensions between the two groups lay very close to the surface. But perhaps more worrying was the apparent lack of working closeness between the two client bodies. Each Progress Group member had been given a name card to place in front of themselves on the table. At this point, they had been working with the SPCB for nearly sixteen months.

With its 'two minutes' up, the film team was hurried from the meeting so fast there was no time to pack up, or even retrieve any microphones. Before long, Linda Fabiani would emerge puzzled. 'Why did we get chucked out?' a furious Stuart Greig asked her. 'I don't know,' she responded, ''cause I thought that's why you were in there.' No explanations for the sudden decision had been forthcoming from the SPCB, but it seemed the film crew's speedy departure had triggered horror. 'They found that you'd left the wee [microphones] taped to the table,' Fabiani giggled, 'and they were in a complete panic that it was being broadcast. And I'm like, "They're no' plugged in yet!" [But they said] "Oooh, they could be remote, they could be remote!" And they're all pulling at the batteries!'

If the meeting had proved unpredictable, however, the run-up to it had been equally bizarre. A month earlier, the team had had a phone call from the Parliament's Press Office. The SPCB was concerned about the date of broadcast. Would the programmes be shown close to the elections, or might they over-shadow the opening of Holyrood itself? Worse, there had been a threat of legal action if the 'Labour administration' was made to look bad. It seemed a clear attempt at editorial control, something the film team were never going to consent to. But if the SPCB's behaviour had proved frustrating and unpredictable, what was about to happen would almost beggar belief. 'If you can say your national parliament's debating chamber is predominantly accessible to disabled people,' explained the Progress Group's John Home Robertson, 'that conveys quite an important message. And . . . I was disappointed and frankly bloody angry when David Steel and the [SPCB] decided to overrule us on that. And I haven't a clue why they've done it; you'd better ask them. I just think it's barmy.'

On 19 December 2001, the Progress Group travelled to Rosyth. A mock-up of the debating chamber had been constructed there, and the client body was going to take a look. From the beginning of the parliament project, the ethos behind Holyrood had been inclusion. And for Margaret Hickish, head of the access consultants advising on the building, it was an exhilarating and challenging aspiration. 'Well, Donald was always someone who was terribly keen that everyone – every single person in Scotland – had access to this new parliament,' she explained to the film team. 'He was always very excited about the whole idea . . . the concept that disabled people would be able to come along – quite freely – without having to make appointments, without having to . . . make any special arrangements . . . and the idea was that they should have access to democracy just the same way as anyone else could.'

It was an aim that had been enthusiastically shared by architect Enric Miralles. From Margaret Hickish's own experience – and what the film team itself had witnessed – the designer had responded boldly to the problems of disabled inclusion. 'He was very, very keen,' Hickish remembered, smiling. 'I remember him getting very, very excited about the idea of the grand lift and the grand stair arriving at the same point, and having the same degree of grandeur if . . . you were arriving for an important occasion. He got very, very excited about people feeling just as important whether they had a disability or not – that they had to have the same sense of awe about the building, and anticipation about the building.'

During the troubled redesign of Holyrood's debating chamber in 1999, disabled access had clearly been at the forefront of the architects' thinking. And for the new client body the SPCB, it soon became apparent that for it too the issue had caused a positive reaction. 'The SPCB gave a very strong steer about disabled seating at the last meeting,' John Gibbons wrote to Miralles on 20 August 1999. 'Disabled access to the front row and a middle row was thought to be desirable. The SPCB thought it unwise to use the last or back row for the disabled.' Four days later, the message would be equally strong. 'Sir David remains particularly interested in the disabled access issue,' Gibbons confirmed in a fax to Barcelona, 'he reiterated the need to allow access to any disabled members to the front and middle seats in the Chamber and was emphatic that the back seats should not be identified as "for the disabled".'[2]

With 100 per cent disabled access making the chamber too straightened out and leading to design problems, a revised layout would be approved, and an agreement made to build a 'mock-up' to test the key issues in practice. It was the sensible option to go for, but, as always, was open to risk. In October 2001, Bovis' Alan Mack would sound a by-now familiar warning. 'There's an argument that it's great to have a mock-up . . .' he told the film team wryly, 'but the argument here is you produce a fancy debating chamber . . . and you're gonna have 129 people tripping through saying, "Oh, I don't like that. Oh, I don't like that," and we're back to square one again . . . Time for debate is over. If you want an end result, and you want it in [the timescale], stop fannying with it.'

For the documentary team, however, it had now become clear that almost any decision on the Holyrood project had the potential to blow into a petty and embarrassing crisis. From November 2001, concerns about the PR situation surrounding the building had been increasing. A press officer was moving on, the media office was seriously understaffed, and political and media opponents remained as hostile to the parliament project as ever. With one press officer now assigned to the

Holyrood building part-time and the media office soon recruiting, a pro-active approach was suggested, and some positive stories arranged. The mock-up – an obvious 'good news' piece – seemed a sensible story to start with, and in mid-January a responsible exclusive was run in the *Herald*.[3] With the mock-up constructed from MDF and costing £24,000, those in charge had been warned it was a tactic that could end in trouble. As events turned out, however, it seemed that even the experience of some on the inside track could not prepare them for what the story was soon to unleash. The *Herald* piece would bring the mock-up to the attention of the SPCB. And its reaction to it would trigger the bitterest fallout between Progress Group and Corporate Body that Holyrood had yet witnessed.

On 16 January 2002, the Progress Group gathered for a meeting. A day earlier – according to the SPCB's minutes – the senior management group had met and 'noted that a mock-up of the Chamber was now available, [although] some concern was expressed that this had not been reported to the SPCB earlier . . .'[4] As the Progress Group meeting unfolded, a familiar problem emerged. The SPCB, it was said, was 'up in arms' that it hadn't known the chamber mock-up was happening, although according to one insider, 'In Corporate Body terms it was 5 on a scale of 1 to 100.' A visit had been arranged for David Steel and his colleagues, and a trip to Rosyth was taking place. 'There have been one or two disturbing signs recently of the [SPCB] wanting to move back into the scene and to reassert direct control,' John Home Robertson had told the film team back in October. 'Now this is a complicated enough job as it is without having different branches of the client saying different things to different people at different times.' The debating chamber, centre of Holyrood's aspirations, would be the scene for another fallout. And this time, some of the parliament's founding principles would be at stake.

With both SPCB and Progress Group now having seen the chamber mock-up, two opposing views of the layout had emerged. 'Essentially, to get the high degree of disabled access that we have – eightly-one positions in the seating arrangements for MSPs are accessible to wheelchair users – we've really had to spread the spacing out,' explained John Gibbons, standing underneath where the Holyrood chamber was being constructed. 'That design was accepted over a year ago – approved over a year ago by the [SPCB] . . . subject to . . . seeing how [the mock-up] worked in practice. When the Progress Group saw the mock-up, I think they were quite happy with sightlines, with views from the Presiding Officer's desk and with the general arrangement. The [SPCB], when they saw it, were not happy. And there was concern . . . amongst the members of the [SPCB] that in catering at the level we have done for disabled access we had moved too far in the direction of spreading the chamber.'

Essentially, the issue was one of priority. Was an 'intimate' chamber for politics more important than access for all? For Margaret Hickish, the SPCB's position would provoke fury. 'Donald Dewar's aims were to have a completely accessible parliament building, and that included the debating chamber,' she would explain to the film team with passion. 'And when we were at the mock-up in Rosyth and Sir David Steel was talking to us, he did say that this was the MSPs' debating chamber – I always thought it was the people's debating chamber – and I was very angry at the prospect of disabled people being excluded under any terms within that.' To John Home Robertson, the entire situation was simply extraordinary. 'At an earlier stage there were some problems with the architects in particular changing the design as it went along and that was giving rise to costs,' he confided, frustrated, 'so we had to read the riot act with everybody saying, "Look, no more changes; this is costing money, it's taking time. We need discipline in this thing." And that was agreed and endorsed by the [SPCB]. So it was all the more frustrating when they of all people should come in and impose changes – particularly . . . a controversial change of this nature.'

For some observing the problem from the inside, the situation now unfolding seemed almost farcical. Having been furious about the Progress Group's failure to consult it on the Barcelona trip, it now seemed the SPCB was reversing the roles. On 5 February, the group had agreed to review the spacing between the seats in the chamber, potentially bringing the back row just 677mm closer to the Presiding Officer. On the 13th, the news that the SPCB had decided to go ahead with the change – without going through the appropriate consultations – was broken to the Holyrood Progress Group. John Home Robertson and Linda Fabiani were incandescent. 'The optimum design of the chamber, which the Progress Group and the [SPCB] came up with in conjunction with the disabled access users' group . . . was that as far as possible we should have the maximum number of wheelchair [options] in the chamber,' Fabiani would explain to the film team frankly. 'Unilaterally, without even, I have to say, a report from the disabled access user's group and the consultant that we employ for that reason, the [SPCB] appears to have made a decision that they are going to change the design of the chamber.'

To David Steel, the decision was justifiable. 'We looked at it and we came back a second time and I think a third time,' he would explain to the film crew at the mock-up, 'and eventually said, "No; we must close up these rows." And we still have 60-odd places which are accessible, which we think is enough. But of course the problem was that people said, "Oh, you're reducing it." No, we're not. We're increasing it from zero at the present time to 60.' It was an argument Linda Fabiani wasn't buying. 'It's an equality issue, and it's a choice issue,' she told the film crew firmly, 'and if we can come up with a design that allows the maximum possible, that's what we should stick with. You do not then reduce it. Unacceptable in every way.'

For Margaret Hickish and John Home Robertson, meeting in the mock-up to discuss the problem, the situation now facing them was quite astonishing. 'I believe that if you watch now the Scottish Parliament, you can see that the ministers sit in the front row, that deputy ministers or junior ministers sit in the second row,' Hickish explained with feeling. 'And my view, as I expressed it very clearly that day, was that that meant that disabled people – unless they were in those positions – would be in the back row. Which is abysmal, it's something that we thought we'd moved on from.' So what had the SPCB gained? Speaking later, John Home Robertson was blunt. 'All that they've gained out of it is . . . they've reduced the gap between the furthest back bench and the Presiding Officer's chair by twenty inches,' he explained candidly, 'and in the process they've sacrificed one whole row of twenty seats which would otherwise have been accessible to disabled people . . . [and brought] the furthest backbench member – for example Margo MacDonald – twenty inches closer to David Steel. Well, I rest my case!'

On 26 February, the Progress Group made a principled stand. Despite an expectation that they'd be told to 'bugger off', John Home Robertson wrote directly to David Steel formally dissenting from the SPCB's decision, and pressing for the group to reconsider. In return, he received not a brush-off, but an apology and a suggestion that the two groups should visit the mock-up together.[5] The visit did not go well. If anything, the two men left more firmly entrenched in their opposing views than ever, although a proposal had been put forward that the problem could perhaps be resolved by decanting the disabled into smaller than average wheelchairs. By 27 March, this suggestion had been discounted. 'I think pretty quickly, on reflection, everybody who'd thought about that recognised that . . . it was just not a good thing to do in principle, because people shouldn't have to move out of their own wheelchair in order to go into the chamber, but it also was hardly going to be . . . a vote-winner from the disabled lobby,' explained Project Director Sarah Davidson.

Again, however, consultation had led to more problems. 'The access consultant had been asked to go away and give some more thought to that,' Davidson continued diplomatically. '[But t]here seemed to have been some misunderstanding at yesterday's [SPCB meeting] about whether or not further advice was awaited. And I suspect that what actually happened is that the [SPCB] thought that the negative comments that we were making about the small wheelchair proposal meant that we didn't think there was any point in waiting for further advice. Anyway the wires were crossed and the [SPCB] went ahead and . . . made a confirmation of their early decision, that they should just go ahead and remove this extra row of seats.'

The impact on internal relations was immediate. 'When John [Home Robertson] telephoned me last night he was seriously considering his position,' Linda Fabiani admitted twenty-four hours after the decision. 'He felt very, very strongly about it and he was on the point of saying, you know, "my position as convenor is untenable if the [SPCB] will just take this unilateral decision after we had agreement to get a report from the disability consultants". And I was really worried about that, because if John . . . felt that he had to resign, I would have to look at my own position as well, especially over this issue.' A pre-Progress Group meeting had been called to address the matter, and, for one member, resignation of the whole political contingent looked like it might be on the cards.

As always, though, the crisis was wrestled back from the brink. Discussions with David Steel concluded that the decision be deferred for a fortnight, at which point another meeting would take place at which the client bodies could discuss the situation. It was a diplomatic solution to the problem. On site, however, with everyone pushing for the May 2003 end-date, frustrations were surfacing again. 'It's a pain, isn't it, obviously?' Alan Mack argued late on in April. 'It puts tremendous pressure on a job that's already under pressure. From a point of view of programme, from a point of view of cost, the world and his wife is constantly looking at us and we want less pressure not more . . . Personal level: this is the continuance of the client from hell. This is the client from hell and with all the ramifications and continuance of party politics and political agendas that each person has, it's no wonder. I mean, I guess people will maybe want to debate issues just to be seen to be debating issues. Meanwhile, work goes on. But what they don't realise is that every time they procrastinate on a decision, it costs time, it costs money.'[6]

For Margaret Hickish, the impact of the SPCB's actions –

which would be pushed through at the April meeting with the Progress Group – was simply 'gut-wrenching'. 'I still feel very, very frustrated,' she would confide nearly two years later. 'I feel that having continued to work on the parliament, and continued to work with an exciting and dedicated design team who are striving all the time . . . to achieve a really high level of accessibility, to have had that thwarted within the debating chamber, where it was so important . . . is just so diabolically difficult to express without using language which I wouldn't want to use. It makes me so angry . . . because I really do believe that it was an error to have changed it for such a small distance over such a large area. It just seems so unbelievably wrong to have disadvantaged people with disabilities in that way. There are 830,000 disabled people in Scotland. I have to say, for a politician to have decided that seems perhaps a little bit of an error in judgement.'

So why on earth had the SPCB done it? For Hickish, the answer would be straightforward. 'I have to say that I actually think that it was something about asserting some authority on a design,' she confided frankly. 'It was about stamping an authority on a design and wasn't necessarily about disabled people or the 20 inches . . . The chamber wasn't quite as I think they had . . . understood it to be, and to an extent they weren't going to be able to go back and change all of it. They wanted to make a change. That was absolutely clear – that the change was about putting a stamp on it and an ownership. And some of the discussions I had with the [SPCB] were just that. It was about there being an ownership with the MSPs, rather than with the Scottish people.'

Notes

1. Interview, 18 June 2002.
2. John Gibbons to Enric Miralles, Fax, 20 August 1999, http://www.holy roodinquiry.org; John Gibbons to Enric Miralles, Fax, 24 August 1999, ibid.
3. Annette McCann, 'A model chamber for Scotland', *Herald*, 15 January 2002.

4. *Minute of Scottish Parliamentary Corporate Body Meeting*, pt 8, 15 January 2002, http://www.scottish.parliament.uk

5. John Home Robertson to David Steel, Memo: Holyrood Debating Chamber Layout, 26 February 2002, http://www.holyroodinquiry.org; David Steel to John Home Robertson, Letter, 28 February 2002, ibid. At this stage, the SPCB's decision remained to be implemented.

6. The SPCB had been advised that its rethink was not likely to have a prohibitive impact on cost or programme (Paul Grice, *Chief Executive's Report*, 5 February 2002, ibid, *Minute of Scottish Parliamentary Corporate Body Meeting*, pt 6, 26 March 2002, ibid; *Minute of Scottish Parliamentary Corporate Body Meeting*, pt 17, 16 April 2002, ibid. The SPCB had also, however, been informed of the dangers inherent in its decision. '[W]e have been firmly and publicly committed to introducing no further client changes to the design at this point,' Chief Executive Paul Grice had warned diplomatically. 'There is always a risk associated with design change and I would have to advise the SPCB to consider any client-initiated change very carefully to be certain that the benefits to be accrued outweighed the potential risks'. Paul Grice, *Chief Executive's Report*, January 2002 (delivered 5 February 2002), ibid. By mid-April, Bovis was reporting that the decision had become time-critical, and if the issue was not resolved immediately, cost and programme would begin to be impacted ('Holyrood Chamber: Seating Layout', *SPCB(2002) Paper 34*, pt 2, 16 April 2002), ibid.

20

An Impossible Building

'When we build the House of Lairds, it'll be a box!'
Progress Group member, 5 December 2001

WITH THE PROBLEMS between Holyrood's architects patched over, the row between Progress Group and SPCB brewing, and April 2003 looking an increasingly unlikely target for completion, Holyrood's ability to see almost any potential problem turn into a real one continued to frustrate everyone concerned. On 18 October, Alan Mack had called for 'sea-change' within the project to create impetus for positive decision-making.[1] By mid-December though, the Progress Group was questioning the quality of its programme information, unhappy with its cost reporting, concerned that the design team wasn't functioning correctly, and disappointed that the question and answer sessions they had been running for their colleagues consisted only of 'the usual suspects plus people we've whipped in'.[2] 'I just think that we're . . . past the stage of doing dramatic things that would . . . show that we are absolutely in control of the cost . . .' worried Progress Group mandarin Robert Gordon. 'I think we just have to assert control wherever we can because . . . the scary thing is that an awful lot of effort has gone in . . . to control this, but . . . we're just working with something that seems uncontrollable sometimes.' The events of late 2001 to summer 2002 were about to prove just how impossible Holyrood had now become.

On 13 November 2001, the first quarterly report on the Holyrood building had been made to the parliament's Finance Committee. At that stage, a 'snapshot' of the costs had put them at £211.2 million, with £21.67 million allowed for out-standing construction and design risk, and £8.1 million for inflation yet to be incurred. The grand total, as it could then be calculated, had been £241 million. 'Can we have it on the record,' asked Labour MSP Richard Simpson, 'that the wild cost estimates of £300m that some architects have published in certain books can now be put to rest as fantasy?'[3] As the history of Holyrood had long demonstrated, it was probably wise not to tempt fate.

Less than a month later, the project was again hitting serious problems. On 5 December, the Progress Group was told that the costs of the foyer frame had shot skywards. The architects were blamed for rejecting potential savings, but a fortnight later it seemed this was not the case. It now appeared that the team had made a series of attempts to help bring the costs down, but the onerous bomb-blast requirements had seen savings wiped out. By 19 December, two potentially cheaper cladding options were off the table. The materials needed more testing – not an option when programme was tight. 'Are we getting a good building? Is it value for money? Has it gone on too long? [Has it not]?' the film team's Stuart Greig would ask cost consultant Ian McAndie. McAndie's assessment would be worrying. 'You had a building at one price; you're getting a building at another price. You have to pay more for a bigger building; we needed a bigger building. You have to pay more for a building with flair; you've got a building with flair – so you'll pay for that. But you'll also pay on top of that because of the complexity of design and the lateness of design – which puts pressure on a programme that people are trying to meet, which may turn out to be impossible to meet. And therefore we might pay twice for something, because we might pay for a compressed programme which is not compressed and becomes extended.' Was that likely? Greig asked him. McAndie hesitated. 'I should think so.'

By 18 December, the project was back before the Finance Committee. At the last meeting, the SPCB had advised it was awaiting a detailed update from the Progress Group, which would 'assess the issues facing the project in its final key stages'.[4] When the update arrived, there was an £18.5 million increase in risk monies – accounting for potential costs related to design programme overruns. To observers, it looked like Holyrood had rocketed by £18 million in only a month – and, more damningly, had broken the *quarter of a billion* pound barrier. But if the mood on the outside was angry, on the inside the problems went on. By 11 December, it was being reported that Parliament Chief Executive Paul Grice had investigated the costs of plastic finishes rather than Caithness stone in the toilets, and there were fears that he might now also try to target the oak floor in the parliament's information centre. Attempts were being made to halt this 'Grice audit' in its tracks before he moved on to other areas, and there were worries that the building's veneers could now end up white plastic.

Yet again, the tension was between art and economy, and it highlighted a problem the project had faced from the start. Building a bespoke building – or even a simple box – for a political client was fraught with uniquely depressing problems. Already, MSPs were getting excited about their offices, and it looked like an 129-person client might soon be on the cards. One MSP, it was said, had asked for a partition wall between her researcher and herself to be removed from her office. The fallout would have impacted on ventilation, acoustics, privacy and potentially risked the client wanting to revisit the flooring. By late February 2002, the architects had agreed that signage would be in Gaelic, English and Braille. Now, it seemed, there were political moves on for Scots to be included too. By March, there were rumours that middle-ranking civil servants were finding out who was designing what – and trying to have a word with them direct. And increasingly, it looked like there wouldn't be uniform client agreement about anything. The Scottish Parliament's political and bureaucratic atmosphere was a virtually impossible environment in which to create even the simplest building. And whatever the Miralles concept was at Holyrood, it was certainly not simple.

As the first half of 2002 unfolded, so too did the difficulties in Holyrood's often pioneering design. The number of contractors capable – or willing – to take on the work was minimal, and it seemed some of them were having to enhance their prices due to the risks of taking on the job. 'Clearly, we seem to have difficulties . . . in getting good tenders,' Brian Stewart would tell the film team. 'Maybe it's the environment – the publicity surrounding it. Maybe it's the complexity of the building. Maybe it's all of these things that make it difficult to get a good tender list. It's just so highly charged.' Months later, the problems would be biting. 'It's not helpful, some of the publicity,' he argued, worried. 'Really not helpful in the process at all . . . [We had] fantastic co-operation [with one of our contractors] . . . and a week or two ago there was some criticism of them . . . in the press. What happens? Immediately they become more formal . . . They're a bit more, "Oh, hold on," you know? "We don't want our business to be [the] focus of attention here, as if we're failing the process" . . . Everyone – politicians included – should be aware of that . . . What they say has quite a significant impact on the way people react and behave, and the willingness of people actually to become engaged in the process.'

Yet if the tenders were proving a problem, there were still other worries as well. After months of protracted negotiation, talks with the favoured specialist glazing contractor had fallen flat. 'Obviously, this is the biggest . . . issue at the moment,' Brian Stewart would confide later. 'It impacts on a whole series of issues . . . I think we'd reached the point where the client was saying, "Well, this is gonna prejudice the project if we . . . can't get something finalised here," so they decided to . . . look at alternative ways of proceeding.'

By the autumn, discussions would be underway with the new contractor to see if the design period could be condensed to meet the programme, but it was clear that this single problem could have massive repercussions. With the need to get areas wind and watertight before finishes could be put in, the change was bound to impact on the sequence of work. 'It

. . . is making us look at the programme very carefully,' Stewart explained. 'What we're saying at the moment [is] we probably can't be absolutely firm on [programme] until we know what [the new contractor] can do in relation to the specialist glazing.' And in terms of cost? 'I mean we could throw figures around but I don't know if that would really be sensible,' he volunteered. 'Clearly, we're concerned that there is further risk . . . and risk is potentially money, and I think it could be significant money because . . . you're compressing all of the services co-ordination, the fit-out, all of the finishes . . . into a much shorter period of time . . . We start to work double shifts . . . you can just see there's a big impact and there's a potentially big cost related to that.'

But while the complexities of the project itself continued to complicate, within the Progress Group, still more worries were brewing. The apparent resolution of EMBT/RMJM's internal problems had bred a hope that everything would return to a more even keel. It didn't. At the end of January, the Progress Group was unhappily focused on the performance it was getting from everyone: architects, Bovis and cost consultants DL&E. 'The more it costs, the more we have to pay EMBT/RMJM, the more we have to pay Bovis, the more we have to pay DL&E,' one Progress Group member protested. 'Less the money we recover from them at the end,' corrected another. 'If they're still alive at that point,' came the reply.

With decisions to be made whether to accelerate or postpone completion, 'forensic programmer', Steve Briggs, had been brought in to interrogate Bovis' programme. And by March it looked like relations between architects and cost consultants were under serious strain. 'Really, basically we were very concerned that . . . design proposals were being put forward without any cost evidence from DL[&]E as to whether they were do-able . . .' John Gibbons explained on 22 March. 'It is a classical argument that develops on every building between architects and quantity surveyors. Quantity surveyor will argue he . . . hasn't got information so he can't cost the design. And the architect is developing the design . . . often not in the form that the quantity surveyor can cost. It's more complex in this case because we have a design . . . which is not in any way standardised or typical . . . [And t]hey can't actually sit down and estimate how much things will cost because the . . . construction marketplace in Edinburgh at the moment is horrific.'

Linda Fabiani would be less forgiving. 'Perhaps you have the contractor saying that they're waiting on design information and that that's delayed, but there's no problem to the strategic programme,' she reflected. 'We then perhaps see the cost consultants, who say that they've not been getting all the information from the architects in time to do an accurate costing. We then speak to the architects, who will say that they supplied all the information necessary and that it's rubbish that a proper cost . . . estimate couldn't be achieved. Very difficult, because these people should all be working together . . . I have concerns that they don't seem to be working as one team, but seem to be playing off against each other at various times, and it is really not good enough . . . It would be far too easy to say somebody's not doing their job because these people are all fighting against each other, but it's really not that simple. And there have been many, many times where we've reached this point; things start to go a bit better for a while and then they fall apart again.'

A 'rather bad-tempered and lively meeting' had been held to assess the current risk situation, 'which . . . more or less continued with a . . . certain amount of aggression that'd developed between DLE and the architects at the Progress Group meeting.'[5] 'I think there were very, very entrenched views being expressed,' John Gibbons remembered. 'There was talk of having gone beyond the pale of joint working . . . and we were struggling to get home the fact that . . . we were not interested in their arguing or their bickering, but we were interested in getting unified advice.' With the pressures only increasing, the strains on everyone within Holyrood were now becoming intolerable.

However, if the client was now concerned with its consultants' performance, it was fair to say that there were questions to be raised about its own. In January, it was said that the

Progress Group was getting angry with one member, who was not attending briefing meetings. In March, a heated row was triggered when some of the Progress Group members launched into an attack against the architects – despite John Gibbons' warning that only one side of a story had been given. 'You ordered a Rolls Royce,' Brian Stewart exploded, furious. 'The tyres are the last things to go on and you're asking to make savings. It's impossible . . . I will not have it recorded that we are profligate.' 'I was quite disappointed at the way the Progress Group dealt with that last meeting,' admitted Linda Fabiani. 'I think up till now we've been fairly good at keeping the peace and keeping people working together. But I think at the last meeting it became a bit antagonistic and actually left Sarah as director with quite a lot of ground to make up. It was a natural thing about your frustrations boiling over when you feel you're not getting the right information . . . I felt that that should be investigated, but certainly not in public. And sadly . . . it just became a bit of a dogfight, if you like, and forced people into corners and the recriminations were flying.'

'Who's in charge of this project?' the film team would ask Alan Mack on the site at the end of April. 'Who's in charge?' he laughed. 'That's a good point. Obviously we have a client body . . . the [SPCB], but to all intents and purposes they are totally remote. Most of the principals who are involved in the day to day of this link in . . . to the Holyrood project team and the Progress Group, but it's quite a protracted process of decision-making . . . it's very vacuous. I think about eighteen months ago, two years ago, I said it was like working for a ghost. Nothing's changed except the ghost is more ethereal, you know, it's just a big body, it's an amorphous mass . . . You can't pin it down to . . . any one person.' But didn't that make the job difficult? Mack was blunt. 'Extremely difficult – because as I say, people will want to keep working the issues, even if there's nothing to work. The agendas just keep moving, and that does cause problems. It delays real decision-making at this level.' He smiled. 'It's an experience. Not one I wanna repeat!'

*

In March 2002, the SPCB made another quarterly report to the Finance Committee. '[The total] is complicated by what we were talking about in relation to risk,' Sarah Davidson explained to the film team, 'but if you add together the construction commitment so far, the original value of the packages that have yet to be tendered, fees and VAT and all those other additional items, inflation and the outstanding risk monies, you come to £266 million, I think. Give or take a few pence.' In the outside world, entrenched opposition continued. 'I note that the estimate for the fit-out . . . has barely moved since the inception of the project,' Margo MacDonald pointed out to the meeting. 'The building has almost doubled in size since then and today we have heard your estimates for inflation in the industry, so I am intrigued by how you have managed to keep [the] estimate for the fit-out at almost the same level.' 'I am grateful for Margo MacDonald's positive comments . . .' started Paul Grice, before he was interrupted. 'I will not be positive,' Margo replied, 'until I hear your answer.' Labour's Tom McCabe's reaction was brief. 'You were positive, Margo,' he stated, 'You just did not mean to be.'[6]

As March 2002 moved forward, the impact of Holyrood's problems were beginning to tell on the programme. As far back as December, one of the project's central players had told the film team that there was 'no hope' of the May 2003 date being hit – and that he was very unhappy at being told not to protest too loudly. A month later, Alan Mack had described the date as 'extremely tough – so what's new?', although exceptional measures of extending working hours or changing working patterns remained 'in our back pocket'. By late March, however, Sarah Davidson was confiding that it wouldn't be unreasonable to suggest that there was 'maybe . . . a 10–20 per cent chance of getting it finished and a . . . 80–90 per cent chance of not getting it finished in time . . .' although 'what I think's important . . . is that until . . . that probability becomes nil you keep on working as hard as you can towards it; or else until the cost attached to achieving it becomes – either politically or from an accountable officer point of view – unacceptable.' 'Saying that you *can* achieve it,' she explained frankly, 'is a very different thing from saying that you will achieve it.'

By late May though, a paper drawn up for the SPCB by Paul Grice would sound an unmistakable warning. The end-date, it was said, remained achievable, as long as everything panned out to plan. Given the history of Holyrood so far, this likelihood was noted to be far from certain. A request had gone out to the cost consultants to assess the impact of finishing in April, as currently aimed for, or five months later in September.[7] And on 18 June 2002, the SPCB and the Progress Group would meet for a Holyrood session. With them, for the first time since filming began, would be the *Gathering Place* film team.

On 18 June 2002, over three years after its first letter to the SPCB, the film crew was granted full access to a joint Progress Group/SPCB meeting. Despite the limited access that the management body had offered over the years, the session would prove a fascinating insight into both the SPCB itself, and its attitude to others within the project. Although understanding within the group was clearly varied, the meeting was a worrying insight into the client's management grip. And on this occasion, the Progress Group was delivering particularly bad news. Pressures on Holyrood had now led the Progress Group to report that full operational completion of the building by May 2003 was 'virtually nil', and with the recent risk appraisal timed in order to meet the schedule of the Finance Committee, this cost assessment itself could only be regarded as an 'interim review'.[8]

With uncertainty continuing over specialist glazing, bomb-blast requirements and the letting of fit-out packages, updated figures would need to be given in the autumn. But as things now stood, the current estimated total – including potential risks – came to £294.5 million – perilously close to the watershed £300 million figure. 'I suspect there'll be some sort of predictable posturing on it,' John Home Robertson had stated ahead of his arrival. 'But frankly . . . they are no more or less angry and frustrated than I am about it, and my colleagues on the Progress Group. They can fulminate about it, and probably go back to their respective parties and say, "We've . . . kicked up a fuss." We've got to get on with the job.'

As the film team would now witness, getting on with the job would prove something of a frustrating challenge. Andrew Welsh, the SPCB's SNP member, clearly had very little faith in the report that was being presented, and aggressively questioned issues requiring the most basic understanding. 'Paragraph 21, this work . . . should have gone out to tender in early October 2001,' he protested, 'where in fact was only tendered last month. So why are we learning about this now? . . .' 'We were warned about this at our last meeting,' David Steel explained, measured. 'We were fully informed of this at our last meeting. [But] we've had more detail now – where it's got to up to the present point.' Appreciation of crucial issues – for some members – appeared less than solid. And even Steel himself, who retained a steady hand through proceedings, would surprise observers with one astonishing statement. Nearly two months earlier, DL&E's Ian McAndie had revealed that the cost consultants hadn't met the SPCB for two years.[9] On 18 June, a comment by Steel would speak volumes. 'Mr Fisher, do you want to say anything on the . . .' he started, before halting, 'Sorry, I beg your pardon. I'm looking at the wrong person.' David Steel didn't seem to know what the cost consultant looked like.

As the session drew to a close, Project Director Sarah Davidson remained confident. 'I actually felt that today's meeting – by and large – worked in the way that these meetings are meant to . . .' she confided to the film crew. 'These are the kind of meetings I'm quite nervous about in advance but actually certainly today's meeting went much better than I'd expected. I'm positively relieved right now.' The resolution, ultimately, had been straightforward. Although they were being told that – technically – construction could be finished by the beginning of May, the likelihood was seen as so small that plans for using the building were being moved back to September. And as for cost: 'In theory we should be making a report to the Finance Committee at the moment telling them what was in the latest risk register,' Davidson explained. 'At the moment what our cost consultants are saying to us is that they can't give us total certainty. Paul Grice, Robert Brown and I would have to go to the Finance Committee next week and in response to almost every single question about the numbers in the risk register say, "We just don't know" ... The best thing at the moment is to give an interim report to the Finance Committee to tell them that we've had information but we don't yet trust it enough to share it with them, and that we'll come back and give them more information in September.'

For Brian Stewart, though, the September date for full usage raised another issue. 'If you say "we'll complete in September", I'm not sure that the picture will be any clearer, or your planning could be any clearer,' he would tell the film team in late autumn. 'What you're relying on is good management on a day-to-day, week-to-week basis here, and an integration of the designers, the construction managers and the contractors. And that's the only way we'll complete this project now anywhere close to the programme.' And as for the cost? A year earlier expert John Spencely had uttered a warning. 'The reality is that they are in the grip of the market ... and if the market says, "This is a project with a bad name, a lot of aggravation, very complicated, we're going to put a price premium on,"' he explained frankly. 'And especially when there are very few people able to do the work, you know. It's inevitable ... I'm not saying it's reasonable, it's inevitable, it's unavoidable, it always was.'

Notes

1. Alan Mack to Sarah Davidson, Letter, 18 October 2001, http://www.holyroodinquiry.org
2. John Home Robertson, Progress Group meeting, 19 December 2001.
3. Richard Simpson, *Finance Committee Official Report*, col. 1513, 13 November 2001, http://www.scottish.parliament.uk
4. *Quarterly Report by the SPCB to the Finance Committee*, November 2001, ibid.
5. Interview, John Gibbons, 22 March 2002.

6. *Finance Committee Official Report*, cols 1926–7, 12 March 2002, http://www.scottish.parliament.uk

7. SPCB (2002) Paper 57, pts 2, 3, 5. 21 May 2002, http://www.holyrood inquiry.org

8. SPCB (2002) Paper 69, pts 7, 13, 18 June, 2002, ibid. By this time, Labour's Des McNulty had been replaced by Duncan McNeil.

9. Interview with Ian McAndie, 30 April 2002.

21

Foot to the pedal

'Number one – keep people optimistic. I mean, it's dead easy to become pessimistic. It's so easy to say, "Oh fuck all of this, it ain't gonna happen," and we just walk away from it . . . It is achievable. But it's achievable within a series of caveats.'
Alan Mack[1]

O N 27 SEPTEMBER 2002, an exhausted Alan Mack met the Holyrood documentary team for a regular update. Usually relaxed, humorous and refreshingly good company, Mack's appearance was a shock. His eyes were sunken, his skin grey and his customary bounce had been replaced by an expression of strained weariness. The previous night, he and some of his managers had held a workshop to discuss the problems still emerging at the east end of the Holyrood site – home to the parliament's all-important debating chamber – ahead of a programme presentation to the Progress Group. 'It was a frank exchange of views across the table to say right, you know, what are the concerns we have?' he explained. On such a complicated project, with little time and multiple competing considerations, it was clear that Holyrood was still facing considerable difficulties. 'You're constantly like Paul Daniels here,' he said bluntly. 'You keep coming up with another rabbit, another rabbit, another rabbit. But eventually you get to a point [where] there are no rabbits left, you know. Then it's, "This is it: I'm sorry."' Alan Mack was now under intolerable pressure. And Holyrood itself was poised for yet another delay.

In the public domain, however, the preceding months had

seen a public relations blitz to promote the new building. A survey report commissioned by the SPCB had predicted that expected visitor numbers for Holyrood could place it among Edinburgh's top three tourist attractions.[2] Two areas of the site had been rated 'excellent' in terms of environmental impact in a Building Research Establishment interim report, and the Press Office had proudly trumpeted that an advert had been placed to find a contractor for the formal opening celebrations.[3] As all involved should probably have anticipated, such a stream of good news stories was bound to end in trouble.

Within a month of the environmental puff piece, the *Sunday Herald* revealed that a World Wildlife Fund draft report had alleged that Holyrood's procurement system for purchasing timber was 'flawed and inadequate'. Coupled with another report from Edinburgh University's Eiko Nemitz, which claimed that work on site had actually increased the city's carbon-dioxide levels, Holyrood's green credentials were now publicly under fire.[4] Plans for the proposed opening ceremony, just three and a half months after they had been announced, were formally stood down. The complex would not be available in the timeframe predicted, and all celebration appointments had been put on hold.[5] And as for Holyrood becoming a tourist attraction, key critic Margo MacDonald, quoted in the *Evening News*, was scathing. 'Are we trying to build a new tourist attraction or a parliament that works and is not a standing affront to those who pay for it every time they pass?' she asked. 'I could not care less how many people visit the parliament. I do care how much it costs and whether it is value for money.'[6] For one tourism academic, the predicted visitor numbers raised quite a different issue. 'The only way they would get these kind of numbers,' he mused, 'would be to offer the chance to pillory a few MSPs. They could put them in stocks outside and let the public chuck wet sponges at them.'[7] Beyond Holyrood, press and public hostility was clearly still rampant. But within the project, quite another set of problems was emerging.

*

David Steel's letter to the Finance Committee in June had stated that there would be no change to the April 2003 target construction completion date, with the SPCB confirming that it 'still expect[ed] to take delivery of the completed, fitted out building in time for 1 May 2003'.[8] It was, it appeared, an attempt to keep everyone's foot to the pedal. Yet despite the stated intention, the report marked an important shift. At a 'risk review' meeting five weeks earlier, the message for the client had been stark. Steve Briggs, the 'forensic programmer' brought in to assess the project thought that chances of achievement were 15 per cent and falling. A working chamber, he believed, could not be achieved by the targeted end-date, and his 'gut feel' was that construction completion would run till the following June. The client, however, still required the building as soon as possible, and judged that relaxing the pressure at this stage would be a mistake.[9] The target remained 1 May. The pressure – for Bovis – was on.

By June, with the SPCB being briefed for its visit to the Finance Committee, more bad news was coming in. Information about testing the building was now much fuller, and it seemed that testing the chamber alone was likely to run right up to the end-date. A fully working parliament by May 2003 now looked almost impossible, and – in line with the risk-review thinking – it was suggested that construction completion and operational completion should now be split. Handover for the building would continue to be 1 May, but an up and running complex could be delivered after the recess.[10] David Steel's letter to the Finance Committee would reflect this, but at the sharp end the job was getting harder.

On 31 May, Alan Mack had written to the project team, explaining that a requested programme review had been concluded, a number of assumptions applied in order to produce it, and that some 'major threat[s]' still lay in Holyrood's path.[11] The programme, he had told the Progress Group on 22 May, was already under pressure, and a great deal of work was needed with the new glazing contractor get matters back on track. The Group was convinced that – already – the end-dates were not do-able, and all involved now faced an unpleasant choice. 'Do we accelerate and throw money at it to try and finish it,' explained John Home Robertson to the film team, 'and run the risk of not doing it very well? Or do we prolong the construction phase, which gives rise to difficulties . . . the new MSPs, when they're elected next year, won't be able to move in straight away.' With too many issues still outstanding for a final programme to be available, it was clear Alan Mack and his team had their work cut out. Within weeks, the job would get even tougher.

By early September 2002, a letter was sent from Bovis to the project team. Too many impediments remained outstanding for the final programme to be concluded, and the feedback from key contractors suggested that the programme itself could not be delivered until 27 September.[12] Four key areas which could impact on the programme were being reported, and it was said that failure to resolve outstanding problems could mean that construction of the chamber would not be completed until June or July the next year.[13] Already, the urgency for completion was becoming clearer. 'If we do not complete by 30 April,' cost consultant Hugh Fisher had told the SPCB in June, 'unfortunately [we are caught between] the archetypal rock and a hard place. It costs about £650,000 a month to keep this site operating without a single bit of work being done . . . So . . . if a decision was taken to extend the working period by three months – you've spent £2 million before you've actually done anything.' With trade contractors able to claim for costs of running longer, the end result could be a very large sum indeed. The response Alan Mack would get from the project team would be unflinching: the potential end-date was unacceptable, and all options must be 'vigorously pursued' to achieve completion in April 2003.[14] The pressure to deliver the impossible had just been increased.

By 27 September, Alan Mack was determined. He and his team had reported to Project Director Sarah Davidson on the current ten-week delay at the east end, and 'Once we'd given her smelling salts and lifted her off the floor,' he joked, 'no . . .

I think she understood the issues, and . . . is gonna have to decide how she is gonna promote that information up the chain.' Ideally, Mack needed 'between probably two to four weeks now to bottom it out properly', but he remained focused on what had to be done. 'If you said to me right now . . . "Is that it dead?" – my answer to that is '"No,"' he told the film team from the top of the Holyrood chamber, 'because the four individual contractors that are currently kinda sitting on the fence, have to be explored, and examined . . . Can we accelerate the design now? Can we accelerate the manufacture? Can we accelerate the construction? I've got three questions, and no answers. So why should I automatically assume that . . . all those answers [are] "No, no, no" . . . It's our job to find the yeses, let the client know what the yeses may or may not cost, and what's the benefit.'

So could the situation be reined back in? 'The difficulty now,' Mack explained frankly, 'is to understand how critical the bits that are gonna get worse are. If we can't do anything about them, can we sterilise those areas? And can we still provide a working environment to the client with perhaps a couple of bits out [of] the equation.' Despite his determined focus, the pressures of Holyrood – nearly four years in – were starting to show. 'I've worked in the industry now for thirty-two years,' he confided to the film team smiling, 'and this is as complex a project as ever I've been involved in. I don't want to be involved in anything this complex anymore, because it's too tough.'

On 1 October, an updated programme revision was delivered to the Progress Group. With key information still outstanding, a definitive programme to completion still could not be issued, and Alan Mack had signalled that it would not be till the end of the month that the likelihood of occupation in September 2003 could be confirmed. Mack was giving – according to one Progress Group member – very clear warnings about programme and cost.[15] A week later, the SPCB reported again to the Finance Committee. No more politically expedient 'fixes' were available: the bullet would have to be bitten. Holyrood's total estimated cost – including risk – was now £294.6 million, an increase of £28.2 million since March. It was almost exactly the figure reported to the SPCB some months earlier. The *Evening News*, *The Scotsman* and *The Guardian* all made the point that arch-critic David Black had long ago predicted that the £300 million figure would be hit. None of them, however, questioned what Black's original £300 million prediction had been composed of.[16] For Margo MacDonald and the Scottish Tories, there was now only one way forward: yet another Holyrood debate.

That Margo was frustrated by how Holyrood had arrived at this point did not seem to be in question. If a £28.2 million increase was the latest cost rise, she told the film crew, that was not likely to be the end of the story. Faces were being saved, the entrance date was being obscured, and 'absolutely futile explanations' had been given to the Finance Committee, 'but then we don't expect anything else now.' 'The Progress Group, I have no doubt, meant well,' Margo argued. 'But why was there a Progress Group appointed in the first place? It was to oversee the project in the interest of the parliament . . . on behalf of the [SPCB] . . . They themselves told us time after time, their job was to bring in the project on time and on budget. Well, it's way over time and it's way over budget: goodbye, Progress Group, thank you very much for trying your best. You were futile.'

On 29 October, the Progress Group met once again. Following the meeting on 1 October, Bovis had been advised that 'the revised completion date continued to be unacceptable to the Client'.[17] Six crucial packages were identified, and 'Trade Contractor Senior Management were requested to provide advice on "best possible programme performance" using whatever means available to better . . . the revised completion date.'[18] By the 29th, the situation had finally crystallised. 'The last time that we all met together,' Sarah Davidson told the Progress Group, 'Alan . . . put on the table . . . a programme which showed what Bovis thought and hoped might be able to be achieved by negotiation with contractors – but they yet had another round to go. That showed a final handover date in terms of construction and construction commissioning . . . of the end of September. He's now putting on the table what they're now calling "Final Programme 6B", which reflects all the discussions he's had with consultants and provides what Bovis refer to as their best programme, which has basically bought a month.'

The new programme, Alan Mack made clear, was an 'up against it' one, and for the dates to be achieved 'everything – *everything* – is gonna have to drop into place'. There was no float, no leeway, and, according to one source, Bovis was advising that the qualifications were so extensive that the programme should not be issued in its entirety. Pressure on stone delivery was now so intense that Portuguese granite was again being suggested as a possible alternative, and there were explicit warnings about what was needed to get the job done. 'What's in front of [our contractors] is a tough enough challenge to install in the knowledge that there will be no changes,' Alan Mack told the Progress Group, 'let alone with a history that things might happen that . . . could just slow us up again' . . . Obviously what we're talking about doing here . . . is to make serious commitments for human resource and plant and equipment, extra supervision . . . You know, the impact of making changes during an accelerated process are even more damaging than just the normal flow, and far more costly.'

For the Progress Group, it would not be welcome news. Despite Bovis' intensive work on the programme, the result as far as it could see was a four-month delay beyond April. 'What I'm very clear about is there's no danger whatsoever of the parliament operating there in September,' worried one attendee, 'and I think October's beginning to look quite iffy.' Worse still was the situation with costs. 'In broad terms,' cost consultant Hugh Fisher explained to them, 'the prolongation cost impact of the slippage on programme 6A is in the region of £5 million. The cost implications of changing from a slipped programme 6A to 6B and pulling back the time is a figure between £6 million and £7 million . . . Those figures are not either/ors . . .

That is £12 million that does not currently exist within the . . . risk monies that have been reported [to] this group before.' But worse was yet to come. 'If you don't commit to Programme 6B,' Fisher continued, 'the likelihood is that you will over-run further on programme 6A. And if you over-run further on programme 6A, you will incur additional cost beyond the £5 million that I've already said . . . Broadly, you will pay to accelerate and you will pay if you don't.' With the plans to move into the building now under pressure, the problem would have to be discussed with the SPCB. And that had never been good news.[19]

On 19 November 2002, the SPCB and Progress Group met, not at their usual rendezvous venue, but at a deliberately neutral site, the Apex International Hotel in Edinburgh's historic Grassmarket. Yet again, the documentary team had requested access, and yet again it had been refused, this time in a personal letter from David Steel.[20] For the people meant to be telling Holyrood's inside story, it seemed another morning was to be spent hanging around outside a closed meeting trying to snatch guarded comments, which the SPCB did its best to avoid divulging. And on 19 November, the pressures on everyone were beginning to take their toll.

Even in the three weeks since October, Holyrood's unfolding situation had got worse. Bad news was hitting the papers, Margo had tabled a motion of no confidence in the Progress Group and Sarah Davidson, and a routine SPCB meeting had only led to more bad blood between the two client bodies. In the absence of David Steel, whose father had died, the SPCB had called a meeting, which seemed to signal that trust had broken down. A planned 'brainstorming' session between the two client bodies had been postponed only for the Progress Group to discover that it had gone ahead without them, and the implication seemed to be that the SPCB had to speak to the consultants directly because the Progress Group could not be trusted.

Again, the SPCB was bypassing the reporting process, and

again the Progress Group was unhappy about it, with convenor John Home Robertson writing another letter to David Steel.[21] With the Progress Group publicly – and unfairly – in the firing line, it had been suggested that the SPCB could be cut adrift by the Progress Group's mass resignation. 'I'm sometimes amazed by what I see as their naivety in dealing with this,' confided Linda Fabiani, 'and they also panic. It seems to be if there's a bad report in the newspapers they instantly go into panic mode and they run about and don't deal with it very well. Yes, they have ultimate responsibility. Yes, they have to report to the parliament. But there's no point in panicking... It leaves you with the feeling that if they're more prepared to believe what it says in a tabloid newspaper than they are to believe either the Project Director or the Progress Group, well I think we've got a fundamental problem.'

Fundamental problem or not, the joint meeting between the SPCB and Progress Group did not go well. Unknown to the Progress Group, David Steel and John Home Robertson had sorted out the two bodies' differences in private the night before, leaving Linda Fabiani feeling unhappy, frustrated and concerned that a serious issue of trust had been massaged over as 'a little aberration', something history suggested it clearly wasn't. An unenforceable cost cap of £310 million had already been raised as an option, and there was now talk of yet another independent review being carried out. For Fabiani, this kind of discussion raised only one question. 'When are they gonnae get to the point that they are gonnae take responsibility for themselves?' she demanded. '[The SPCB] took [Holyrood] over in June '99, Progress Group didn't arrive until, I think it was June 2000 – a year later – and here we are another couple of years down the line ... [and] they're still talking about, "We need somebody independent." Well, wait a minute. There comes to a point where you have to either admit to yourself that you don't understand what the heck's going on and you need somebody else to help you, or you say, "We took responsibility for this, we've got responsibility for it and we have to run with it."'

Holyrood's consultants too were angry. Referred to insultingly during the meeting as 'those people at the end of the table', there was now talk of a letter of complaint being put forward as a result of their treatment by the SPCB. Tired, but back on form, Alan Mack's assessment of the meeting was this: 'It was a bit like being involved in [a Fellini film] as an extra,' he joked. 'It was kinda strange. At any moment you expected a dwarf to come running in with somebody's head on a plate, you know . . . it was kinda surreal. It really [was] surreal. I don't know, I'm getting too cynical.'

As 2002 drew to a close, yet again the project was facing serious problems. But whatever the current issues causing concern, around the corner was another threat that would place the project under a more intense political spotlight than it had ever been before. The year 2003 would see an election and, with politicians keen to use Holyrood as a political weapon since its beginning, there was no indication that the situation would get any better. What nobody yet realised, however, was just how nasty things were about to become.

Notes

1. Interview, 27 September 2002.
2. 'Holyrood predicted to become one of Edinburgh's top attractions', *Parliamentary News Release* no. 060/2002, 22 August 2002, http://www.scottish.parliament.uk
3. 'Holyrood underlines its environmental credentials', *Parliamentary News Release* no. 056/2002, 26 July 2002, ibid; 'Parliament advertises for formal opening event contractor', *Parliamentary News Release* no. 058/2002, 14 August, 2002, ibid.
4. Rob Edwards, 'Holyrood fails to match Jack's green dream', *Sunday Herald*, 11 August 2002; Toby MacDonald, 'New Scottish parliament doubles capital's pollution', *Sunday Herald*, 7 July 2002.
5. 'Plans for joint opening ceremony formally "stood down" by SPCB', *Parliamentary Press Release* no. 088/2002, 27 November 2002, http://www.scottish.parliament.uk
6. Quoted in Ian Swanson, 'No debate: tourists will like Holyrood', *Edinburgh Evening News*, 22 August 2002.
7. Quoted in Ian Swanson, '700,000 tourists? Only with MSPs in stocks', *Edinburgh Evening News*, 27 August 2002.

8. David Steel to Des McNulty, Letter, 20 June 2002, http://www.scottish.parliament.uk; 'SPCB updates Finance Committee on Holyrood latest', *Parliamentary News Release* no. 046/2002, 21 June 2002, ibid.

9. *Notes to Accompany Project Director's Report: HPG Meeting*, 22 May 2002, http://www.holyroodinquiry.org

10. *Holyrood Project: Cost and Programme Risk Review*, SPCB (2002) Paper 69, 18 June 2002, ibid.

11. Alan Mack to Paul Curran, Letter, 'Interim Programme Review 6A,' 31 May 2002, ibid. Evidence to the Fraser Inquiry explained that this programme revision was 'essentially a draft document produced to promote discussion within the full Project Team on the achievability of meeting revised targets and sequence for the production and release of design information release dates'. Alan Mack, 'Precognition', para. 3.3.2.1, 2003, ibid.

12. Eddie McGibbon to Paul Curran, Letter, 3 September 2002, ibid. The Queensberry House and MSP block elements had been issued on 9 and 24 August 2002. 'On-going technical issues and the potential for continuing Design Changes were cited as the main risks to programme. All members of the project team considered that these issues could be "managed out" within the timeframe allocated.' Alan Mack, 'Precognition', para. 3.3.3.1, 2003, ibid.

13. *Minute, Holyrood Progress Group, HPG/02/17/M*, 17th Meeting, 2002, pts 14, 15, 11 September 2002, ibid.

14. Paul Curran to Alan Mack, Letter, 'Scottish Parliament Building, Holyrood: Programme', 18 September 2002, ibid. Project Manager Paul Curran would argue, 'The complex design translated into a construction duration and methodology that . . . did not appear to be reflected in the BLL [Bovis Lendlease] Programme', Paul Curran, 'Precognition', para. 22, 2003, ibid.

15. *Minute, Holyrood Progress Group, HPG/02/18/M*, 18th Meeting, 2002, pts 9, 29, 1 October 2002, ibid.

16. 'Expert puts the final cost of Holyrood at £350m', *Edinburgh Evening News*, 5 October 2002; David Scott, 'Parliament costs set to hit £350m', *The Scotsman*, 5 October 2002; Paul Gallagher, 'Welcome to the Holyrood numbers game', *The Scotsman*, 5 October, 2002; Kirsty Scott, 'Scots' £300m seat of power', *The Guardian*, 5 October 2002.

17. Alan Mack, 'Precognition', para. 3.3.4.2 http://www.holyroodinquiry.org

18. Ibid.

19. '[T]he advice we have had from Bovis has always been given in the context of understanding the pressures on the programme and the logistical difficulty of managing the site. Bovis has always been open with us about the programme and given us a great deal of information to back up what it has said, which the project managers in my team scrutinize and advise us on. I have no reason to believe that the programme

advice is not based on sound information that Bovis receives from individual package contractors.' *Scottish Parliament Finance Committee Official Report, Meeting No. 25, 2002*, col. 2418, 17 December 2002, http://www.scottish.parliament.uk

20. David Steel, Letter to film crew, 15 November 2002.
21. John Home Robertson to David Steel, Letter, 14 November 2002, http://www.holyroodinquiry.org

22

Election

'An election is coming. Universal peace is declared , and the foxes have a
sincere interest in prolonging the lives of the poultry.'
George Eliot, *Felix Holt: The Radical*

ON 28 JANUARY 2003, the Progress Group gathered for a
meeting at RMJM's offices in Bells Brae. The preceding
months had seen a distinct shift in temperature at Holyrood.
On 19 November, following their meeting at the Apex Hotel,
the SPCB had announced publicly that the parliament's move
would now not take place over summer 2003 as planned.[1] With
the end-date standing – at best – at August 2003, a decision on
acceleration pending and a tentative figure of £310.5 million
reported, the pressure was now showing on everyone. Bovis
had stressed the need for 'fundamental . . . changes to the production and management of design information', the architects had issued a strong rebuttal, and for one member of the
Progress Group there were now fears that 'defensive' behaviour
would hinder the job getting done.[2]

For Alan Mack, speaking in September, the pressure was
increasing but everyone was focused. 'It's very much the team
as a whole . . . still working together,' he had explained to the
film crew frankly. 'It would be cynical of me to say . . . I sometimes think the client actually would love to divide us all,
because then they've got someone to start saying, "Well, it's
him, or it's him, or it's him." But that's just, you know that's
just . . . maybe the way people think. But as a team game, it's
still there and it's still holding. Yeah, people are having spats
and fights . . . "he says, she says". But it's still a team of people

who've still got a common aim and are still doing their best. And that will continue.'

By New Year 2003, the end-date had slid to November. Estimated costs stood at £324 million, and – as always – absolute certainty could not be known. Benedetta Tagliabue had provoked worry with an unplanned appearance on *Newsnight*, and an exclusive with her in *The Scotsman* had – in the words of one insider – sent an overworked Brian Stewart 'in[to] orbit'. The furniture procurement had gone off course, John Home Robertson had walked out of an interview with the film team, and a 'good news' story about the parliament's reception desk had provoked an outraged response among opponents. 'The casual observer must have seen the stress and the tensions that exist now as we move towards the completion of the project,' John Gibbons confided in February. 'We're in the final year, the end is in sight, and any delays are crucial and critical. And I think . . . amongst a group of people who've always got on very well on an interpersonal basis . . . the difficulties are beginning to surface more clearly for the first time . . . We've got to get over that. We've got to depersonalise them again. And that, in a sense, is the activity that's taking place at the moment.'[3]

Yet whatever the problems emerging within Holyrood, it was *outside* – in the political arena – that the real harm was starting to unfold. With 2003 being an election year, and with Holyrood a vote-losing albatross, it was certain that some move to limit the damage would have to be made. Already, one Progress Group member, it was said, had gone into 'pre-election stupid mode', and it seemed clear Labour convenor John Home Robertson was under enormous stress. Press opposition continued, and now even pictures of the building emerging were provoking aggression. 'Well, [here are] some rather nice photographs of the MSP building [and] . . . the Enric design lattice work in front of the windows,' explained John Gibbons, holding a copy of the morning's paper, 'a very nice set of photographs, very eye catching. And then the usual diatribe of other aspects of the building, the cost of the building, the cost of the reception desk. So it's a really snide, nasty article behind some very attractive photographs, with very little mention to what I would see as the positive aspects, or not even a rational explanation of why these things are like this.' With Holyrood a perennial bad news story, the Scottish Executive would clearly have to do *something* ahead of the election. The question now occupying everyone was – what?

By late January 2003, as the Progress Group gathered at Bells Brae, one option was looking more likely than any other. As far back as November, it had been clear to the film team that the pressures on Sarah Davidson were increasing. And by January it appeared that political knives were already starting to come out. 'I have heard various scenarios about what could happen to save this project and look good for the electorate in relation to Labour and the Lib Dems,' a disgusted Linda Fabiani would tell them frankly, 'but I've actually had a couple of Lib Dems say to me that they think Sarah Davidson requires to be a sacrificial lamb to save this project. Well, you know, Sarah . . . can look after herself; I'm not gonna . . . make any great defence of Sarah – but she doesn't deserve that.'[4]

What was apparent to the film team was that Holyrood – yet again – was in serious danger. In the New Year, according to one source, the press was being sounded out as to whether Davidson's removal would be treated as a positive or negative story, and, with press problems compounding frustrations caused by the SPCB's apparent confusion, there were fears that the Project Director might walk away. 'I mean we're well aware of what is being said,' John Gibbons explained frankly, 'and . . . you're always . . . more aware in a political environment that solutions to problems will be political solutions to problems, and so you get into issues like finding scapegoats; short-term solutions to problems which are nothing really to *do* with the problem, but as far as the presentation of what you've *done* to the problem, it gives you some short-term solutions.' With the parliament project on the home straight, any change now was bound to have catastrophic consequences, and the risk was that decisions would be made without possession of all the facts.

This being Holyrood – and this being politics – one thing was certain. If there was any course of action guaranteed to cock everything up and cause total and damaging chaos, *that* was the course of action that would go ahead.

In November 2002, with another delay hitting the headlines and speculation of a £400 million total bill, it was Scotland's First Minister, Jack McConnell, who would set the ball rolling. On 19 November, he declared the rising cost of the building 'probably . . . the single biggest disappointment in devolution', arguing that this was 'one of the key factors that has affected people's confidence in the new parliament and in devolution as a whole'.[5] 'My job as First Minister,' he stated, 'is to make sure that other major projects in the public sector never go this way.'[6] For the Progress Group's Linda Fabiani, his stance would provoke anger. 'It's ridiculous,' she fumed in indignation, 'when I heard Jack McConnell sitting on TV – First Minister of this country – talking about our parliament building and saying it's the biggest disappointment since devolution, I was extremely angry. I mean I think the biggest disappointment since devolution is the death of Donald Dewar, you know, let's get things in perspective, and then we lose another First Minister for other reasons. That's a big disappointment in the first parliament. And I'm really, really getting very annoyed at how this is going.'

How this was going, it appeared, was towards the election. Four years earlier, First Minister Donald Dewar had been the building's champion. Just one term in, it seemed his successor was turning his back. 'When Jack took office a policy decision was made to distance from the project,' John Gibbons explained to the film team with great pragmatism. In his view, McConnell had had little to say about the project until he came out with something taking the side of the critics. For Brian Stewart, on the project's frontline, the mood was unsettling. 'I had never [doubted the project] – not for a minute,' he agonised, 'and maybe it was the leadership that it had in the early days, you know . . . the intellect that was applied to that, and the meaning of it and what it was going to be. I'd never doubted the project for a minute. Any element of it. Nothing.' Now, however, all that was starting to change.

As Stewart sat among the debris following the Progress Group meeting, the worries and self-doubt about Holyrood came spilling out. An article published in the *Telegraph* had triggered intense self-examination. And this, coupled with McConnell's stance, had shaken the foundations of what he had believed. 'I just feel that the project has reached a stage now that there are so many doubts being expressed by so many people that it shakes the passion,' he argued, 'you've got to stop, you think, you know, is it right? Are you right?'

With the project now being blamed for the public's view of the parliament, a central question for Stewart was being asked. Where did that opinion leave the architects? 'It's not good enough to say, "Well, you know we're trying to satisfy a brief,"' he argued, '"we're trying to create something which is worthy of the institution." When everyone is back there saying, "But it's not actually what we wanted."' The issue, for him, had raised questions about both politics and Scotland. And with the First Minister apparently standing back, the impact on morale and confidence had been immense. 'Well, it's [like] standing in line and all of a sudden, you haven't heard the command but everybody's taken a step back,' Stewart confided honestly, 'and you're standing out in the front. It's . . . kinda lonely, because all of a sudden the focus can heavily come on to us. "The history of the Scottish Parliament is bad for architects",' he read from the newspaper cutting. '[If] people keep saying it often enough, the general public'll believe it. "Tarred again with the presumption that innovative architecture leads necessarily to massive costs and time overruns". There's no question mark.'[7]

For Linda Fabiani though, an electoral agenda by McConnell was almost certain. 'I have a real concern that all this slagging us off, putting us down, is about Jack riding in on his white charger and saving the day before the election,' she argued. 'I think it's no more than electioneering. The problem

[is] Labour's, they picked the site, they picked the architect, they picked the design. They picked the kind of procurement, prior to the parliament even being set up. So now to try and stand back and shirk all responsibility as First Minister, when you were Finance Minister right at the start as well, I think is just appalling behaviour for anybody in that position.' Already, she had written to David Steel to explain what she believed she saw happening. A copy of the note had gone to John Home Robertson, and another to the parliament's Chief Executive Paul Grice. '[There was] panic stations,' she explained, 'which is fine: gives them something to think about. I'm convinced that's what they're gonnae do,' she continued, 'absolutely convinced.'

On 19 April, just as Fabiani had predicted, an electoral white charger rode into sight. As Holyrood's arch-nemesis Margo MacDonald celebrated her sixtieth birthday, a fax was handed to her from First Minister Jack McConnell. 'Over the last four years, every so often . . . I have spoken to Jack . . . quite often before he was the First Minister – really as just a pal, somebody that I knew,' Margo explained to the film team, '– saying to him, "Look Jack; there's something not right with this project – why are you lot refusing . . . to have any sort of investigation into it?" And usually Jack laughed, tapped his nose and walked on.' On this occasion, however, the First Minister's reaction had been quite different.

Following a rift with the SNP, Margo had chosen to stand as an Independent candidate for election. And on 8 April she had launched Holyrood to the front of the campaign. 'Some time ago when I was re-reading the Auditor General's report I noticed that the name Gardiner and Theobald was mentioned . . .' she recalled frankly, 'and I therefore wrote to the various committees of the parliament and eventually to the Auditor General himself, asking if I could see [Gardiner and Theobald's] report . . .' The answer she had received back had clearly surprised her. 'He virtually said, "Go away; you're not getting to see this because I don't think you need to see it and

I don't always publish reports which don't agree with my final conclusion,"' she remembered, 'Something to that effect.'[8] Yet the relevant parts of the report had found their way into her possession. And 'there were a number of things . . . which made me very, very concerned that the process had been corrupted and that some of the people who had been party to that were still taking the decisions on the contract now'.[9]

For Margo, the response had been to make the leaked report public. 'This document makes devastating reading and justifies my criticism of this project since its inception,' she stated publicly. 'The report reveals the project was fundamentally flawed from the very start and it has grave implications for the whole of our public life and Executive spending.' If she was re-elected, she promised, 'I will campaign tirelessly for this major scandal to be fully investigated by a truly independent figure who will lay the truth bare.'[10] 'The public think that the parliament as an institution has made a mess of building this project and that we couldn't be trusted to build a dog kennel,' she told the film team in her campaign office. 'And that's bad. That's bad for democracy, it's bad for the parliament. So, therefore, when I produced something that said, "It may well be that the public is absolutely right to suggest that things are not well; here's a report which says so from a very reputable company. I think you should investigate it," Jack to his credit came back and said, "Right, we will investigate it."'

To several observers, however, McConnell's decision may not have been as straightforward as Margo suggested. According to one source, the SNP, which had been doing well in the polls, had been furious that Margo had distracted attention from the unpopular war in Iraq. And for one observer, the move was 'widely seen as a calculated boost to the MacDonald campaign and a manoeuvre to discomfit the SNP leadership'.[11] 'Exactly who is Jack McConnell trying to kid here?' asked Scots Tory leader David McLetchie. 'We have been exposing the failures of "Follyrood" for four years – Jack McConnell has been doing it for about four minutes. It seems to be a remarkable coincidence that he has suddenly decided to launch an investigation with less than two weeks to go before a Scottish election, after four years of voting in parliament for the shocking cost increases and signing blank cheques for the project.'[12] For the SNP's John Swinney, there was a further issue. 'Jack McConnell faces some very difficult questions,' he argued. 'As finance minister he was responsible for signing the cheques yet did nothing to stop the spiralling costs. His late conversion to an inquiry does nothing to remove the responsibility he must bear for the lies that were told and the money that has been spent.'[13] Margo, however, had achieved what she had hoped for; what would become the Fraser Inquiry into Holyrood was going ahead. She was, it was reported in the papers, 'absolutely delighted'.[14]

For those inside Holyrood though, the mood would prove considerably less celebratory. With pressure on the project now intense, yet another political spanner had been launched into the process. 'Through all of the media criticism and all of the problems that the project has suffered there's been quite a cohesive objective,' Brian Stewart would explain to the film team in November, 'that everyone's still carried on, believing that there was something good at the end of it, believing that the building would be good, that people would be proud of it, it would raise the standard of the politician... Then you introduce the Inquiry and all of a sudden that isn't that important anymore – it's not the prime focus. Because immediately... everyone needs to go back in and needs to look at their role in it... because they're going to have to be examined on it and they're going to have to be able to explain it... That clearly takes you away from the prime objective. And to do it... when you're just literally five metres from the finishing line, just doesn't make sense.' Yet again, politics was interrupting getting the job done. And if things had been difficult to this stage, they would get worse. Holyrood was about to enter an entirely new phase of problems. And it would expose the project's key players like never before.

Notes

1. 'SPCB sets out latest Holyrood information', *Parliamentary News Release* no. 087/2002, 19 November 2002, http://www.scottish.parlia ment.uk

2. Bovis, *Development Programme Review 6B*, 28 October 2002, http://www.holyroodinquiry.org; Brian Stewart to Sarah Davidson, Letter, 6 November 2002, ibid; *Minutes, Progress Group Meeting, HPG/02/21*, para. 27, 12 November 2002, ibid.

3. Gibbons seemed to be referring specifically to tensions between the architect and construction manager, although it was clear to the film team that as the atmosphere became increasingly political, the tensions within the project were becoming far more wide-ranging.

4. Political unhappiness with Davidson seems to have stemmed from a comment she made in a November 2002 interview with the *Herald*. Asked whether a mistake had been made in starting the parliament project too early, Davidson told journalist Ron McKenna, 'It might have been the most sensible thing they ever did to start when they did. At least then they had a Secretary of State who said, "I want it done this way." The idea of waiting for the parliament to begin and negotiating with 129 MSPs over what kind of building they want is an interesting one. I would be astounded if they had even selected a site by now'. Quoted in Ron McKenna, 'On your heads be it . . .' *Herald*, 16 November 2002.

5. Quoted in Tom Peterkin, 'Holyrood setback forces MSPs to sit in pub', *Daily Telegraph*, 20 November, 2002; Eddie Barnes, 'McConnell's despair at soaring Holyrood costs', *Scottish Daily Mail*, 20 November 2002; Neil Rafferty, 'McConnell admits Holyrood should have been PFI deal', *Business am*, 20 November 2002.

6. Quoted in Neil Rafferty, 'McConnell admits Holyrood should have been PFI deal', *Business am*, 20 November 2002; David Scott, 'Holyrood saga shatters Scots' illusions', *The Scotsman*, 20 November 2002.

7. Quoted in Giles Worsley, 'There shall be a Scottish Parliament. Yes, but when?', *Daily Telegraph*, 25 January 2003.

8. This was Margo's précis to the film team of the Auditor General's reply. Her press release on 8 April quoted the Auditor General as saying that he refused her request as his own report 'represents a balanced and comprehensive assessment of all the evidence available about the state of the project at that time'. Robert Black, quoted in Margo MacDonald press release, 8 April 2003.

9. It should be noted that Margo was not suggesting any individuals were corrupt. She continued, 'Now, that is not to say that they are corrupt people. It means that the processes which are supposed to be upfront and transparent and were supposed to provide a model for the parliament's

business and were supposed to provide the ... pathway for how the parliament would do business in future and so on, that these had been subverted or corrupted.'

10. Quoted in Ian Swanson, 'Report damns Parly project', *Edinburgh Evening News*, 8 April 2003.
11. Robbie Dinwoodie, 'Inquiry promise could backfire', *Herald*, 21 April 2003.
12. Quoted in Matthew Knowles, 'Labour to probe cost of Holyrood', *Sunday Times*, 20 April 2003.
13. Quoted in ibid.
14. Quoted in Douglas Fraser, 'McConnell: I'll probe cause of Holyrood overspend', *Sunday Herald*, 20 April 2003.

23

Taking Control

'Run a moist pen slick through everything and start afresh.'
Charles Dickens, *Martin Chuzzlewit*

O N MAY 7 2003, during an unusually eventful ceremony,
Scotland's second intake of politicians was sworn in. It
was, by any standards, a colourful occasion. A week earlier,
according to the *Mirror*, Jack McConnell's former colleague
Tommy Sheppard had declared that the four main parties had
run a 'boring election' and needed 'a good "kick up the arse"'.[1]
On 1 May, that was exactly what they got. Turnout was low, the
SNP's results were disastrous and a kaleidoscope of party
colours were returned to office. 'We're going to bring colour,
imagination and all sorts of diversity and attitude to the parliament . . .' declared the Scottish Socialist Party's Rosie Kane.
'They're going to be amazed at all the madness and craziness
that's happening in there.'[2]

Given the newsworthy protest delivered by her colleague,
the SSP's Carolyn Leckie provided a rather sweet objection to
swearing allegiance to the Queen. 'Like all my comrades, I
think that the Parliament should be accountable and loyal
only to the people,' she stated. 'I believe in an independent
socialist republic, so I take the oath, which is to a woman who
has inherited privilege, under strong protest. Apart from anything else, I do not even know the woman. I apologise to my
mother, who is actually a great fan of hers, but that is not for
me, thank you.'[3]

Whatever the changing atmosphere within the parliament,
however, at Holyrood the complications remained as difficult

as ever. In January, David Steel had written to the Finance Committee. 'At this stage in a project, programme uncertainty is the biggest threat to costs,' he had explained. 'The significantly increased programme certainty we are now discussing allows the cost consultant to be similarly confident about the accuracy of his current estimates and he has assured us that he is comfortable that this estimate of £324 million represents the funding now required to complete the project.'[4] As always with Holyrood, emerging problems were certain to have an impact. And on 18 June Brian Stewart would raise a concern. 'Now, I don't know how surprised they were about the costs moving on and the programme, you know, still being tight,' he pondered, looking back over the events of the summer. 'I don't know how much they knew. Maybe they knew more than they were giving the impression . . . Think about all of the logic about a new parliament, how does it present itself? If day one it's saying, "Here is another issue, another problem arising through this building," that maybe it was the logical thing . . . to deflect the responsibility to the professional people. We will never know. All I'm concerned about is this business.' By 4 June, Holyrood had been estimated at £375 million. And new Presiding Officer George Reid had been very publicly livid.

On 5 June 2003, the parliament's Press Office had issued a news release. 'I am furious and dismayed at this latest report,' George Reid had stated firmly, 'especially in view of the assurances given to the [SPCB] only four months ago that the estimated completion costs were £338 million. I share the anger and frustration which MSPs and the Scottish people will understandably have at news like this coming out of the blue. All the key members of the design and construction team have been summoned to a meeting with the [SPCB] on Tuesday. I have demanded a full breakdown of the reported costs and the current programme. There are questions which require immediate answer including why our professional advisers failed to spot, and report the increase sooner.'[5] For Brian Stewart, it would signal a change of direction. 'From here on [they're] going to be seen to be much more direct . . . have things under control,' he would tell the Holyrood film team, 'and if that was perceived as being an important element of it, then you can understand why there would be a strategy to look at what are the major elements at the moment that are affecting that. Uncertainty still with cost and programme – how do we present that to the public, that we've taken control of that? So there is a logic. I mean, there is. I don't like it being at RMJM's expense. That's what I don't like.'

The 10 June meeting with the SPCB – and its spectacular fallout in the papers – would mark a watershed. More damagingly, it would signal the start of a spiralling deterioration of relations between Holyrood's consultants and their political client. 'I mean the whole tenor of the newspaper coverage of the project has developed quite dramatically in the last three or four months,' John Gibbons would explain, sitting, sleeves up, in his office near the building, 'and particularly I think since the First Minister described it as a fiasco . . . It's become a bit of a witch hunt and . . . the politicians that made the key initial decisions are being targeted as in some ways being guilty for the actions that followed, and obviously the key advisors at that period of time have been targeted in much the same way.' Holyrood's consultants too were now in the firing line. And as usual, political opinion remained ill-informed. 'People have had enough of their pockets being picked to pay for the new parliament,' SNP leader John Swinney would publicly state of the price rise. 'It is long past time to call a halt to these cost increases. A cap should be introduced and not a penny more spent on this project. Enough is enough.'[6] For Holyrood's consultants, the fallout from the meeting would be horrifying.

On 10 June, Brian Stewart, Alan Mack and Hugh Fisher had arrived to meet the SPCB as requested. 'Well, it was an inquisition, and it was all structured in that way,' Stewart remembered to the film team, 'and the press prior to the session was indicating that . . . politicians were angry, that the latest revelations on cost – and potentially programme – were unexpected, and the members of the team were going to be cross-examined or taken to task on the reasons behind. So it was set up in such a way. It was "summon[ed]" – all these words were used – "demand that they come and talk about this on Tuesday", and so you could sense what was going to happen. And that was predictable, and that's how it happened.'

The meeting itself had been civilised – although it sounded intimidating. 'It was obviously run by the [SPCB] and by George Reid,' Stewart remembered, 'and he was winged by members of the [SPCB]. There [were] members of the Holyrood parliament team, behind, there [were] media and other parliament officials, and behind on the left hand side was the Progress Group. And on the other side from George Reid of this long table, there was a solitary seat – there wasn't quite a solitary seat but effectively there was no one else – and clearly . . . we were invited to take position there.'

For Hugh Fisher, a dry-witted Scot with a strong sense of fair play, arrival at the meeting had been unpleasant. 'Well, it was an unpleasant experience because even walking through the assembled press on the way into the building was an unpleasant experience,' he recalled pragmatically, 'and having aggressive questions shouted at you on the way in. But going into the meeting itself . . . I didn't mind, really, being in individually. That didn't matter because you were only responding to questions and telling the truth . . . One of the difficulties is that the [SPCB] is a Hydra-headed beast, and everybody has slightly different angles and slants on things, and the questioning reflected that. So it wasn't pleasant, but I recognise it had to be done. It's a political project.' However, what was about to happen would alter his view dramatically.

As the 'inquisition' drew to a close, the three men were asked to stay behind till the meeting was finished. 'The implication was that we might be asked to go back in,' Brian Stewart remembered. 'That wasn't what evolved . . . Paul Grice and others from the parliament team came in and told us that George Reid would be making some statement to the press. It was kind of obvious 'cos there was a huge scrum as we arrived and clearly there was a huge scrum actually inside the building.' Outside, the new Presiding Officer was speaking to the media. 'I put to all the participants that they should consider in the public interest, because it is a matter for the public purse, a reduction in the money they receive', he stated. 'I'm happy to say we have today secured the agreement of all the consultants to cap their fees to the end of the project. In the public interest that cap will include a reduction in fees in respect of the latest projected increase in costs.'[7] The reaction to his words would be a feeding frenzy.

On 10 June, Alan Mack's wife Janice had gone to visit her mother. 'And as I arrived at her flat, the news suddenly came on and there was a shot of Alan walking in – and then a shot of you all walking out again,' she remembered. 'And I realised then, 'cos Alan had sort of prepared me for the fact that . . . there was going to be a lot of hassle at this meeting.' The next morning, however, had delivered an enormous shock. 'I walked into the newsagent – and all I saw was Alan's face on the front of the *Daily Record* with "Fat Cats",' she recalled, 'you know, the implication being that the massive escalation in costs were somehow down to the ridiculous profits Bovis were making! . . . And . . . of course a couple of days later it was . . . the photograph of the house – which I actually saw the photographer taking . . . I ran towards him and he immediately jumped back in his car again . . . I said, 'What do you think you're playing at taking a photograph of my house?' He says, 'I'm a freelance photographer and I was sent by the *Daily Record*.' [And] I said, 'You don't want to know what I think of the *Daily Record*.'

In the *Mirror*, the 'fat cat contractors' were the 'Three Wise Men.'[8] In the *Scottish Daily Mail*, 'Holyrood's gravy train finally hits the buffers.'[9] Hugh Fisher had appeared in the tabloids with the Millennium Dome on his head, and all three men had had their homes photographed and published under the headline, 'Lifestyles of the rich and infamous'.[10] For Alan Mack, the triggered headlines had been 'absolute shite'.[11] 'But it's consistent with the shite that's been put out in the papers to date', he argued, angry. 'I mean, the next one the next day was "Queensberry House Sinking". And then you get this, you know, let's dive into the site business. I mean, what can I say? I've had reporters driving round my house, in my garden taking photographs . . . What does my wife know about all this nonsense? . . . I bought the house in 1985 for Christ's sake.'

In the fallout from Reid's announcement, both Mack and Brian Stewart had had their salaries published in the tabloids. The method of finding the figures had provoked disgust. 'What they did was they actually phoned up, and . . . in Brian's case, pretended to be from the Inland Revenue,' Mack told the film team, appalled. 'Now I thought there was a law against impersonating . . . people like that . . . He said he was from the Inland Revenue, and . . . Brian was due a major tax rebate and we just want to check what his . . . flat rate is. And they probably did the same for me . . . They got it to the button. Got it to the button.'

His colleague, Ed Parry, had witnessed the impact. 'Hugh Fisher and Alan were here that day for a meeting . . .' he remembered. 'I [saw] the fear in Alan and Hugh, the way they were getting treated by the press. And whilst Hugh and Alan were sitting with us in Alan's office, his phone rang, and it was his wife upset on the phone that there was a photographer in his garden . . . Alan was trembling when he came off that phone, you know, with anger . . . They just didn't know where it was going to lead.' A week later, Mack was still voicing horror. 'What am I, a paedophile or something, you know?' he asked the film team, angry. 'Shit I'll be going on a register soon. I build buildings: keep away from that man.'

To Brian Stewart though, the stories had been unavoidable. 'In my view this is inevitable that it would get to this point,' he argued frankly, 'because we've gone round everybody else. Today it's Donald Dewar's fault. You know, there will always be this search for blame. It's a very sad culture . . . Instead of people thinking constructively about what is being done – albeit, that, yes, it's an expensive building and, yes, it's taking longer. But it isn't about this month and next month and next year. It's what will it be and where will it be in fifty years' time?'

More used to press criticism than his colleagues, Stewart's response to the tabloid stories had been to laugh. Crammed into a gravy boat on the cover of the *Record* with Mack and Fisher and labelled a 'Bisto Boy', he had gone to the shops and bought a packet of gravy. 'Well, we don't ever use Bisto. Actually, we make our own . . .' he laughed. 'I tried to get a [gravy] boat as well, but it was too late, the shops were shut!'

For Hugh Fisher, however, a good-humoured and hard-working Scot, the impact of the stories had been different. 'I was horrified to see it,' explained colleague Ian McAndie. 'So you know, within minutes I was able to reach Hugh on the telephone, and he was in a terrible state. When you think that . . . you work on a project from something like October 1997 to now, delivering cost information on a fortnightly basis, in a thorough way, in a way that's been perfected over decades with the LICS, by me who's been with the company for thirty-two years. We know how to do this process – we ask people what they want, we translate it, we pop it down. So if somebody chooses to deliver a message in a certain way, which finds its way into the media . . . you know . . . I mean [the word] hurtful's not really strong enough. I mean it's absolutely infuriating to see what was delivered in the press there . . .'

Fisher himself was still disgusted by the stories two weeks on. 'I don't really want to touch them,' he asserted, picking up the papers the film team had brought with them. 'I think it's disgraceful. I think it's an absolutely appalling way to treat us as individuals, although we can live with that. But it's a disgraceful reflection on the people who have been working very hard on this project for the last four or five years. It's potentially damaging to their jobs. And if that's journalism then, you know, I'm glad I'm a cost consultant.'

For new Presiding Officer George Reid, speaking to the film team in the corridor of the Holyrood MSP block, the news stories provoked had been 'thoroughly unpleasant. But that was nothing to do with me. If you want an answer to that question you must go and ask the red tops.' 'Remember it was the start of a new parliament,' he argued. 'Could you really in a new parliament say, "Och, it's away again for another £37 million [and] nothing's happening?" I think that that would have put a terrible damper over the first months of a new parliament. That's why it had to be done.' So did he believe that the consultants had been profligate, the film team asked him. 'No,' Reid replied. 'I think all the consultants are people of very high skill working on a very complex building. This was a matter of issue management which *had* to be addressed. And I cast no aspersions whatsoever, quite the reverse, on the professional skills of the architects and the builders.'

If that was the case, however, 'Bisto Boy' Brian Stewart would raise a very important question. 'Well, you know, where are we?' he asked the film team on 18 June. 'A week further on? There's been no public statements made in relation to the way the press have dealt with the respective businesses and the individuals who have been involved. So there's nothing public been said. I have written to George Reid, and, I believe, others have – the other two who were subjected to the same sort of issues.' Although disquiet had been conveyed behind closed doors by the client about the personal focus of the stories, Stewart was convinced that nothing would be done publicly to protect them. 'I don't think that'll happen,' he pondered. 'It won't happen, because . . . when the fee issue is being presented as one which is being addressed now by this new regime as getting to grips with the problem . . . they're not then going to say, "Well, hold on a minute, these chaps are squeaky clean, they're white knights," you know, "they're in there doing . . . everything that they can. There are people working very long hours, working under extremely difficult circumstances, to deliver something worthwhile" . . . They're not going to say that. Why would they say that? 'Cos they'll immediately switch the pressure back on to themselves.'

Certainly, by 21 August, when George Reid made an appearance on *Newsnight Scotland*, it didn't look like he was rushing to safeguard reputations. 'I didn't say I was going to sort things out,' he explained, 'I said I'd be transparent, and I said I would get a grip hopefully on the problem that's dogged this right from the start and that is that every time the project took longer, every time the costs went up, people got richer. One of the things we have got a grip on in eight weeks is to end that; the fees are now capped, we know where the costs of the consultants will be through to the end – and that's why we've got a £5 million reduction this week in terms of the overall budget.'[12] 'The implication is that there was gonna be some massive windfall that we were going to give up,' Brian Stewart had told the film team in June, 'which is really non-sense, and anybody who knows anything about what we do knows it doesn't work like that . . . You know, if you have thirty, forty, fifty staff working on it, they all need to be paid. The professional indemnity insurance to cover the project has to be paid. The accommodation that they're in has to be paid. There's a massive cost related to running a business . . .This is something which has been ongoing with us and I'm sure with all the others – looking at what finances are needed to complete the project in a relatively open-book way with the client . . . It was conveyed [as a windfall], I think there was a clear view before that that was how to present it, and it was a way of shifting responsibility.'

So what, exactly, was the gulf between what the outside world believed had happened at the meeting, and the reality of what had been achieved? As they sat with Brian Stewart in his office, the film team would hear a rather different version of events than the stories making all the headlines. Already, Hugh Fisher had written to Reid, declaring 'This business will not be made a scapegoat to political expediency,' while Bovis Managing Director Harry Thorburn had done the same, '[taking] exception to the erroneous and misleading content of your letter and press release'.[13] Brian Stewart, too, was unhappy with what had been announced. '[Paul Grice] read [the relevant portion] and asked us if we would agree to that statement being made,' he explained. 'My immediate reaction was, "No, I'm not going to agree to that statement being made," simply because to give the impression that we were reviewing fees only after today's meeting being "hauled in to account" and all of that was quite wrong. Because I've been having discussions on fees for quite some time – for over a year.'

Fisher's explanation, too, would paint a differing picture. 'At the end of the meeting, George Reid said, "In the interests of the public purse," or whatever . . . "would we be willing to discuss a cap on our fees?"' he confided. 'And my response to that was that I was perfectly willing to discuss converting our fee to a lump sum – which is the same thing – maybe a less emotive way of putting it, but it's the same thing. The fact is that our fee and the calculation of our fee is based on a series of work stages . . . so the basis of the calculation of our fee had already been . . . "capped" in calculation terms on four of the five headings under which our fee is made up, so what we're talking about is agreeing a lump-sum conversion of the final bit of that fee. And I'm perfectly happy to do that and I told them I was. It didn't really amount to a question of conceding that there would be a reduction in fee or something like that. We were looking at a means of drawing the fees to a conclusion, which I suppose has the benefit of giving everybody certainty as to where they're going on that part of the budget.'

Yet if relations with Stewart and Fisher had been badly damaged by the episode, in the case of their construction manager, Alan Mack, the client had shot itself firmly in the foot. 'It's very, very critical when we've reached the stage when we're now reporting back so closely on each step,' John Gibbons had explained to the film team back in February. 'And Alan particularly . . . has been put very much in the driving seat, and more of the responsibility is on Alan and Bovis . . .' Given what George Reid's statement had triggered, it seemed the client had just landed itself with an enormous problem. 'Next move is to get all my gear together out of the office, get in the car and go off on holiday,' Alan Mack confided in the film team, utterly demoralised, 'and while I'm away on holiday, no doubt my good lady and I will have a chat about whether I'll bloody well come back or not. Simple as that.'

Notes

1. Quoted in Mark Smith, 'Jack's no leader, he's just not interested or inspirational; exclusive – former pal lets rip', *Scottish Daily Mirror*, 1 May 2003. Sheppard had been McConnell's deputy as General Secretary of the Scottish Labour Party from 1994 to 1997.
2. Quoted in Andrew Denholm, 'SSP pledge to shake up parliament', *The Scotsman*, 3 May 2003.
3. *Scottish Parliament Official Report*, col. 5, 7 May 2003, http://www.scottish.parliament.uk
4. David Steel to Tom McCabe, Letter, 16 January 2003, ibid.
5. *Parliamentary News Release* no. 040/2003, 'Further Holyrood Costs: Reid "Furious and Dismayed"', 5 June 2003, ibid.
6. Quoted in Hamish Macdonell, 'Price of Holyrood Parliament rises once more as bill soars to £375m', *The Scotsman*, 6 June 2003.
7. Angus MacLeod, 'Holyrood consultants agree cap on rising fees,' *The Times*, 11 June 2003. The transcript of the meeting records the following exchanges between George Reid and the consultants: '[GR:] I am anxious to resolve this in a civilised fashion and complete a building to be proud of . . . In the public interest, will BLL [Bovis Leaselend] waive or set aside at least part of charges relating to current increase? [AM:] We would be happy to convert to a fixed contract. We are prepared to convert the current percentage to a lump sum at this stage . . . [GR:] Would you be prepared to waive scale fees in relation to latest incur? [BS:] I can only speak for RMJM, although I would hope to carry EMBT on this issue. I have already indicated to HPT that I agree to cap fees; I've made that commitment. I don't want to ring-fence the £18.75 million as that suggests culpability, but I'm certainly willing to discuss the terms of the cap . . . [GR:] Would you waive scale fees relating to latest cost increase? [HF:] I am perfectly willing to have discussions about a lump sum. Can't be more definitive than that at this stage.' Transcript, SPCB/HPG meeting, 10 June 2003, http://www.holyrood inquiry.org
8. Mark Smith, 'Three Wise Men', *Scottish Daily Mirror*, 11 June 2003.
9. Eddie Barnes, 'Holyrood's gravy train finally hits the buffers', *Scottish Daily Mail*, 11 June 2003.
10. 'Lifestyles of the rich and infamous', *Daily Record*, 16 June 2003.
11. Alan Mack stressed during this interview that the opinions expressed were personal views, and not those of Bovis Lendlease.
12. *Newsnight Scotland*, 21 August 2003, BBC Scotland.
13. Hugh Fisher to George Reid, Letter, 16 June 2003, http://www.holyrood inquiry.org; Harry Thorburn to George Reid, Letter, 13 June 2003, ibid.

24

The Fraser Inquiry[1]

'I am confident that I have sufficient powers to secure the co-operation of all those I invite to give evidence to the Inquiry and I will not hesitate to "name and shame" anyone who does not take up my invitation. To fail to co-operate with the Inquiry is to thwart the will of the Scottish Parliament and I do not believe anyone would want to do that lightly.'
Lord Fraser of Carmyllie[2]

ON 8 JULY 2003, at the Macdonald Hotel in Edinburgh, details of the Fraser Inquiry into the Holyrood 'debacle' were announced. 'The people of Scotland expect the truth, they deserve the truth and I am determined that they will get the truth,'[3] Lord Fraser of Carmyllie told the press. For Stuart Greig and I, sitting amongst the gathered throng of journalists, the situation was raising some serious questions. Given what we'd seen of the Inquiry's origins, could Lord Fraser really manage to deliver what he was promising? And after years of misinformation and political spin surrounding Holyrood, did he have any idea of the scale of the task he'd taken on?

A short time earlier, we'd arrived to meet John Gibbons in his office. By mid-May, there had still been no word on the intended Inquiry's format, and descriptions seemed to range from 'review' to 'report' to 'investigation'. Privately, Jack McConnell was said to have given assurances that nothing would be done until Holyrood was completed, and one source had suggested that a debate was one idea to get the First Minister 'off the hook'. By 4 June, the Inquiry's remit remained uncertain, and there had been no decision on who was going to preside. And on the 26th, we asked John Gibbons a very direct question. 'Do you think [this] Inquiry is just totally pointless?' Stuart queried. John thought. 'It depends how it . . . actually work[s] . . .' he responded. 'I think one could make sure it isn't pointless by the right approach to it. If the approach is to learn lessons from things that went wrong, and that's what the Inquiry does, then it would be very important to learn these lessons . . . It's entirely pointless to me if there is a view either to find the guilty people or name and shame as though something dreadful has gone wrong. I mean, I've been very close to all aspects of this project. There's nothing of that nature in the project that I'm aware of at all. It's all been honest endeavour.'

From where I was standing, the Inquiry was raising clear worries. On 12 June, McConnell had written to the Presiding Officer. Details of the investigation remained unfinalised, but Lord Fraser of Carmyllie had been invited to head the process up. According to one insider, the ideas had been put together 'in a hell of a rush', and the manner of announcement had itself raised further questions. Just seven days earlier, George Reid had been furious at the latest cost estimate, and within days the fee cap had spawned pages of tabloid abuse. The First Minister's letter had been copied to Margo MacDonald prompting an understandable question from inside the Progress Group. If Margo had been given a copy of the letter asked one member, why had the courtesy not been extended to them?

For an informed observer, the entire process was prompting searching questions. Holyrood raised important issues for investigation. But could an Inquiry called during an election really point the finger at the parliament itself? By early July, the signs did not look healthy. Investigating Holyrood itself was a daunting prospect – and after six years of public misinformation the dangers of mixing myth with fact were simply huge. Early indications already raised several concerns. Despite stating that he came to the Inquiry with an open mind, Lord Fraser had included a 'whistleblower's' button on his website. It was intended to 'encourage those who may fear pressures from within their own organisation or company',[4] but what it suggested to some was a potential presumption of guilt.

By 24 July, more than 20,000 people were reported to have got in touch on it, although some claims, said an Inquiry spokesman were 'a bit vague and it was hoped people would return and be more specific'.[5] The Inquiry appeared to have tapped a vein of public disillusion, and its website itself recycled one of Holyrood's most damaging public myths. Lord Fraser had been appointed to conduct an Inquiry into Holyrood, the homepage declared, 'which is now two and a half years behind schedule with costs running approximately ten times more than the original estimate of £40m'.[6] Yet despite these problems, it seemed Lord Fraser was proceeding with good intentions. 'Since the First Minister announced his invitation to me,' he declared at his preliminary hearing, 'I cannot walk through Edinburgh, sit on a train or go to any event anywhere in Scotland, public or private, without being asked about the inquiry or being told in no uncertain terms how I should conduct it.'[7] Twelve days later, within Holyrood, the following exchange: 'Who's advising Lord Fraser on this inquiry?' asked one insider. The response to his question? 'People on trains.'

From my own perspective, the Inquiry had become a serious worry. For years Stuart and I had been the only observers 'inside' Holyrood, and hundreds of hours of research and filming had been amassed. Constant discussion had led to a comprehensive grasp of Holyrood's key issues, and we had filmed countless interviews and meetings, and spent years beside the project's central players. With Lord Fraser determined to 'leave no stone unturned',[8] we were now in a difficult position. The BBC did not allow voluntary access to untransmitted footage, when doing so would prejudice the ability to gather material in the future. And to compound matters further, our research had been conducted on a confidential basis. All material was embargoed until the project was completed, and promises to contributors had been given to that effect. Yet if Lord Fraser was determined to reach the truth behind Holyrood, one thing seemed absolutely certain. The Inquiry team would definitely get in touch with us, to discuss how Holyrood had reached its current point. Wouldn't it?

By late September, Lord Fraser's Inquiry was beginning to gain momentum. A letter from the team had been sent to the Holyrood consultants, and for Brian Stewart the potential impact was huge. 'I came in here on a Sunday and [there] was the first letter from the Inquiry and I just . . . looked at it and I thought . . . how the hell are we going to handle this?' he told us in his office. 'It was setting down broadly what the Inquiry was going to do . . . it was asking for every bit of information on the project . . . And I didn't do anything on the Sunday other than look at this and . . . start to try and understand the scale of it . . . The scale of it is massive; it's two container loads of paper . . . I may as well have not bothered: the day was written off and it's not got much better.'

The request had been for information by 15 October. It was, according to one insider, a 'ludicrous' timeframe – and 'if Lord Fraser requires everything he indicates, I would suggest that he needs to change the year'. Yet as things evolved, further concerns were emerging. 'In a way, if it's a proper inquiry they should be looking at absolutely every piece of paper,' Brian continued, 'But instead it's now developing into what, in our opinion, is important. I'm not sure that's the right way to deal with it.' 'Pick and mix', Stuart volunteered. 'Pick and mix . . . is a term that I've used,' Brian agreed, 'because, you know . . . we're making the judgement on what's relevant. And I'm not sure that's correct . . .'9

Within the project itself the Inquiry's effect appeared enormous. Its announcement seemed to have sparked panic in one member of the Progress Group, and by 10 July it was said that neither the Executive nor the parliament had agreed to pay for it. With every document sent to the Inquiry needing to be duplicated, material costs of providing Lord Fraser with evidence could run into thousands of pounds for Holyrood's consultants. Had the Inquiry offered to pay?, we asked Brian Stewart. 'No, no they haven't,' Brian confided. 'I think that the Inquiry may have some funds to cover some expenses. I'm not clear . . . how their budget's formed . . . It's a big factor, so it's there, quite near the top of the agenda every time there is a discussion about this.' It was a point Brian had also made to the client. 'It's a bit like a ping-pong,' he argued, 'don't come to us, go to them; no, no, no that's them, they're responsible for that. But it's a factor that is quite important to . . . a business of our nature that if this starts to run into six figures, which it could well do, that could have quite a serious effect on the business. It certainly can't be ignored, it certainly can't just be . . . funded and certainly not on an open-ended basis.'[10]

By 24 September the consultants had a worrying message for the Progress Group. A possible inquiry had been on Alan Mack's 41-page list of programme caveats. Now, they were warned, it was the number one risk. In the public domain, it had been made clear that the Inquiry mustn't delay the building. But, according to one source, the disruption over the previous fortnight had been considerable. Meetings had been cancelled because the consultants were attending Inquiry sessions, and a discussion on quality matters had ended up being almost all about Fraser. 'Well, it's obviously quite distracting,' argued architect John Kinsley in November, 'just from the point of view of the physical hours involved in putting [our timeline] together. It's taken me personally away from site when obviously there are burning issues that need to be resolved down there. I think the Inquiry as a whole is obviously impacting. We can see it impacting, not just from the amount of time that we're having to spend on it but clearly there are issues that come up in meetings on site that need client input. And there are people from the client side that are not available to make those decisions at the moment because they're also being prepared for the Inquiry as well.'

But concerns raised provoked a contradictory reaction from the client. 'Well, at a meeting last Friday with the client, I said I felt the impact was massive,' Brian told us in November, 'and I was stopped there. "What do you mean massive? . . . You've got contract obligations in relation to the delivery of the building." It is massive. Clearly it is. It's not just the times spent sitting reading and going through the history. It's the nervous energy you're using when you're not even working . . . it's the constant going through your mind, getting the events in the right place and getting the facts assembled. It's just on your mind all the time. So clearly it has an impact on us. I think it's massive.'

And what had been the client's response to his worries? 'That it shouldn't have a massive impact,' he replied. 'That's the parliament point of view at the moment: that the Inquiry should not have a massive impact on our activities in relation to the delivery of the building . . . You can't [concentrate on the building to distraction] and then on the other hand be asked to co-operate with an Inquiry that potentially could damage the health of your practice,' he stated. 'It's divisive. Everybody now is preparing their own case; they're preparing their own case almost to the point of everyone's forgotten that there is a building . . .'[11]

By late October, the massive impact would shift focus. As early as June, political voices had been calling for the film footage. 'The documentary must be made available,' Margo MacDonald had declared. 'The interviews in particular should be made available to Lord Fraser because it might very well be in the public interest . . . Wark Clements shouldn't have any problem if there is an undertaking that the raw contents are not made available for public viewing.'[12] 'Unless this evidence is seen,' agreed David McLetchie, 'no-one can judge whether or not it is relevant to the inquiry. The only people qualified to make that decision are Lord Fraser and his inquiry team.'[13] For Stuart and I, the calls had raised a very simple question. It was certainly true that nobody could judge whether our tapes were relevant. And that was because no one had asked either of us what the footage contained.

By autumn, the battle for the tapes had hit the headlines. 'The official inquiry into the Holyrood fiasco was effectively derailed before it started,' the *The Scotsman* argued on 25 October, 'when BBC managers last night refused to hand over potentially vital documentary material collated over the past five years . . . The BBC's decision not only threatens to undermine the inquiry, but is likely to put the corporation in direct conflict with Jack McConnell.'[14] In the parliament, the reaction was unsurprising. For the SNP's Fergus Ewing, the situation was a 'total outrage', while for David McLetchie, the credibility of the Holyrood Inquiry was 'now at stake'.[15] 'When the First Minister announced the Inquiry, I recall that . . . he said that anyone who refused would be named and shamed,' Ewing argued. 'It appears that the BBC has a shame deficit.'[16]

In fact, we were locked in a battle to protect our central sources. Correspondence between the BBC and the Fraser team had recently emerged in public – and what it appeared to be suggesting that the Inquiry intended was causing us great alarm. 'We would welcome the opportunity to view those sections of the film covering the late Donald Dewar and the late Enric Miralles,' a letter to BBC controller John McCormick had stated. 'If, on viewing such footage, it was felt that extracts from the interviews could benefit the inquiry, it would be our intention to show such footage during a public evidence session of the inquiry.'[17] Viewing any footage through the eyes of 2003, let alone viewing it out of context, ran an extremely serious risk of misinterpretation. But to then broadcast extracts into a hostile political arena threatened to make the situation even worse.

Still we had had no approach to ask what the tapes recorded, and the unfolding Inquiry continued to raise serious concerns. 'I think that the approach to this whole Inquiry is evolving almost on a day-to-day basis,' Brian Stewart would tell us in November. 'You know, what to focus on, and where to expend energy.' For John Gibbons, speaking in January, the process raised another crucial issue. 'I think the treatment of all of the witnesses was so variable,' he would explain to us in his office, 'That's a sort of general observation. Some of the witnesses . . . the attitude towards them was one of great respect, whereas to others there was almost the reverse – no respect whatsoever . . . There was an attitude I felt towards Barbara [Doig] that was different. There was an attitude towards Alex Salmond that appeared to be deferential and very different.'

By mid-October, Stuart had had a traumatic meeting with one source in the Marks and Spencer's food hall. 'I will not be found dead in the woods,' the source had stated – a reference to government weapons expert Dr David Kelly – before bursting into tears. With Lord Fraser's decision to broadcast evidence publicly, the stress within Holyrood would prove incalculable. Day after day, Inquiry evidence would dominate the headlines, and for Stuart and I the situation was causing massive strain. Heavily pregnant with my second child, I would end up in hospital three times in a single week. Yet in the political world, the pressure remained overwhelming. 'The BBC's position is breathtakingly arrogant,' Fergus Ewing argued on 26 October. 'I urge the Presiding Officer, George Reid, to consider using the powers of the parliament including, if necessary, court action to demand delivery of the documents.'[18] From the Inquiry, the message coming back sounded ominous. 'The focus right now is on getting the inquiry under way and amassing the evidence,' a spokesman stated. 'If the BBC continues to refuse to hand over the tapes then we would consider it. But we are not at that stage yet.'[19]

But on 29 October, the tape battle would take a turn that prompted fury. The SNP's Fergus Ewing had become a vocal force in calling for our footage. And on the 29th, he would raise a Point of Order. 'The [BBC's] justification now appears to be that there are in existence legal undertakings and confidentiality agreements that are, I presume, signed by the contributors,' he told Presiding Officer George Reid. 'I ask you to indicate whether you are aware of such documents having been signed by any Presiding Officer of the Parliament, any member of the [SPCB], any member of the Holyrood Progress Group or any member of the parliamentary staff.'[20] Reid's response was this: 'I can hardly go through four years of documentation. However, to the best of my knowledge, no such collective agreements have been entered into. Therefore one must look at the issue as a matter of contractual agreement between the individual who takes part in the programme and the film makers. I have to say that, when I did the interview for Wark Clements, I was given no guarantees, nor was I asked about the subsequent use of the footage.'[21]

For Stuart and me, the reaction was absolute outrage. Straight on the phone to each other, and rushing to our computers, we searched our e-mail to dig out our correspondence with George Reid. Unable to fight back publicly, our key concern had been maintaining filming access. Now, however, the credibility of the programmes was at stake. Within minutes, we had found what we had needed, and Stuart began an e-mail to the BBC. Regardless of whether he remembered, our message to George Reid on 9 June had been unambiguous. All our material was locked inside a bank vault, and everything filmed remained embargoed until Holyrood was finished, and our completed films broadcast. In a reply, personally addressed to Stuart, one thing was clear. Back in June, George Reid had not only received an undertaking. He had acknowledged it.[22]

On 27 November 2003, the BBC board of governors backed BBC Scotland's decision not to release the Holyrood tapes. For me, exhausted and embattled, it was a decision that would prompt tears of relief. With the pressure intense and mounting, and the BBC already under pressure over Hutton, we had presented a watertight case to back our position. A huge amount of filming and research time had been lost as we trawled through notes, transcripts and tapes, and hours had been spent constructing a letter and briefing document to go to the governors. If anything would demonstrate the impact the Inquiry was having on Holyrood, it would be this. To our immense gratitude – and despite what was being played out in the papers – some of Holyrood's key figures had written to the BBC to state that they were not releasing either of us from our promise, and one had even rung his lawyer to get a sworn affadavit. The message he had given us was unequivocal. A promise means very little until it comes under pressure, we were told firmly. That is when it becomes important.

Yet in spite of Lord Fraser's determination to get to 'the truth' behind Holyrood, there was one stone he never attempted to turn. Despite countless years at the heart of the parliament project, neither Stuart nor I would be invited to the witness stand. As early as 17 November, the BBC had offered a viewing of redacted tapes of Dewar and Miralles – an offer the Inquiry would finally accept in its final phase.[23] And in late April 2004 – just a month before the Inquiry's closing submissions – Inquiry QC John Campbell would finally contact Stuart direct. But while the Inquiry battled for the tapes of *The Gathering Place*, they ignored a source that was every bit as vital to understanding. Following years of painstaking research, I possessed volumes of detailed contemporaneous notes. I never received a single phone call from Lord Fraser's Inquiry.[24]

Notes

1. The account of the Fraser battle with the BBC over the *Gathering Place* tapes is drawn from my own experience, and represents my own views and not those of any other person or organisation.
2. 'News and Updates', 8 July 2003, http://www.holyroodinquiry.org
3. Ibid.
4. 'Inquiry Objectives', http://www.holyroodinquiry.org
5. Quoted in Murray Ritchie and Frances Horsburgh, 'Architect's widow at centre of political row over her firm's Holyrood fees', *Herald*, 24 July 2003.
6. 'Introduction', http://www.holyroodinquiry.org
7. Lord Fraser, 'Preliminary Hearing', 12 September 2003, ibid.
8. 'Inquiry Objectives', ibid.
9. This modified approach appears – at least in part – to have been an attempt by RMJM to help put some sequential order into an enormous volume of information.
10. Interview, 4–5 November 2003. Brian's total also appears to include the cost of legal representation. At this point, it seemed that the consultants were having to pay for their own representation, while the Executive, Scottish Parliament and SPCB were funded by the taxpayer. This suggested strongly that the consultants were paying twice.
11. Ibid.
12. Quoted in Liam McDougall, 'Documentary footage may be called in Holyrood probe; film may reveal history of parliament blunders', *Sunday Herald*, 29 June 2003.

13. Quoted in ibid.
14. Hamish Macdonell, 'BBC war with Holyrood inquiry', *The Scotsman*, 25 October 2003.
15. Quoted in ibid.
16. Fergus Ewing, 'Points of Order', *Scottish Parliament Official Report*, col. 2634, 29 October 2003, http://www.scottish.parliament.uk
17. Derek Bearhop, Inquiry Secretary, to John McCormick, BBC Scotland controller, 22 October 2003, quoted in 'They gave undertakings about the contributions', *Herald*, 25 October 2003.
18. Quoted in Murdo MacLeod, '"Holyrood tapes" legal battle looms', *Scotland on Sunday*, 26 October 2003.
19. Quoted in ibid.
20. Fergus Ewing, 'Points of Order', *Scottish Parliament Official Report*, cols 2634–5, 29 October 2003, http://www.scottish.parliament.uk
21. George Reid, 'Points of Order', *Scottish Parliament Official Report*, col. 2635, 29 October 2003, http://www.scottish.parliament.uk
22. E-mail to, and response from, George Reid, 9 June 2003.
23. The background and timescale of this is discussed in the closing submission by Inquiry QC John Campbell, and the submission by BBC Scotland Solicitor Advocate Alistair Bonnington. Closing submission, paras 38, 308, 312–13, 334–41, 25 May 2004, http://www.holyrood inquiry.org
24. The Inquiry had made an attempt to discover my contract details, but – having been told I was on maternity leave – appear not to have followed the matter up.

25

The End?

*'Well, I mean . . . you know, six years? Can't come quickly enough . . . The
Inquiry finished, the building finished, people in enjoying it . . .
It's good to see it like this.'*
Brian Stewart[1]

O N 9 OCTOBER 2004, the new Scottish Parliament building
at Holyrood was declared open. For those involved, it was
the end of an exhausting and exhilarating journey. 'Nobody
said in 1997, "Would you consider working on a building for
six years with two clients, that's going to increase in size by
twice . . . [that's] probably gonna cost too much money and by
the way, the architect's gonna die half the way through . . . the
principal client is gonna die half the way through and you're
gonna have two inquiries . . . how do you fancy it?"' an emotional John Gibbons had confided in the summer. 'You know,
you'd say, "Thank you very much but I think I'll stay doing
what I'm doing." It wasn't like that.'[2]

The weeks before the opening had seen a clear shift of mood
within Holyrood. Speculation about who the Inquiry would
'finger' had been growing steadily, and tensions were high as
those inside waited for Fraser's results. Letters had been sent
out to all those potentially subject to criticism, and, for some
involved, there were strong and wounded reactions. 'It says,
"I'm driven to the conclusion that . . . [the directors of
EMBT/RMJM] *consistently* failed to see the greater good for
their own sectional interests,"' Brian Stewart had told the film
team, angry. 'Now, what an outrageous thing to say. I mean, I'm
embarrassed for him, actually. Because he doesn't understand

what we've been doing for six years. In the face of extreme adversity and massive challenges, the one thing that we have been is professional, and I resent it. I really, really resent it . . . Questioning professionalism in this organisation is just outrageous, and I am furious.'[3]

For John Gibbons, the passing months had raised different worries. With his health suffering due to stress and overwork, the situation had been compounded by press allegations. 'One of my daughters told me that she'd seen a . . . headline which said "Chief architect to be accused of corruption",' he told the film team in September, 'and then I had a press reporter on the doorstep who said was I aware that the Chief Constable was about to take action against me . . .?' The impact had been enormous, and for Gibbons, after years of commitment, it had meant reassessment. 'As we've moved closer to [completion], I think . . . the balance between whether to stay or whether to finish you look at quite differently,' he'd confided in July, 'and I've certainly looked at it quite differently on a personal level as to whether this is the way to spend your time. I suppose there's a feeling of whether the effort that's been put into it is being acknowledged or recognised, I suppose. Not personal, but corporate. You feel that very much if you spend your time with some of the folk working [on the project team] . . .'

With the report's publication, however, the reaction – from most of the project's key players – had been relief. Brian Stewart's robust corrections seemed to have tempered conclusions, and, for Hugh Fisher too, the results of Lord Fraser's report had been 'reasonable'. 'I mean, I haven't read it fully,' Stewart told the film team frankly in mid-September. 'You just look for the sections you think impact and affect the practice. I think that it's "bland", sounds as if it's a critical word but it is a reasonable assessment of the evidence. There is criticism; maybe I thought the strength of that criticism would be stronger in some areas. [But] I think as far as we're concerned, the professionalism is not coming into question . . . [The brief's] been delivered – through all the challenges and all the twists and turns, that has carried on, and that focus has remained.'

At Bovis, however, Alan Mack had been disappointed. 'Initial first views are, I don't think there's anything there that surprised me,' he explained flatly. 'We had received a letter . . . a one-page letter, and it annexed certain views that Fraser had about our programming – "optimism of programming" I believe. And we responded to that in about seven pages of detail, and we based our seven pages of detail not on anything new, but on evidence that he was given . . . And it's fair to say that *some* of that response I think he must have reviewed and believed it had constructive comment, because he took some of those initial views out of the end document.'

For Mack, what Lord Fraser had missed had been the team's passion. 'I guess, you know, he's written something that fits . . . a lot of agendas . . .' he stated, 'but it doesn't portray the picture, it doesn't portray anywhere near the blood, sweat and tears that people have put into the building.' Hugh Fisher, though, had raised another issue. 'The . . . thing that I find *slightly* surprising about it is the almost total lack of criticism of the body politic,' he observed, 'both generally and in certain individual cases in the report because, well, I think that doesn't really reflect the impact that politicians and political wishes had on the project.'[4]

After years of trauma, the Holyrood building was finally in the hands of the parliament. And for Lord Fraser of Carmyllie, his hopes for the future of the institution now seemed clear. 'The Scottish Parliament has a building that meets the vision that I believe Donald Dewar and his colleagues set for it,' he stated. 'I express the hope shared by many that the excellence of the parliamentary activity within the building will reflect the quality of the structure, and that the painful lessons of its pro-curement are not lost on those privileged to serve there as rep-resentatives of the Scottish people.'[5] It was certainly a bold vision. The question was – was it possible?

From what I'd observed, Lord Fraser's statement raised a number of key issues. In 1997, hopes had been high for Scotland, and Donald Dewar's vision had been distilled into

Miralles' bold design. Holyrood would be home to a new politics, an open and accessible form of government that could rise above the sniping of party debate. 'There was a vision . . .' Brian Stewart explained with passion. 'There were people looking at creating something exceptional. And you can't go halfway and stop, you can't go halfway and stop. You can't dumb down, halfway through. You can't have columns on cantilevers halfway through. You must follow that vision to the end. Because if you stop in the middle, you've got nothing. You have to go right to the end. And you have to put your – damned – effort right in, to the end. It's the only way, and then we'll see.'[6]

As Stewart stood in the foyer of the building he had fought for, Scotland's politicians met for Holyrood debate number six. Since filming began, four sessions had been held on the building itself, one had been conducted over the BBC tape battle, and a further debate was now taking place in the wake of Fraser's report. 'You asked me what I feel . . . about the debate,' Stewart argued with feeling. 'It's really quite vivid . . . there are a lot of MSPs, individuals in there, who are saying: "We're stopped in the street, [by] the taxi driver," what was happening during the last election was this building was the worst thing and it affected the institution. Now, really, if they stopped to think about it, it's their behaviour, it's the way that they have wanted to present the building, denigrate it, every element of it, every aspect of it. They've treated it as a key political issue. And *that's* the thing that's affected the credibility of the institution. It's the fact that they have been so extreme in their views about it . . . it's their behaviour, and the way that they have presented it, or the way they've criticised it; they've mauled it . . . it's just been in extremes. And those extremes are quite difficult for the public to manage.'

The Holyrood building had been born as the symbol of a new Scotland. What it had become over the years had been a catalyst exposing Scotland's flaws. 'The building that we are talking about will not make us a Parliament,' Mike Russell had argued in 1999, 'All the comments that we have heard so far suggest that we will miraculously become a Parliament in two years' time and that the problems we have with the new politics and the style of debate will change because we have a new building. That is not true. We must think about what we should be doing and how we, as men and women, should make ourselves a Parliament and not imagine that a building can do that for us.'[7] With Holyrood open, that challenge had now become reality. And the future of Scotland lay in the Parliament's hands.

For Alan Mack, speaking in March 2004, the signs for the future had not looked hopeful. 'I don't know I'm becoming even more cynical about our amazing . . . democratic process,' he had argued at the height of the Holyrood Inquiry. 'I'm gobsmacked that we seem to be surrounded by people who can spend their whole lives actually never being responsible for anything . . . and yet we look up to them as something special. And at the end of the day . . . it's what you do and the responsibility you take for your actions. It appears that many of our amazing ministers take no responsibility for their actions whatsoever, which is pretty shitty.' For Jack McConnell though, at the parliament's opening ceremony, it seemed the vision for the future of Scotland would be clear. 'It is we who are elected to serve who form the human institution that is the Scottish Parliament,' he declared firmly. 'It is how we perform our duties, how we advance or inhibit the progress of the nation, in our conduct and the decisions we make, that will chart the future course of Scotland.'[8] The question was then – and still remains – a simple one. Can the Scottish Parliament now meeting at Miralles' building, at last rise to match the standards of its home?

Notes

1. Interview, 31 March 2004.
2. Interview, 21 July 2004.
3. This would be Brian Stewart's primary concern with Fraser's provisional conclusions. The others, he stated, were 'not actually too difficult to deal with'. 'I think there's just a lack of understanding of the whole process,' he continued. 'I mean, the Inquiry doesn't have

technical advice there, so . . . I think there hasn't been a full grasp of how a project emerges, how it evolves, the reiterative process that takes place.' Despite this, however, the Inquiry did manage to scotch several of the myths surrounding Holyrood, although these were not necessarily translated into press reporting of the project.

4. Fisher had also had reservations about Lord Fraser's comments on the construction management method chosen to procure the building. 'I think it's slightly unfair to the procedures followed under construction management, because there's nothing inherently unsatisfactory about them,' he argued. 'I think the nature of this particular project, looking back on it with hindsight, has meant that it quite rightly has contributed to the cost, 'cos that's the nature of the contractual agreement. But there's nothing wrong with the procedure.' Interview, 16 September 2004.

5. Lord Fraser's speech, Publication of Holyrood Inquiry Report, 2004, http://www.holyroodinquiry.org

6. Interview, 18 June 2003.

7. *Scottish Parliament Official Report*, vol 1, no.10, col. 531, 17 June 1999, http://www.scottish.parliament

8. Jack McConnell, Speech, 9 October 2004, http://www.scotland.gov.uk

Index

Index

Index

Index